MAOISTS IN NEPAL
FROM INSURGENCY TO POLITICAL MAINSTREAM

MAOISTS IN NEPAL

FROM INSURGENCY TO POLITICAL MAINSTREAM

B.C.Upreti

Publications

KALPAZ PUBLICATIONS
DELHI-110 052

Maoists in Nepal: From Insurgency to Political Mainstream

Rs. 750

ISBN : 81-7835-687-2

Published in 2008 in India by
Kalpaz Publications,
C-30, Satyawati Nagar,
Delhi-110 052
Phone: 9212729499
E-mail : kalpaz@hotmail.com

Laser Type setting by: Isas System, Delhi
Printed at: Sangal Print Media, Delhi

Contents

Preface

The Nepali politics is passing through a critical phase. With the Maoists joining the political mainstream the prospects for republican state and inclusive democracy have brightened in Nepal. The objectives are still to be realized but the country is steadily moving towards that direction.

The withdrawal of insurgency by the Maoists has indeed given a new dynamism to Nepali politics. Why did Maoists agreed to join the path of multi party-democracy is a significant issue. This particular development has necessitated looking at the Maoist insurgency in Nepal in a broader perspective.

The present study is an attempt in that direction. The basic objective here has been to understand the factors and forces that gave way to the Maoist insurgency in Nepal and also the circumstances and factors that encouraged the Maoists to join the path of multiparty democracy.

In the pursuance of this study I have been benefited by the writings of a number of scholars. I would like to express my gratitude to all of them.

I would like to express my sincere thanks to my colleagues in the South Asia Studies Centre for their encouragement and help. My thanks are also due to my students and research scholars in the centre. I would also like to extend my thanks to the staff members of the South Asia Studies Centre library and the central library of the university of Rajasthan for their help in procuring the source material.

I have no words to extend my sincere gratitude to all my family members who have always encouraged and helped me in my academic pursuits, and also to my friends and well wishers who have appreciated my academic ventures. I have also to express my thanks to M/s Kalpaz Publications for taking interest in the publication of this book.

I have tried my best to make an objective assessment of the events, forces and factors that this study has dealt with. However, I alone am would be responsible for any short of omissions and commissions.

Jaipur **B.C. Upreti**
1 December 2007

1
Communist Movement in Nepal: Historico-Political Context

Marxism and Leninism started gaining popularity in many countries in Europe and Asia as a form of governance, as a political ideology and as an alternative to capitalism after the establishment of communist regime in the Soviet Union. The foundation of communist party based on the principles of Marxism and Leninism was considered to be the first step towards raising communist movement in a country. The communism was viewed as an international movement. So the countries like Soviet Union considered it one of their primary objectives to encourage expansion of the Marxist ideology elsewhere in the world.

In Asia three factors were important in the context of the rise of communism: The rise of nationalistic movement against the feudal-autocratic political order; struggle against the colonial rule leading to the transfer of power to indigenous political elite and the establishment of democratic political order and the external support to the growth of communist organizations, particularly from the neighbouring countries.

The communist movements thus taking shape in many countries have had different destinations. In many countries the communist party succeeded in establishing its rule, while in many others it survived but failed in founding a communist regime. In many countries including the Soviet Union communism collapsed after a certain period of time. There have been some countries where communist organizations succumbed to the rise of fundamentalism, authoritarian regimes and strong foundation of liberal capitalist regimes. There are countries like India where communist organizations have succeeded in sharing power at the level of state governments and a supporter to the government at the centre but not beyond that.

Nepal provides an example where after nearly 46 years of the foundation of communist party, a strong Maoist insurgency based on the ideology of Marxism-Leninism-Maoism took roots. It has to be noted here that the political history of the country has not been all that uni-lenear. The democracy came to Nepal in 1950 but it failed in taking roots in the way it was expected. After 1960 far a long span of 28 years, there was panchayat system that did not allow organized political activities in the country. So the political environment of the country was not at all favourable for the growth of a communist movement for most of the time. Than the country faced insurgency at a time when it was struggling hard for the institutionalization of democracy. It naturally raises a plethora of questions. As a preliminary exercise towards finding causes and ramifications of the Maoist insurgency it would be desirable to took into the growth of communist organizations and activities in Nepal. How and under what circumstances the communist movement took shape in Nepal? What courses it followed during different political regimes and what lead to the growth of a radical Marxist ideology in that country? These are some of the issues that are significant in the context of a study of the Maoist insurgency in Nepal.

Rise of Political Extremism in Nepal: An Overview

Before coming to the rise of communist movement in Nepal let us briefly look in to the growth of political extremism in Nepal. Nepal has been a feudal state and a fragmented society ever since the foundation of the kingdom in 1769.

The highly centralized and authoritarian political order did not allow political dissent. Therefore, there was hardly any scope for the growth of political extremism within the country. It is true that there were several instances of palace conspiracies, intrigues, murders and so on in the history of Nepal.[1] But these were of a different nature based on the feudalistic power struggle and factionalism.

The Political extremism of the modern era began to take shape in Nepal towards the decade of the nineteen thirties and it was, by and large, based on external sources. The main objective of these political extremists was to fight against the authoritarian rule in Nepal. But due to the prevailing political conditions in Nepal they were compelled to keep their organizational activities based in India and operate from the Indian soil. The various social reform movements taken place in India over a period of time and the National Movement of India, became primary sources of inspiration to these Nepali political extremists.[2]

The Nepalese settled in India and the Nepalese students studying in the Indian educational institutions played a major role in the rise of Nepali political extremism. The Nepali solders serving in the British army were another important source. The social reform movements, Indian National movement and the ideas of Mahatma Gandhi and the other Indian political leaders influenced the Nepalese living in India. In 1920 some of the Nepalese like Tulsi Mehar, Chakra Bahadur, Amar Raj Joshi and Krishan Prasad Koirala launched Arya Samaj Movement in Nepal. They also began to spread ideas of Mahatma Gandhi in Nepal. The Rana rulers strongly opposed such activities, as they did not believe in any kind of social transformation in the country.[3]

In 1931 Prachanda Gurkha was established by Nepalese living in India like Umesh Bahadur Shah, Khadga Man Singh, Matrika Bahadur and Ranga Nath Shah.[4] They demanded an end of rule of the Ranas and the establishment of a democratic system in the country.[5] The Prachanda Gurkha tried to follow revolutionary tactics. But they were strongly dealt with by the Rana rulers. In 1935 Tanka Prasad Acharya along with Dasarath Chandra, Ram Hari Sharma, Pushkar Nath Upreti, Bal Chandra Sharma, .etc founded Praja Parishad. They, however, also met the same fate as Prachanda Gurkha. Sukraj Shastri constituted a Nagarik Adhikar Samiti in 1937. The idea was to generate consciousness among the masses.

These developments clearly indicate that the Nepalese were gradually becoming conscious of the tyrannical rule of the Ranas and a revolutionary thinking was developing aimed at abolishing the Rana autocracy and the establishment of democracy in the country. These developments formed a background for the growth of leftist ideology in the country. The Indian National Movement played a significant role in the growth of left ideology in Nepal as well. They derived ideological inspirations from the Bolshevik revolution in Russia but their ideological linkages were with the revolutionary movement in India.[6] It may be pointed out here that the Communist Party of India was against that Rana rule in Nepal. They considered Ranas as supporters of the imperialist forces.[7] This influenced those Nepalese who too were against the Rana rule.

The likeminded Nepalese were also educated by the activities carried out by the Indian socialist and communist leaders near India-Nepal border or on the Nepali side of the border. Jai Prakash Narain, a socialist activist founded a Guerrilla camp in Nepal Tarai.[8] Some of the communists like Sibban Lal Saxena, Bishwanath Dubey, Jamil Ali established camp in Nepal Tarai and organized their activities from this camp.[9] Nepal Tarai was also used as an hideout by the Indian socialist and communist leaders like Jai Prakash, Ram Manohar Lohiya, Baidyanath Jha, Achyat Patwardhan, etc. It was obvious that their activities also left some impact on the Nepalese, some of whom were attracted towards the communist ideology in due course.

The roots of the communist movement in Nepal can be traced back to the beginning of the decade of 1930, when Khadgaman, a Nepali student of Calcutta University founded a political organization in Kathmandu. He advocated launching a struggle against the rule of the Ranas. He was arrested by the Nepali government and sanctioned 20 years imprisonment.[10] Man Mohan Adhikari worked for trade unions in Patna. Similar was the case of Pushp Lal Shrestha. These young Nepalese were attracted towards the Indian Communists and the Soviet Communist movement was their source of inspiration. Some of the young Nepalese like Pushp Lal Shrestha, Shambhu Ram Shreshta, Surya Bahadur Bhardwaj, Prem Bahadur Kansakar, etc. who were influenced by the communist ideology formed a Nepal Prajatantrik Sangh in 1944. The organization was soon banned and its activities were declared illegal. Man Mohan Singh Adhikari and many others joined Biratnagar Jute and Cotton Mill strike in 1947. Two things are clear here: The young Nepalese who were either studying in India or living here were gradually attracted towards the communist ideology. They were looking for the opportunity to give an organizational basis to their activities. It is also clear that all their activities were surrounded the Rana rule in Nepal. Their main objective was to overthrow the Rana rule.

In 1948 when All India Nepali Congress was constituted in Varansi, most of these young Nepalese influenced by the socialist and communist ideas joined it. But they were soon dissatisfied with the working of the party. They alleged that the party was following an attitude of conciliation with the Ranas and was trying to accommodate feudalistic elements in the kingdom. It was clear that they would not remain within the party for a longtime. But the formation of All India Nepali Congress had induced in them an idea of forming their own independent organization. In July 1949 Pushp Lal Shrestha, Niranjan Govind Vaidya, Durga Devi, Nar Bahadur and Narayan Vilas formed the Communist Party of Nepal (CPN) at Kolkata. Pushp Lal became Secretary of the party. Earlier in April 1949 he had translated the Communist Manifesto into Nepali language. Thus, he had already established his credentials as a strong follower of communism. The formation of CPN was a significant development. In 1950 All India Nepali Congress was reconstituted at Calcutta as National Nepali Congress. It soon declared an armed struggle against the Ranas. The CPN hailed the decision of the Nepali Congress. It also issued statement supporting the armed struggle but the Nepali Congress was not willing for active participation of the CPN in the struggle against the Ranas. The CPN too was in a dilemma as it apprehend that the Nepali Congress could compromise with the feudal forces at some point of time. Nevertheless, CPN declared its support to the armed struggle against the Ranas. In early 1951 CPN shifted its head-office from Kolkata to Kathmandu. CPN termed the Nepali Congress as a stooge of India.[11] It began to search alliance with parties and groups that were opposed to the Nepali Congress.[12] CPN also denounced the New Delhi agreement concluded between the Nepali Congress Ranas and Monarchy.[13] CPN hailed the revolt of K.I. Singh and his associates against the Ranas. The Nepali Congress government banned CPN for 4 years. Thus, lines were clearly drawn between the Nepali Congress and the Communist party of Nepal. One was considered to be pro-India while, the other anti-India.[14] The communists went underground till 1956. During this period they concentrated in the eastern region of the country under the banner of Akhil Nepal Kishan Sangh[15] and worked for the welfare of the rural people.

In 1953 the first congress of the party was organized. It endorsed the leadership of Man Mohan Adhikari by electing him as General Secretary of the party in place of Pushp Lal Shrestha. The Praja Parishad government was formed in 1956 under the leadership of Tanka Prasad Acharya. CPN agreed to work under the constitutional monarchy in a peaceful manner. In 1956 ban on CPN was lifted. In 1957 CPN and NC together launched a Satyagraha Movement, demanding establishment of democratic system in the country. King did not agree to the demand of a Constituent Assembly but agreed to frame a new constitution and hold general elections. CPN also agreed to it after a formal protest. There was a change of leadership of the party. Keshar Jung Raimajhi became the General Secretary in the Second Congress of the party in 1957. The party took part in the February 1958 elections and won 4 seats out of a total 109 seats of the parliament. It indicated that the party did not have a strong social base in the country. King Mahendra abrogated the parliamentary democracy in December 1960. Keshar Jung Raimajhi who was a staunch loyalist supported the king's action. As a result conflicts began to surface within the leadership of the party.

Leadership Conflicts and Factionalism

It was not very late that differences began to erupt between the central leadership of the party. This process had indeed started towards the middle of the decade of the fifties. The main issue was relationship of the party with the Nepali Congress and the feudal forces represented by monarchy. Pushp Lal Shrestha one of the founders of the communist movement in Nepal and a dedicated communist leader was of the opinion that the Communists could work with the democratic forces in the country to fight for the establishment of democracy. Thus, he believed in organizing a joint people's movement for the restoration of democracy. But the hardliners in the party did not agree to him. They believed that the democratic parties, like Nepali Congress, were following reconciliatory approach towards the feudal forces. The Party's pro-India approach was also a matter of criticism for the hardliners. They later called Pushp Lal Shrestha as a stooge of the Nepali Congress **(Congress ra Puchhar)**.[16]

On the other hand leaders like Keshar Jung Raimajhi were strong supporters of the royalty. He believed in feudalistic nationalism. He supported Panchayat System established by king Mahendra in 1962, and as a reward of his pro-monarchy approach he was appointed Chairman of the permanent committee of the Council of State.[17]

Split in the Party

Pushp Lal Shrestha who had strongly criticized king Mahendra's action to abrogate the parliament system and was not happy with the pro-royalty approach of Keshar Jung Raimajhi moved to Varanasi. They began to criticize the party leadership for its reconciliatory approach. In 1962 the third congress of the party was held in Varanasi. The conflict within the party reached to its climax. Raimajhi and his supporters were expelled from the party. Disciplinary action was also taken against some of the followers of Raimajhi. Tulsi Lal Amatya was elected as the General Secretary of the party.

The panchayat government introduced land reforms in 1964. The Communist Party mobilized peasants in many parts of the country against these reforms. Similarly the students also became active. They formed Free Students Union in University and colleges. But the central leadership of the party failed in organizing these activities and providing leadership to them. As a result these groups began to depend on the local leadership of the communist party. This paved a way for the localized activities of the party and consequently the emergence of local units of the party. This indeed became a primary factor in heading the party towards a split.

Pushp Lal Shrestha was the first to break away from the party. Actually, as pointed out earlier, Pushp Lal was of the opinion that it was not possible to establish a democratic system in Nepal without waging a protracted war.[18] Other leaders like Mohan Bikram Singh, Nirmal Lama agreed to it. But the point of difference was that Pushp Lal advocated collaboration with other democratic forces, while the other radicals did not agree to it. Pushp Lal formed his own party in 1968 and remained its General Secretary till his death in 1982. The party leadership was than taken by his wife Sahana Pradhan.

Pushp Lal's break from the party was an important development in the communist movement in Nepal. Actually, after this incident the local leadership of the party particularly in the areas where local units of the party were active also began to think in terms of following the Pushp Lal's way. Consequently, there were more groups to come out of the party.

Rise of Maoism

The second half of the decade of the sixties was marked by significant developments in the International Communist Movement. China was passing through a strong cultural revolution to clean up the communist party from the revisionists' forces. In India CPN (M) launched the peasant movement in 1967. A strong and violent Naxalbari movement began in West Bengal. The Naxalite movement in India and the ideology of Charu Majumdar influenced CPN units in the adjoining areas of Jhapa and Morang in Nepal. Leaders like Mohan Chandra Adhikari, Radha Krishan Mainali Chandra Prakash Mainali were interested in launching a movement like that of Naxalbari. It came to be known as the Jhapa Uprising. In 1969 Man Mohan Adhikari and Sambhu Ram Shrestha were released from jail. They went to Biratnagar to work with the local leaders. In 1971 Mohan Bikram Singh formed a Central Nucleus. The Central Nucleus following the Fourth Congress of the party in 1974 formed a party called CPN (Fourth Convention), led by Mohan Bikram Singh and Nirmal Lama. The party believed in violent tactics and its main objective was to launch a people's movement that could be developed into an armed struggle later on. The greatest contribution of this faction has been to provide leaders to the Maoist insurgency.[19] The Panchayat government took strong action against the party. A number of its leaders and workers were arrested or killed. The party was successful in the sense that it generated seeds of extremist Maoism in Nepal. But it had to stop its activities. It now gave attention to three aspects: to understand Nepali conditions to envisage strategies and action plan suitable to the Nepali conditions and to work among peasants and workers so as to strengthen its organizational base. In 1977 CPN and other leaders called for Fourth Congress of the party at Varanasi. Tulsi Lal Amatya, Pushp Lal, Man Mohan Adhkari and Sambhuram Shrestha did not attend it. The party passed a political resolution to launch a mass struggle. It criticized the Jhapa group for its altra leftist activities.

After a gap of 4 years on December 1978 Mohan Bikram Singh and Nirmal Lama formed the Communist Party of Nepal (Marxist – Leninist) (CPN ML). The Party made it clear that it was not sufficient to import ideology of revolution.[20] The local conditions were also important. It was necessary to take socio-economic and political conditions in view in the context of Nepal's march to socialism and communism. The party concentrated more on underground activities, so as to strengthen its social base.

The decade of 1980's was highly significant from the point of view of communist movement in Nepal. It witnessed the rise of a number of communist splinter groups, the consolidation of radical communist ideology and the communist parties joining the struggle for the establishment of multi-party democracy in the country. In 1984 Nirmal Lama broke out from Mohan Bikram Singh to form CPN (Fourth Convention). Actually differences were brewing between the two leaders for some time. Nirmal Lama wanted to recognize the leadership of Deng Hsiao Ping after death of Mao, while Mohan Bikram Singh denounced him as a counter-revolutionary. Lama was also advocating participation in the panchayat elections, which the party rejected. Mohan Bikram Singh and Mohan Baidya formed CPN (Masal). In 1984 Man Mohan Adhikari who had formed his own party in 1980, joined Sahana Pradhan to form CPN-Marxist Party. Tulsi Lal Amatya who was in self-exile in India for the last 19 years returned back to Kathmandu and he formed a new party called CPN (Amatya). CPN (Manandhar) of Bishnu Bahadur Manandhar expelled Keshar Jung Raimajhi from his party in 1984. Raimajhi joined CPN (Varma) of Krishna Raj Varma but he was also expelled from there.

In 1986 CPN (Masal) bifurcated in to two CPN (Masal) lead by Mohan Bikram and Babu Ram Bhattarai and CPN (Mashal) lead by Mohan Baidya. Pushpa Kamal Dahal (Prachanda) became General Secretary of CPN (Masal) in 1989.

The various communist groups were gradually preparing for a struggle against the panchayat system. These groups including the Nepal Majdoor Kishan Party of Rohit and the Revolutionary Workers Party of Roop Lal Viswakarma, Krishna Das Shrestha of the Marxist.-Leninist Party were ready to join the multi party democratic mainstream. The Nepali Congress was already preparing to launch a movement for democracy. The communist groups were in a mood to support the democratic forces. On 15 January 1990 seven communist groups consisting of CPN-ML, CPN-M, CPN-Manandhar, NKMP-Rohit, CPN-Varma, CPN-Amatya, CPN-Lama formed a United Left Front (ULF). ULF joined the Nepali Congress to launch the democratic movement. The Nepali Congress and ULF along with other democratic forces agreed to the king's decision to abrogate panchayat, system prepare a new constitution and hold general elections. The altra-leftist did not agree to king's decision and pledged their commitment to people's war. In the interim government that came into being in May 1990, under the leadership of K.P. Bhattarai of the Nepali Congress. CPN ML (2 Members) and CPN Manandhar represented ULF. This was something frustrating to the other constituents of ULF. So the four dissatisfied groups CPN-Amatya, CPN-Varma, NKMP-Rohit and CPN-Lama broke out from ULF. It was a big shock to the communist unity. It also indicated that these communist groups were also desperately looking for sharing the power.

CPN (M), CPN (ML) formed CPN United Marxist Leninist Party (UML) in 1990. Later on, CPN (Amatya) also joined it. The party was agreed to participate in the 1991 elections.[21] It emerged as a moderate communist party accepting the constitutional monarchy.[22] Another important development in the communist camp was the formation of CPN Unity Centre by the hardcore communists. CPN (Fourth Congress) CPN (Mashal) joined it. Prachanda became General Secretary of the party. Later on CPN (Masal) (Babu Ram Bhattarai) also joined it. UC decided to participate in the 1991 elections as the United People Front of

Nepal (UPFN). Babu Ram Bhattarai became its convener.[23] UC was a revolutionary political forum. It had serious objections to the constitution making process, yet it decided to participate in the 1991 general elections under the banner of UPFN. The Unity centre secured 9 seats in the elections and stood as the third largest party after NC (109) and UML (69). It indicates that despite its revolutionary postures the party had believed in constitutional-democratic processes till 1991. It was only in the post 1991 period that the Unity Centre gradually lost its interest in the constitutional-democratic process and turned into a hardcore violent organization by 1995. So the period between 1991-95 was highly crucial for the rise of Maoists in Nepal. Two factors were quite significant in this regards: The Nepali Congress government considering that the communists had emerged as a considerable political force began to follow a hostile attitude towards them, particularly towards the radical communists, who were not happy since the formation of the interim government.[24] Secondly, the radical communists began to realize that the elected government of the Nepali Congress was not capable of meeting the challenges that the country was faced with. In the first Congress of the Unity Centre held in December 1991, it was agreed to follow the ideology of Marxism-Leninism-Maoism. The party also decided to launch protracted war from the rural areas by following the Chinese model of rural to urban insurrection. It was also decided that the Unity Centre would go underground while UPFN would remain active over-ground.

In 1994 the Unity Centre got bifurcated into two groups: one CPN (UC) under the leadership of Mohan Bikram Singh and Nirmal Lama and the other CPN (Maoist) under the leadership of Prachanda. Subsequently, the CPFN also faced a split: one group of Niranjan Govind Baidya supporting Mohan Bikram Singh and Nirmal Lama and the another group lead by Babu Ram Bhattarai supporting Prachanda. Mohan Bikram Singh and Nirmal Lama decided to participate in the 1994 elections while Prachanda decided to boycott it. The election Commission recognized Baidya faction of UPFN. CPN (Maoists) finally decided to abandon all its democratic political activities. In March 1995 it was renamed as CPN (Marxist). It got membership of the Revolutionary

Internationalist Movement (RIM). In September 1995 the party took its historical decision to wage a protracted war in the near future. It selected the western hill districts of Rolpa and Rukum as its main areas of activities and began to prepare for a guerrilla war against the Nepali state.

Summing Up

The rise of the communist movement in Nepal is contemporary to the rise of organized political activities and political parties in the country. Another important aspect is that like the Nepali Congress the Communist Party of Nepal also emerged in the Indian soil. The Indian National Movement along with various social reforms that took place in India from time to time provided the necessary background for the emergence of organized political activities in Nepal. So while the international communist ideology provided the necessary ideological input to the young Nepalese activists the Indian environment provided opportunity for the shaping of organized Nepalese political activities. The fact remains that the autocratic Rana rule in Nepal did not allow any socio-political reforms and organized political activities within Nepal. It could only grow outside the country. No other country would have been a better place than India to provide such an opportunity, which itself was undergoing a strong anti-colonial movement at that point of time.

The Communist Movement has undergone several stages during the last half a century in Nepal. The internal socio-economic and political conditions have influenced it to a considerable extent. The alignment and realignment of communist forces have followed the development of international movement as well as the internal political dynamics.

The Communists of Nepal have broadly fallen into three categories. The royalists who had associated themselves with the monarchy accepted the political moves of the monarchy and sought benefits form the monarchy. The liberal or moderate communists whom accepted the constitutional monarchy and have believed that the social transformation is possible through constitutional and democratic methods. The third category of communists is the hardcore communists who believe in complete social and political transformation based on the Marxist ideology. There has been a gradual and steady growth of the extremist ideology in Nepal. There is no doubt that the communists of the extremist ideology had existed in the country ever since the foundation of the Communist Party of Nepal. Because for instance the demands like formations of the Constituent Assembly had been raised by the communists as early as 1950. Similarly the Communists raised voice against feudalism since the beginning. However, all of them were within one umbrella at that time. The radical communist ideology began to grow towards the beginning of 1970's when there was lot of defections in the communist camp, the central communist leadership became weak and the local leadership of the communist groups began to grow. For another 20 years there was a process of synthesisation of the communist forces and the Marxist ideology. It was also a time when hardcore Marxists tried to strengthen their organizational base, particularly in the rural areas. They also tried to influence the peasantry and the youth. The Jhapa insurrection was a significant development in that direction. These uprisings were consolidated in the form of a strong communist party of the radical Maoists towards the end of the decade of nineteen seventies. The decade of the eighties was also marked by the realignment and fragmentation of the communist partics. But it provided an opportunity to the radical Communists to further consolidate themselves. Even the radical communists participated in the 1990 movement for democracy and in the democratic process subsequently. But they were soon frustrated with the political process in Nepal. The governments formed by both the Nepali congress and the United Marxist – Leninist failed in realizing the aspirations of the people, streamlining the politics and administration and maintaining law and order in the country. The radical communists also realized that it was not possible to attain their objectives by following the constitutional and democratic methods. So they began to consolidate the extremist forces to ultimately follow the path of a revolution.

References

1. For Some detailed explainations about the formation of Nepali state and power politics see, Bhuwan Lal Joshi & Leo E. Rose,

Democratic Innovations in Nepal, A Case of Political Acculturation, University of California Press, Barkeley, 1966; Ludwig F. Stiller, the *Rise of the House of Gorkha: A Study in the Unification of Nepal,* Munjushree Publishing House, New Delhi, 1973; Richard Burghart, "The Formation of the Concept of Nation State in Nepal", Richard Burghart, *The Conditions of Listening,* Oxford University Press, Delhi, 1996.

2. See for these inter linkages, Kanchanmoy Majumdar, *Nepal and the Indian Nationalist Movement,* Firma K.L. Mukhopadhyay, Calcutta, 1975:21-45.
3. Kanchanmoy Majumdar, *Political Relations Between India and Nepal* 1877-1923, New Delhi, 1973 : 257; Anirudha Gupta, *Politics in Nepal : A Study of Post Rana Political Developments and Party Politics,* Allied Publications, Bombay, 1964:17.
4. See Rishikesh Shaha, *Modern Nepal, A Political History* 1769-1955, Vol.-II, Manohar, Delhi, 1990:126-130.
5. G.P. Bhattacharjee, *India and the Politics of Modern Nepal,* Minerva Associates, Bombay, 1970:22.
6. Satwanta Tiwari Chaube, *Democratic Movement in Nepal and the Indian Left,* Kalinga Publications, Delhi, 2001:47.
7. *N. 6:* 48.
8. *N. 6:* 49.
9. For details see, Kashi Prasad Shrivastava, *Nepal Ka Itihas,* Atmaram & Sons, Delhi, 1986.
10. H. Fukui (ed.) *Political Parties of Asia and the Pacific,* Vol. II, Greenwood Press, West post, 1985: 805-806.
11. Deepak Thapa & Bandita Sijapati, *A Kingdom Under Siege, Nepal's Maoist Insurgency, 1996 to 2003,* Printhouse, Kathmandu, 2003:21.
12. Surendra K.C., *Nepal Ma Communist Aandolan Ko Itihas* (History of Communist Movement in Nepal), Kathmandu, 1991.
13. See Bhim Rawal, *Nepal Ma Samyavadi Aandolan: Udbhav Ra Bikas,* Poiravi Prakashan, Kathmandu, 1990.
14. Bhuwan Lal Joshi & Leo E.Rose, *n.1.*, Anirudha Gupta, *n.3.*
15. H. Fukui, *n. 10:* 807.
16. Shankar Pokharel, *Maovadi Ugravampanth Ra Prajatantrik Nikas,* Kathmandu, 2058:8.
17. Shankar Pokharel, *n. 16:* 9-10.
18. Arjun Karki & David Seddon, "The People's War in Historical Context", in Arjun Karki & David Seddon, *The People's War in Nepal, Left Perspective*, Adroit Publishers, Delhi, 2003 : 11.

19. Deepak Thapa and Bandita Sijapati, *n. 11*; Deepak Thapa, "Erosion of the Nepali World", *Himal South Asia*, April, 2002.
20. Arjun Karki David Seddon, *n. 18*: 10.
21. Nickson R.Andrew, "Democratization and the Growth of Communism in Nepal: A Peruvian Scenario in the Making", *Journal of Commonwealth and Comparative Politics,* Vol. 30, No. 3, November, 1992: 371.
22. See, B.C.Upreti, *The Nepali Congress, An Analysis of the Party's Performance in the General Elections and its Aftermath*, Nirala Publishers, Delhi, 1993.
23. Panchanan Maharjan, "Role of the Extra-Parliamentary Political Party in Multi-Party Democracy: A Stud of the CPN Unity Centre", *Contribution to Nepalese Studies*, Vol. 20, No. 2, 1993.
24. Arjun Karki & David Seddon, *n. 18*: 16.

2
A Movement in The Making: Parties, Governance and Politics Between 1990-1995

There is a general understanding that the road to Maoist insurgency in Nepal began with the split in the United People's Front of Nepal (UPFN) and the consolidation of the extremist Maoist forces in the subsequent years both ideologically and organizationally. After a year, with the formation of the Communist Party of Nepal (Maoist) it was clear that the Maoists were heading on to the warpath. But it was only one dimension of the process leading towards the insurgency. What happened during the first five years of the democratic governance is equally important. In fact, the policies, working and performance of the Nepali Congress and the United Marxist-Leninist government afterwards also provided ample scope for the rise of a radical movement in Nepal. Therefore, the making of the Maoist rebellion can be understood in the context of the working of the democratic governments and the politics within the communist camp and the interaction between the two.

1990 Democratic Movement and the Communists

The 1990 democratic movement was a turning point in the political history of Nepal. It paved a yet fresh way for the initiation of democracy in the country. After a long gap of nearly 30 years the democratic forces got united to pose a serious challenge to the autocratic panchayat system. In fact, there had been a long history of distrust, disbelieve and mutual suspicion between the Nepali Congress and the communist parties. But it was towards the end of the eighties that both groups succeeded in bridging their differences and to work together to launch a movement for the establishment of democracy.[1] Not only the moderate communist parties but the radical communists also supported the movement for democracy. The people of Nepal were dissatisfied with the working of the panchayat system because of their ill performance and failure in delivering goods.[2] The centralization of power and continuation of the feudalistic orientation of the politics and the administration had dissatisfied various communities, regions and groups. As a result, various intellectual, professional and ethnic groups came forward to support the movement. Perhaps, there was a realization among the different political parties and the groups that it was not possible to fight against the authoritarian rulers individually. It required a joint and consolidated effort.

The political developments taking place in the South Asian region at this point of time were also encouraging to the democratic forces in Nepal. Some significant changes were in the offing in the domestic politics of Pakistan and Bangladesh, where the democratic forces were demanding for the restoration of democracy. In India also changes had taken place in the government, thereby bringing up a perceptional change among the political leadership in India towards the political developments taking place in Nepal. The 1988-89 impasse in India-Nepal relations and the resultant economic hardships experienced by the people in Nepal had considerably brought down the prestige of panchayat government. It was held responsible for the stalemate by the Nepali Congress and the other political parties. A number of Indian political leaders expressed their moral support to the democratic forces of Nepal. It was indeed highly encouraging to them. The Indian leaders like Chandra Shekhar participated in the convention of the Nepali Congress party and thus provided a moral boost to their efforts.[3]

Not only that the regional political developments were encouraging to democratic political forces in Nepal, but some of the developments at the international level also supported their efforts. In fact, the end of the decade of the eighties was marked by a strong worldwide wave in favour of democracy. The process of democratization in the eastern European countries, and the quest for democratization and the breakdown of Soviet Union and the emergence of democratic states in Central Asia were highly encouraging factors. It can be said that the 1990 democratic movement was a net result of the polarization of various political forces, the understanding that was developed among them in favour of launching a nation-wide movement for democracy and their efforts supported and encouraged by international and regional events.

Polarization of Left Parties

There were two main streams of polarization of the left political parties before and after the 1990 democratic movement. The moderate communist parties had formed a United Left Front (ULF) under the leadership of Sahana Pradhan. ULF agreed to form a joint front with the Nepali Congress to fight for the establishment of democracy in the country. It joined the interim government headed by the Nepali Congress. They were willing to contest general elections jointly with the Nepali Congress but the Nepali Congress did not agree to it and made it clear that the party would contest in the 1991 general elections independently. ULF realized that there was no more any possibility of polarization of the political forces in the form of a united force in the general elections.

Incidentally, ULF faced a split towards the end of 1990. In December 1990 four of the constituents of ULF, which had not been represented in the interim government namely, Nepal Workers and Peasants Party (Rohit), CPN (Amatya), CPN (Varma) and CPN (Fourth Convention) complained that their interests had been overlooked. They were not happy the way they were ignored in the coalition government. It is true that the coalition government had its own limitation, but these constituents of ULF were disappointed and decided to break out of the front. They suggested for a broad front of the leftist parties including those that were so far not a part of ULF.[4] They also pleaded for equal treatment to all the political parties. Perhaps, they thought that as part of ULF they were not given equal treatment. These political parties were also trying to justify their decision to break away from ULF.

In November 1990 the radical communist groups of Fourth Convention of Nirmal Lama and CPN (Mashal) merged together to form the Unity Centre (UC). There had already been a split in CPN (Masal) in March 1991. Actually Mohan Bikram Singh was not in favour of contesting the elections and had decided to boycott the elections. While Babu Ram Bhattarai and some other leaders were in favour of contesting in the general elections.

The beginning of the movement for the restoration of democracy in the Kingdom may be treated as 18 January 1990 National Convention of the Nepali Congress. It was the first convention of the Nepali Congress party in the last 10 years and it received a nation wide consideration. It was believed to be a powerful show by any political party for the first time in last many years.[5]

The Nepali Congress President K.P.Bhattarai said on this occasion:

"Today a new wave of democracy and freedom is sweeping the world. Despotic and dictatorial regimes have become islands in the ocean of the free world and their days are numbered. This is true of Nepal as well. Even senior leaders of panchayat system are now admitting publicly that the system has achieved nothing. The impact of the deadlock in Indo-Nepal relations has proved how hollow the claims of development made by the panchayat system are".

He further said that:

"The Nepali Congress remains committed to the goal of full democracy and human rights in Nepal. We have convened this conference to decide on the character and date of a nation-wide peaceful movement aimed at the liquidation of the present party less or one party system".[6]

The Nepali Congress convention posed a clear challenge to the panchayat government and also it indicated a determination of the democratic forces to launch a nation wide struggle for the establishment of democracy. The event was naturally disturbing to the panchayat government. The panchayat leaders also tried to demonstrate their strength. They organized public meetings, rallies and processions all over the country. On 18 January 1990, a mass rally was organized in Kathmandu. The government with its wide spread canvassing was expecting a huge turn out. But it had proved to be a failure as there was not much mass support to the rally.[7] The veteran panchayat leaders like Surya Bahadur Thapa and Rajeshwar Devkota did not attend the rally.[8] It clearly revealed that there were internal disputes in the panchayat leadership. The events clearly indicated that:

1. The democratic forces were in a process of consolidation and were preparing for a movement.
2. The panchayat leaders were aware of the situation and so they were trying to reconsolidate themselves.
3. It was becoming clear that the panchayat system was loosing mass support.

The democratic movement was formally commenced on 18 February 1990. The public demonstration, strikes and confrontation with the government officials took place in many parts of the country. The government tried to contain the movement by taking a number of measures. Censorship was imposed on the media. A large number of political leaders were locked up. The communists through their underground network tried to generate mass support for the movement. The atrocities of the panchayat government converted Nepal virtually into a police state. Despite the government suppression there was a steady increase in the intensity of the movement. The movement also became violent. A number of associations such as the Medical Association, the Bar Association, the Teachers Association, etc., joined the movement and it consequently became widespread.

There were certain turning points in the movement. The situation underwent a drastic change when movement started in Bhaktapur. Not only that it became intensive but it also took a violent turn. Bhaktapur indeed played a significant role in taking the democratic movement to new heights.[9] An agitation in the Tribhuwan University campus in Kathmandu was yet another turning point. In fact, it took the democratic movement to its climax.[10]

Interestingly, at a time when the democratic movement was spreading in and outside the Kathmandu valley, king Birendra was out of the capital city. He had camped at Pokhara and was busy in visiting different parts of western Nepal, as if he was not aware of what was happening in the country. He was surrounded by a close group of his associates. At a time when the government was in much need of his support and guidance the king left the government alone to take its own decision. It was indeed difficult for the Prime Minister to act efficiently in such a situation. It is believed that the Nepali Congress leader K.P. Bhattarai who was under house arrest had suggested the king that he could stop further spreading of the violence and the emerging anarchic situation by declaring a reform package while addressing panchayat rally at Pokhara on 16 March 1990.[11] But king did not utilize this opportunity to announce any reforms.

The movement reached to its climax between 1-9 April 1990.[12] The Foreign Affairs Minister of Nepal, S.K. Upadhyay resigned in protest against the repressive measures taken by the government. Meanwhile, the government employees, officials of the Royal Nepal Airlines and civil servants also began to support the movement. The panchayat system had already lost the popular sympathy. On 2 April, the cabinet was reshuffled.

On 6th April Lokendra Bahadur Chand was appointed as the Prime Minister of Nepal. It was decided to open a dialogue with the political parties. King said to the Prime Minister, "if the leaders of the Nepali Congress have clear ideas about political reforms, you should start a dialogue with them".[13] But no dialogues could be held between the government and the political parties because of the fast developments taking place within the panchayat system. Lokendra Bahadur Chand was forced to resign and Marich Man Shrestha was brought in as the Prime Minister. But again Lokendra Bahadur Chand replaced him. These sudden changes had proved to be demoralizing to the government.

On 7th April Tundikhal parade took place in Kathmandu. Curfew was imposed in the city. But people became unruly. The king broke his long silence and declared lifting of ban on the political parties on 8th April and dissolved the government. He said in an announcement.

"Respect for the ideals and values of democracy have always guided us in the conduct of the affairs of state. It was in this spirit that we held a referendum in 1980 to allow the people to choose the changes they wanted in the polity of the country. It is the government's duty also to maintain law and order. Regrettably, since the present council of ministers has not been able to do so, resulting in the loss of life and property, we have in consonance with the popular will and in accordance with the constitution of Nepal, dissolved the present council of ministers".[14]

On 16 April king announced dissolution of the National Panchayat, Panchayat Policy and Evaluation Committee and 6 Class Organizations.[15]

This brought an end to the democratic movement and also the panchayat system. But interestingly, it was the king who emerged as the main actor in the final show and not the joint front of the political parties. It is also interesting to note that the king labeled all blames for atrocities, failures and misconduct on the panchayat government and did not share any responsibility with the panchayat leaders. Ultimately, he took side with the people and in his own explaination was that he did what the people of Nepal actually wanted. The democratic forces accepted the outcome and for nothing king became the hero of the movement.

Working of the Coalition Government

After the abolition of the panchayat system the question of formation of an interim government came up, which would run the administration of the country till a popularly elected government could take its place. To let the panchayat government continue as an interim government was not feasible, as it had become very unpopular among the masses. Moreover, the political parties would not have accepted it for obvious reasons. At the same time king himself would not have been allowed to hold powers as an interim provision because that would have given rise to suspicions about the motives of the monarchy. Therefore, a coalition government of the Nepali Congress and various factions of the communists formed the government under the leadership of the Nepali Congress leader K.P.Bhattarai. The coalition government consisted of four ministers of the Nepali Congress, three of the United Left Front, two nominees of king, and two intellectuals.[16] It was decided that the ministry would be further expanded at some appropriate time in order to accommodate four constituents of the United Left Front who had so far not been given a place in the ministry.[17]

The coalition government had two major tasks to complete: to promulgate a new constitution for the country based on the principles of constitutional monarchy and hold elections. The coalition government came into power at a time when the country was facing a deep economic crisis, largely due to the impasse in Indo-Nepalese relations two years back. Therefore, its for most task was to provide economic relief to the people. Nevertheless, its political tasks were of primary importance as the future of democracy in the Kingdom depended on the successful completion of the above-mentioned two tasks. There can be no doubt that the Bhattarai government fulfilled its duties successfully. Despite many odds the coalition government remained in power almost for a year. It is surprising that the two ideologically opposite political parties could run the government till the end. In fact, the Nepali Congress as well as the communist factions were committed to the restoration of democracy in the Kingdom, and it was clear that the breaking of the coalition government would have disrupted the whole process. Also, an important factor was that both the Nepali Congress and the communists had contributed in the movement almost equally and both were aspiring to form the government individually after winning in the general elections. Hence, they did not want to be labeled as disrupter of the movement by not cooperating in the coalition government. Thus, the coalition of the Nepali Congress and UML worked not for positive reasons that much but in order to avoid the negative connotations related with the breaking the coalition. No doubt that the successfull working of the coalition government was a very difficult task which K.P.Bhattarai completed skillfully. The communists themselves were divided and there were seven factions of the communists in the United Left Front and it was not an easy task to keep them intact in the government.[18] However, the coalition government could not register any significant contribution in the field of socio-economic reconstruction and development. Thus, the immediate economic relief that the common people were aspiring from the Bhattarai Government remained unrealized.

1991 General Elections and the Communists

The second general elections held in May 1991 after a gap of 32 years. In fact, 1991 general elections were important in many respects and it was likely to be a trendsetter for the future course of democracy in the country.

Out of 40 political parties registered with the Election Commission 22 political parties filed nominations in the elections. The Nepali Congress was the only political party that had nominated candidates for all the 205 seats. UML the second largest political party had 177 candidates. The National Democratic Party (Thapa) and the National Democratic Party (Chand) had 163 and 154 candidates each. 219 independent candidates also fought in the elections. There were 1,11,42,638 voters in the 1991 general elections out of which nearly half were women voters.[19] The radical communists decided to participate in the elections by forming United People's Front of Nepal (UPFN). Babu Ram Bhattarai became its coordinator. UPFN had its own objective in participating in the elections. It wanted to use this opportunity to increase its base. The moderate communists were not happy with UPFN. Tulsi Lal Amatya commented thus; "These are those communists who only want to exploit the elections as part of their own strategy. These are not truly democratic. Our main aim must be to prove to the rest of the world that we are truly democratic and as communists we only intend to wield power through elections and maintain democracy after we come to power.

The political parties raised different issues and programmes in their manifestos. The Nepali Congress stressed on democratic socialism as its fundamental objective. The party also emphasized prosperity of people and the nation, human dignity, socio-economic parity, development of rural areas, decentralization, equal opportunities to people and world peace.

UML on the other hand, emphasized planned economic development and pledged its struggle against the economic disparities, exploitation and corruption. The party also talked of a balanced regional development, introduction of land reforms, protection of rights of poor farmers, and labourers. On the foreign policy issues it advocated equal relationship with India and China, revocation of all treaties and agreements signed by previous governments that were unequal, disadvantageous and derogatory to Nepal. National Democratic Party (Thapa) pledged its support to the constitutional monarchy and multi-party system. The party had projected itself as an alternative democratic party that had to play a leading role in the politics of Nepal.[20] The National Democratic Party (Chand) on the other hand, entered the election fray with the slogan that 'Let us save the nation, reconstruct it and safeguard democracy.[21] The party supported constitutional monarchy, mixed economy free education to all up to the secondary standard, heavy industries and close relations with the two neighbours. The Communist Party of Nepal (Amatya) called for the initiation of popular democracy, heavy industrialization, special treatment to labourers, depressed castes and tribal people. It supported equal relationship with India and China.

The Dalit Mazdoor Kisan Party affirmed its commitment to the creation of an egalitarian society based on democracy, secularism and socialism.[22] The Janata Dal (Socialist – Democratic) emphasized up on the struggle for the creation of a socialist democracy.[23] The Rashtriya Janata Dal (H) gave the slogan of 'removal of poverty.[24] The Nepal Rashtriya Jana Mukti Morcha called for democratic socialism and local autonomy.

The Nepal Sadbhavana Party being a representative of the people of Tarai concentrated on the problem of the Tarai region. The party strongly reacted to the discrimination against the people of Tarai.[25] It demanded proper representation of Tarai in the politico– administrative structures of the country, inclusion of Hindi as an official language and abolition of discriminatory policies based on language, region and ethnicity.

There were certain common issues that came up in the manifestos of most of the political parties. The socialist path of development was supported by most of the parties. Similarly, constitutional monarchy, multi party democracy, mixed economy, etc., were highlighted in the manifestos of most of the political parties. The issues relating to political stability and good governance, development of natural resources, national security, etc. were not given importance in the manifestos of different political parties.

The election campaign of different political parties was marked by intra-party and inter-party differences and rivalries.[26] It had aroused more emphasis on personal attacks and abuses than concentrating on the national issues. None of the political parties agreed to any kind of electoral alliance. Their election strategies and campaigning clearly reflected at the lack of electoral experience and the lack of a powerful leadership. The major political parties were more interested in raising issues relating to relations with India, while these issues was not that much important for the elections.[27]

The total voting turnout in the 1991 general elections was 65.15 per cent. The voting percentage was higher in the Kathmandu Valley (75%) and in some parts of the Tarai region. Only 4.4 per cent votes were invalid, which was not a big number keeping in view the low literacy rate and poor voting experience of the people of Nepal.

The Nepali Congress with 110 seats emerged as the winning party though with a razor thin majority. It secured 39.50 per cent of the total valid votes UML emerged as the main opposition party with 69 seats and it got 29.27 per cent of the valid votes. The other parties which got an entry to the lower house of the parliament were the National Democratic Party (Chand), 03, the National Democratic Party (Thapa) 01, the Joint People's Front 09, the Nepal Sadbhavana Party 06, the Communist Party of Nepal (Democratic) 02, the Nepal Workers and Peasants Party 02, and independents 03. The Joint People's Front representing the hardcore communists emerged as the third major political force in the parliament. The Nepali Congress formed government under the leadership of G.P.Koirala.

Problems Before the Government

There were a number of problems, which created hurdles for the smooth functioning of the government. Actually certain problems were bound to creep up. Since popular aspirations had remained suppressed for a long time, with the establishment of democratic government there was an ever-increasing expression of these latent expectations. The left forces tried to raise these issues and take the NC government to task. UC was quite active in this direction. As a result, relations between the radical leftists and NC deteriorated day by day.

Law and Order Situation

The G.P.Koirala government was confronted with the deterioration of law and order all over the country. During the first six months of the Koirala government there was widespread violation of law and order in different parts of the country.[28] A large number of terrorist activities were also reported. There were vested political interests too. Those parties that had not been able to win the elections they wanted to create political instability and chaos. The non-availability of essential commodities and deepening economic crisis had agitated the masses.

Unrest Among Civil Servants

The Nepali Congress government also had to face opposition from the civil servants. In fact, they were aspiring for certain announcements as a reward to them by the new government.[29] Immediately after the installation of the new government they gave a call for an indefinite strike. The opposition particularly the Communists, who wanted to provide a political colour to the agitation, encouraged them. However, the 55 day long agitation of the civil servants came to an end unconditionally in September 1991.[30] The strikes had ended without any success but it also laid seeds of distrust between the radicals and the government.

Problems at the Economic Front

There was a need for immediate economic relief to the people, particularly to control the ever-increasing prices of essential commodities and to make them available. It should be remembered here that the stalemate in Indo-Nepalese relations had given a serious jolt to the Nepalese economy. But there were may other problems as well. The Nepali Congress had advocated a policy of democratic socialism but there were no signs of socialist orientation of the government. There were gaps between party's objectives they and government's strategy. The Nepali Congress government, by and large, followed neo-liberal economic policies generally advocated by WB, MF, etc.[31] It made the government unpopular and leftists tried to take advantage of this situation.

It may be pointed out here that certain social and economic conditions were essential for the promotion of democracy in the long run. And it may also be noted that Nepal was yet to acquire these basic requirements. It is true that the economic and social situation had undergone substantial changes in comparison to the early fifties and sixties. Nepal had been able to build a viable economic infrastructure. Yet, certain issues were still unsolved. Nepal's economy was at a low stage of development. Nearly 60 per cent of Nepal's population was living below the poverty line. The consumer price index had increased by 9.1 per cent during 1991-92 in comparison to 3.3 in 1990-91.[32] Nearly 40 per cent people were unemployed or under-employed.[33] The dual ownership of land was the main problem before the peasant and there were vested interests trying to preserve and perpetuate this system. The radical leftists were demanding to protect the interests of the small farmers and the land less labourers. Nepal's per capita income had been $ 170.[34] The growth rate had been around 3.5 per ccnt, and during 1991-92 it was 3 per cent[35] while the population growth rate had been 2.7 per cent.[36] According to the World Development Report 1991 Nepal was the second poorest country of the world. Nearly 70 per cent of the population was living without social services and basic amenities. These problems required comprehensive long-term development planning as well as its careful implementation. But the government hardly had any opportunity to look into these matters. There were serious differences between the Communists and the Nepali Congress on issues like relationship with India, the concept of common rivers, the status of monarchy, parliamentary system, etc. Although the parliamentary system was acceptable to most of the communist factions and they believed that class struggle was possible through parliamentary system[37], a few of them like the United People's Front and the Mashal group talked in terms of

'*Naulo Janabad*'.[38] The Communists had also held the Nepali Congress responsible for its leaning towards India and had raised the bogey of Indian expansionism. Some Communist groups had also given a call for joint movement against the government.[39] They had organized demonstrations and processions in Kathmandu on July 27, 1991. In February 1992 UC and CPN (Masal) launched a protest against the government. A Joint People's Agitation Committee was also constituted.[40] Thus there was lot of discontent among the radical communists against the policies and working of the government.

14 Point Demand Charter

The Unity Centre, which was not happy with the working of the Congress government, submitted a 14-point demand charter to the Prime Minister on 5 March 1992. These demands included providing relief to the common men by controlling price rise, ensuring availability of goods of daily necessity and checking corruption, black marketing and smuggling. It was demanded to streamline the administration without any prejudices and favours. It was demanded to abrogate all the unequal treaties and agreements concluded with the other countries. The radical Communists also demanded to eliminate injustice, exploitation and discrimination against farmers, employees, dalits, and women, ethnic and regional groups. It demanded action against the corrupt people of the Panchayat regime and to unfold any conspiracy between the king and the reactionary forces.

The demand charter was indeed an expression of the issues on which the Maoists would concentrate in launching a struggle against the government and the system as a whole. They had, in fact, raised such issues, which were becoming trouble some for the government of the day and the government was not in a position to find out, any way primarily during to its own internal difficulties and complexities.

1992 Local Bodies Elections and the Communists

UPFN participated in the local bodies elections held in May 1992. It contested in the elections with 5 other communist parties namely, CPN Masal (Mohan Bikram Singh), NWKP (Rohit), CPN

15 September 1949, CPN (Marxist) and Nepal Communist League. UPFN and the other left parties wanted to enter into a seat sharing agreement with UML but it could not be worked out due to their differences on many issues. However, adjustments were made in some areas. It was clear that there were no possibilities of a broad based understanding between the moderate and the radical left parties. So the possibilities of a left unity ended.

The Nepali Congress acquired top position in the local bodies' elections. The Nepali Congress candidate was elected as Mayor in 22 out of 36 municipalities and Deputy Mayor in 21 municipalities. The party also won 55.8 per cent seats in the Municipal councils and 50 per cent seats in Village Development Commitees. The UML Mayor won in 6 out of 36 Municipality. The party won 20 per cent seats in Municipal Councils and 26 per cent seats in the Village Development Committees.

UPFN could secure only one seat of Deputy Mayor. In Municipal Councils it won in 1.34 per cent seats and 5 per cent seats in the Village Development Committees. In Kathmandu UPFN candidate for Mayor secured only 3.4 per cent votes compared to 52.20 per cent votes to the Nepali Congress and 44.4 per cent votes to UML.

It shows that UPFN performed quite poor in the local bodies elections. It was also clear that the moderate communists like UML had a much better position in comparison to the radicals. In fact, UML was successful in establishing its credentials as a liberal-democratic communist party. It also indicated for to the radical political parties that perhaps it was not possible to realize their political objectives through the constitutional – democratic process. They realized that it was not easy to reach to the masses through constitutional – political bodies.

The radical parties had given an impression since the beginning of the success of the 1990 democratic movement that they believed in the establishment of a 'New Democracy' in the country. They had denounced the way multi party democracy was announced in 1990 and the constitution. UC was also talking in terms of launching a protracted war ever since 1991. In these circumstances it was hardly possible for the radical communists to enjoy any meaningful gain in the democratic institutions.

On April 6 1992 UC and the other radical groups of the communists called for organizing a protest against the government. It lead to violence and clashes between police and the agitators. It is believed that 13 persons were killed in the incidents of violence that took place in Kathmandu and Dhangadi. The left parties demanded resignation of the government. These incidents clearly indicated that the UC and other radical parties were all set for an agitation politics against the government.[41]

Apart from several domestic issues, protest campaigns were launched against the government on international issues, like river water resources sharing with India, 1950 peace treaty, etc. They alleged that the NC government was having a leaning towards India.

1994 Mid Term Elections

The 1991 general elections paved way for a weak government and a strong opposition. But more than the weak position of the government, the intra-party disputes of the Nepali Congress and the leadership conflicts soon came to the surface, making it almost impossible for the government to run the administration. The Nepali Congress party was sharply divided along organizational and government lines represented by K.P. Bhattarai the party President and G.P. Koirala the Prime Minister. UML took advantage of the NC factional politics and joined hands with the dissatisfied group of the Nepali Congress, which was prepared to the extent of going against its own party's government.

It became almost impossible for Prime Minister G.P. Koirala to run the government due to the opposition by its own party members. On 10 July 1994, Koirala resigned and recommended dissolution of the parliament. The king dissolved the parliament and mid term elections were declared for 13 November 1994. It aroused lot of controversy. The anti – Koirala group of NC did not like Koirala's action, while Koirala pointed out that if the Prime Minister were to be removed from the office on the personal wishes of an individual a stable government was not possible. A faction of the Nepali Congress demanded action by the party against the Prime Minister.[42] It was suggested that the Nepali Congress and UML should jointly boycott the mid-term polls.[43]

UML appreciated Koirala's resignation but did not favour dissolution of the lower house. The other communist parties also viewed king's action unparliamentary and undemocratic.[44] However, the two National Democratic Parties and the Nepal Sadbhavana Party welcomed the decision of the monarchy.

Thus the political parties were divided on the issue of holding early polls. However, the events leading to the mid – term polls were indicative of certain emerging trends of Nepali politics:

1. It became clear that the task of political stability and continuity was difficult in Nepal due to intra-party conflicts.
2. It was also evident that the socio-political conditions were not yet much supportive to the process of institutionalization of democracy in the country.

Before the elections there was a split in UPFN. The Unity Centre also divided into two groups consequently. Actually the issue of conflict was party's participation in the 1994 mid-term elections. In 1991 Babu Ram Bhattarai was in favour of contesting the elections while Mohan Bikram Singh opposed it. This time Babu Ram Bhattarai and Pushp Kamal Dahal were not in favour of participating in the elections but Mohan Bikram Singh and Niranjan Govind Vaidya did not accept it. As a result they separated from the party. The election commission recognized the Vaidya faction in place of Babu Ram Bhattarai. Vaidya group contested on 49 seats including 5 of the 9 seats won by UPFN in the 1991 elections.

Mohan Bikram Singh preferred to remain underground but his party CPN (Masal) decided to support some of the independent candidates. CPN (Mashal) did not register itself with the election commission. The party entered into an alliance with the Nepal Janbadi Morcha of Ram Raja Prasad Singh, a former leader of the Nepali Congress who had assumed responsibility for the 1985 bomb episode. The different political parties emphasized upon their future plans and policies in the manifestos issued by them. The Nepali Congress again emphasized upon the policy of democratic socialism and pleaded that the basis of democratic socialism was socio-economic justice. It was possible to fight against hunger, poverty, disease illiteracy, injustice and exploitation by adopting democratic socialism.[45] The party emphasized that there was a need to increase the production and the employment opportunities. The party supported liberalization and privatization. The party also emphasized upon safe drinking water facilities, abolition of dual ownership of land, promotion of Nepal's image as a peaceful and democratic country and peaceful relationship with all countries on the bais of mutual cooperation and equality.

UML party assured that it would provide a clean, healthy and efficient administration. The other aspects that were emphasized by the party in its manifesto were: promotion and protection of the multi – party democracy, eradication of irregularities and corruption, proper utilization of revenues and foreign assistance, reduction of foreign debt, steps towards laying foundation of an independent economy, increase in agriculture production, securing forest resources, socio-economic equality, planned development, land reforms and reorganization of agriculture sector, poverty alleviation through increased avenues of employment in the agriculture sector and friendly relations with all the countries on the basis of non-alignment and principles of panchsheel.[46]

The Communist Party of Nepal (Marxist) reiterated its commitment to nationalism and rights of the people. The party called for the abrogation of all international treaties. It also emphasized upon converting Guthi land into Raikar land, land to land less farmers and minimum wages to farmers and labourers.

The National Democratic Party pledged its commitment to nationalism, democracy and the constitution. The party also laid its commitment to land reforms, reconstruction of rural economy, population control, etc.

The Nepal Mazdoor and Kishan Party criticized the use of money in elections. It called for a struggle against price rise and improving the conditions of workers and peasants. The party viewed elections as a class struggle and that her efforts would be to raise workers and peasants to the status of ruling class.[47]

Nepal Sadbhavana Party pledged its support to the constitutional monarchy, federal system, religious freedom, constitutional rights and duties. It demanded that 50 per cent places be reserved for Tarai and 30 per cent for hills.[48]

It is clear from an overview of the manifestos and electoral declarations of the major political parties that there were a number of common issues. For instance, the constitutional monarchy, multi-party democracy, rural reconstruction, restructuring land system, etc., were raised by most of the political parties. In the 1994 general elections there was an added focus on the socio-economic issues, particularly the problems relating to socio-economic transformations. However, in the electoral campaign and meetings the political leaders concentrated more on attacking the leaders of the rival parties.

It is interesting to note that out of 24 political parties 19 parties failed in securing a single seat in the house of representative. The total votes polled in the 1994 elections were 62 per cent. Thus the percentage of voting had lowered down in comparison to 1991 elections. The outcome of the mid term polls was not at all encouraging as none of the political parties could secure a majority. There was a close contest between UML and Nepali Congress. However, UML became the largest party in the House of Representatives with 88 seats, followed by Nepali Congress with 83 seats. UML secured 42.93 per cent votes and Nepali Congress 40.49 percent. The position of other parties was National Democratic Party 20, Nepal Peasants and Workers party 4, Nepal Sadbhavana Party 3 and independents 7. There was a marginal increase in the member of independent candidates. The National Democratic Party also emerged as gainer as it had a benefit of 16 seats over the previous position. There can be no doubt that the Nepali Congress had to pay for its infighting and leadership clashes. It had a loss of 27 seats over the 1991 elections.

The UML Government

CPN (UML) constituted a minority government on 29 November 1994 under the leadership of Man Mohan Adhikari. It was for the first time that communists came to power in Nepal. However, it should be made clear that UML had an image of a moderate communist party. While UPFN had an image of a party representing the radical communists. UML had already accepted the constitutional monarchy and had been closely associated with the democratic process-taking place in the country after 1990.

UML as an opposition party did face an embarrassing situation when the radical communists decided to launch struggle against the Nepali Congress government. The dilemma was that UML wanted to disassociate itself from the extremist forces so as to maintain its image as a party having faith in the democratic process. But it also did not want to disassociate itself from the communist movement. The party though condemned any hard government actions but did not join the radical communists in agitation politics. So it is clear that UML was conscious about its image as a party abided by constitutional and political norms and practices instead of cooperating with the radical groups. The party was careful about its political carrier. So the point is that UNL represented the moderate communists only and it was clear that the party would not be accommodating the issues and demands raised by the radical communist groups. Initially it was being expected that UML government would bring up some drastic changes in the sphere of Nepal's domestic politics and international affairs. But UML government afterwards took no such policy measures.

In fact, the government was not in a position to take any new economic policies that would satisfy the radical communists. UML government so as to satisfy the common men introduced some consumer subsidies. It constituted a commission to suggest for land reforms. A 'Build Your Village Yourself' scheme was also launched in which RS. 300000 were distributed to each of the 400 village Development Councils. UML followed a policy of patronizing its followers in government and various professional jobs. Large-scale replacement was done in the administration. The party activists were appointed in various positions in the government.

On the whole UML government could not take any such policy initiatives that would have made it different from the earlier government. It did not allow the Nepali Congress government's plan regarding privatization to move further. But could not produce any alternative development strategies. There were several problems. It was a minority government. So there were problems in getting its polices and plans passed through the parliament. Like the Nepali Congress party UML too was faced with internal dissensions and fluids. There were dissatisfied groups lead by leaders like Bam Deo Gautam, C.P. Mainali, etc. The government was also faced with the charges of corruption. It had also to face strong opposition from Nepali Congress and the other political parties.

In June 1995 Man Mohan Adhikari resigned and recommended for the dissolution of the parliament. In August 1995 the Supreme Court declared dissolution of parliament unconstitutional. The parliament was reinstated and the Nepali Congress formed a new government on 11 September 1995 under the leadership of Sher Bahadur Deuba. The working of UML government further made the radical communists apathetic towards the ongoing democratic process in Nepal.

Drive Against Maoists

In September 1995 the Nepali Congress again formed its government under the leadership of Sher Bahadur Deuba. By this time two things were quite apparent: It was clear that the radicals had disassociated themselves from the parliamentary democratic process. The Unity Centre had gone underground after the 1994 mid term elections. They were busy in expanding their support base in the rural areas particularly in the mid Western hills and also making preparations to launch a struggle against the Nepali state. It was also clear that the government and the radical communists had Conflict relationship during the first term of the Nepali Congress government.

The Nepali Congress government began to take tough actions against the activities of the Unity Centre. Police actions were taken in the areas particularly where UC leaders were active. It seems that the government was of the opinion that these extreme leftist groups were scattered and it was possible to crush them by force. But at the same time the government was also apprehensive of their hidden motives. So government did not trust them and wanted to see that their position was not strengthened.

Operation Romeo

In November 1995 the government launched a campaign to

control the activities of radical Communist groups and take into task those who were involved in it. The campaign based on the policy of strong police actions and arrests was named as Operations Romeo. The Operation Romeo focused on the activities of the Unity Centre in the rural areas of mid-western Nepal. Babu Ram Bhattarai in an interview to a Nepali weekly news paper, Independent explained that "under this armed police operation around 1500 policemen including a special trained commando force sent from Kathmandu have been deployed to let loose a reign of terror against the poor peasants of that rugged mountain district (Rolpa) in Western Nepal. So far about 1000 are kept in police custody or sent to jails under fictitious charges while the rest have been released on bail after severe torture." The government's attitude towards the radical communists made it certain that there were no possibilities of any peaceful compromises between the two.

Birth of CPN (Maoists)

The developments taking place in the radical left camp took a final shape in the form of the birth of the Communist Party of Nepal (Maoists). The party was formed after a discussion between Babu Ram Bhattarai and Pushpa Kamal Dahal. It is still not clear when exactly the party was formed. There are different opinions about it. But it seems that the party was formed some times towards the end of 1994 and it was formally announced in the Third plenum in March 2005.

The party declared its goal to establish a new democracy in the country and its strategy as protracted war. It believed in the ideology of Marx-Lenin and Mao. The party viewed Nepali Congress Party as its main enemy. But it also leveled UML as a revisionist party that was protecting the cause of monarchy and other feudal elements. The radical communists also termed CPN (Masal) as a rightist and new revisionist party. The party began to prepare for launching a movement in the country soon after its formation.

The CPN (Maoist) initiated a programme to propagate its ideas among the people, as a part of its objective to launch a movement. The programme was named as 'Sija Campaign' –

after Sisne and Jaljala two significant mountains in Rukum and Rolpa of mid-Western region. It may be pointed here that the radical communists now termed to be as Maoists had already selected this area as its main base.

Summing Up

The post-1990 political process and the prevailing socio-economic conditions in Nepal were important in the rise of the Maoist movement. The Maoists as a political strategist tried to in-cash the conditions in order to move further for the attainment of their political objectives.

It can be said that the political uncertainties that prevailed in the country in the years immediately following the establishment of democracy, created conditions for the rise of the Maoist movement. The outcome of the first general elections (May 1991) was rather disappointing as the Nepali Congress, the largest party, recorded only a razor thin majority and formed a weak government. It was not very late that the conflict of leadership and contest for power began to take place within the Nepali Congress and between the different political parties. The intra-party conflicts became so prominent that Prime Minister G.P.Koirala had to resign and to declare the mid-term polls in 1994.

Again, the performance of the political parties was more disappointing in the mid-term polls as none could secure the majority. UML formed a minority government. The first communist government also failed due to inter and intra-party cleavages and survived till mind 1995 only. The Nepali Congress again came to power in September 1995, with its second rank leadership Sher Bahadur Deuba at the helm of affairs. But the party fluids continued. It was indeed the beginning of weak coalition and insatiable governments in Nepal. None of the incumbent governments could retain power even for a year.

The negligence on the part of the subsequent governments and the political parties on many counts generated widespread dissatisfaction. The formation and reformation of the governments proved to be a drama of power sharing and power grabbing. The functioning of the governments was marked by widespread corruption, favoritism and nepotism. On the other hand, the government took strong action against the hardcore communists in many areas of western region, where they were active and had strong hold in the rural areas. In Rukum and Rolpa the government launched the Operation Romeo against the Maoists. Such type of actions by the government indicated that it wanted to suppress the hardcore communist activists. It indeed gave an adverse message and the Maoists lost their faith on the government.

It was obvious that the government failed in addressing itself to the developmental issues. Nepal was characterized as one of the poorest countries in the 1989 World Bank Report. Out of 120 countries it ranked 115. Nepal's per capita income was US $ 220. The UNDP Human Development Report 2001 stated that 38 per cent of Nepal's popuiation was extremely poor and was not in a position to meet its basic requirements. There was uneven distribution of income and wealth. The democratic government instead of going for the distributive justice strengthened these trends. There were sharp hill vis-à-vis Tarai, urban vis-à-vis rural and caste divides in the distribution of land and economic benefits. There was an over concentration of resources and wealth. Many regions were neglected in the distribution of resources and the development programmes. This was the reason why the Maoists concentrated in these regions to cultivate them for a movement. It can be said that there were sufficient socio-economic and political reasons for giving way to an insurgency in the country.

References

1. Martin Hoften, et.al., *People, Politics and Ideology, Democracy and Social Change in Nepal,* Mandala Book Point, Kathmandu, 1999 : 115.
2. B.C.Upreti, *Nepal, Democracy at Cross Roads,* Kanishka, Delhi, 2007: 23-25.
3. B.C.Upreti, *The Nepali Congress, An Analysis of the Party's Performance in General Elections and Aftermath,* Nirala, Delhi, 1993 : 18-25.
4. Martin Hoften, et.al., *n.1* : 173.
5. Martin Hoften, "The Dynamics and Chronology of 1990 Movement" in Michael Hutt (ed.), *Nepal in Nineties,* Oxford University Press, Delhi, 1994: 17.

6. *Rashtra Pukar* (Kathmanu), January 18, 1990, *Nepal Press Digest,* (Kathmandu), Vol. 34, no.4, January 22, 1990.
7. *Dristi* (Kathmandu), January 29, 1990.
8. Martin Hoften, *n. 5* : 17.
9. Dharendra Purush Dhakal, *Jan Andolan* (Nepali), Kathmandu, 1990.
10. T.Louise Brown, *The Challenge to Democracy in Nepal: A Political History,* Routledge, London, 1996: 122.
11. Rishikesh Shaha, *Politics in Nepal 1980-90,* Manohar, Delhi, 1990.
12. Martin Hoften, et.al., *n.1* : 128.
13. Ogura Kiyoko, *Kathmandu Spring: The People's Movement of 1990,* Himal Books, Kathmandu, 2001: 159.
14. *Gorkhapatra* (Kathmandu), April 7, 1990.
15. Ogura Kiyoko, *n.13:* 153.
16. *The Patriot* (New Delhi), March, 1991.
17. These were CPN (Amatya), CPN (Verma), CPN (Fourth Convention) and Nepal Peasants and Workers Party.
18. The CPN (Manandhar) was also involved in the formation of UML but it later decided to retain its independent identity.
19. B.C.Upreti, *n.3*: 98.
20. *Nepali Patra*, March 15, 1991.
21. *Gorkhapatra*, March 26, 1991.
22. *Gorkhapatra,* April 4, 1991.
23. *Gorkhapatra,* April 3, 1991.
24. *Gorkhapatra,* April 5, 1991.
25. B.C.Upreti, *n. 2.*
26. B.C.Upreti, *n. 3:* 61-62.
27. R.C.Mathur, "India Factor to the Fore in Nepal", *The Hindustan Times,* May 12, 1991; S.D.Muni, "India Factor in Nepal's Election", *The Times of India,* May 6, 1991.
28. Surya Bahadur Thapa, "Nepal; Threats to Democracy", *The Hindustan Times,* June 19, 1991.
29. Ram Pradhan, "The Troubled Nepal Government", *The Indian Express,* June 17, 1991.
30. *The Hindustan Times,* November 10, 1991.
31. Louise T.Brown, *n. 10*: 178.
32. *Gorkhapatra*, January 17, 1992.
33. *Nepal Press Digest*, Vol.35, no.25, April 26, 1991.
34. *n.33.*
35. *n.32.*

36. For details see, Narayan Khadka, *Foreign Aid, Poverty and Stagnation in Nepal,* New Delhi: 1991.
37. *Nepal Press Digest,* Vol.35, no.22, June 3, 1991.
38. R.C.Mathur, "Challenge Before Koirala", *The Hindustan Times,* June 18, 1991.
39. *The Rising Nepal,* January 5, 1992.
40. Martin Hoften, et.al., *n.1* : 189.
41. See for the incidents, Martin Hoften, et.al., *n.1* : 189-191.
42. *Rashtra Pukar*, July 13, 1994.
43. *Kantipur,* (Nepali) July 15, 1994.
44. *The Nepal Post,* July 15, 1994.
45. *The Rising Nepal,* October 6, 1994.
46. *Gorkhapatra,* October 6, 1994 & October 18, 1994.
47. *The Rising Nepal,* October 25, 1994.
48. *Gorkhapatra,* October 11, 1994.

3
Maoist Ideology, Organisation and Strategies

Two issues are important in the context of the Maoist insurgency in Nepal. After the 1991 political change when radical communist parties started agitation politics and began to talk in terms of launching a protracted war in the country with an objective to establish a new democracy, they were treated as a law and order problem. With this perception they were not taken much seriously and were dealt with by the use of police force. Secondly, when CPN (Maoist) declared people's war in 1996 they were again perceived as a splinter group of the rebel communists who could at best create some trouble in the remote areas of the country.

But as the Maoist movement went further it became clear that they had a solid ideological background, strong organizational and support structures and well drawn and long term strategies. The fact that the Maoists continued with a violent movement for a decade and fought against the state army are sufficient enough to suggest that in the course of time it grew into a well thought of and an organized movement.

It naturally calls for an in-depth understanding of the ideological orientation, structural bases and strategies followed by the Maoists.

Maoist Ideology

The role of ideology is important in the context of political organizations and institutions. It reflects upon the objectives, orientation and plans of a political organization. Ideology is particularly important in the context of political parties because the soundness of a political party depends on its ideological base. In fact, various political parties can be differentiated on the basis of ideology.

Ideology refers to the patterns of belief that attain some degree of coherence as ideas and establish certain priorities and principles of rule. It is a set of values.[1] A specific ideology may belong to a particular group or a political elite. In democracy there exists competing political parties and groups having different ideologies. Each group intends to popularize its own ideology.[2] It is the ideology which popularizes a political group among the masses and thus generate a support base for that political group.

Ideology helps in developing a sense of cohesion. It also reflects upon the present perceptions and objectives for the future.[3] There is a closer relationship between ideology and political activities. In fact, ideology determines political activities of the political organizations.[4] The attitude and the perception towards the ruler, ruled, governance, etc are determined by ideology.[5] It is in this context, that one may state that ideology is important for the political parties. In fact, it is through ideology that the aims and the actions of a political party are surfaced. There is a closer relationship between ideology and politics.[6]

The Maoists followed the ideology of Karl Marx, Lenin and Mao. Generally all the communist parties follow the ideas of these three supreme Marxist thinkers and activists. Than one may raise this question as how does the CPN (Maoist) differ from others? Three broad aspects of differentiation come to our mind in this regard;

I. The Maoist tried to combine the ideology of all the three – Marx – Lenin and Mao - with an added emphasis on the ideas of Mao.

II. The Maoists not only propagated the theoretical postulates of Marxism but they also set out clear-cut goals and formulated an action plan in order to attain these goals. Thus the Maoists believed in actualizing the ideas of Marxism.

III. Maoists also tried to provide a local context to the Marxist ideology by ensuring applicability of the Marxist ideology in a particular context. In this way they tried to make their own contribution to Marxism. Whether Prachandapath was an ideology or a strategy is a debatable issue, which we shall try to investigate later on. But the point is that the Maoists of Nepal gave a loud thinking to the suitability of the Marxist ideas in a particular context so that its relevance could be ensured more authentically.

The Maoists of Nepal were highly influenced by the ideas of Karl Marx on dialectical materialism, materialistic interpretation of history and class struggle. Karl Marx believed that the class struggle was the driving force of history. He viewed capitalism as a system plagued by greed and avarice. He viewed capitalism as the most critical stage relating to the issue of social revolution. Kar Marx said that.." At a certain stage of their development that material productive forces of society come into contradiction with the existing productive relationships, or, what is but a legal expression for these, with the property relationships within which they have moved before. From forms of development of the productive forces their relationships are transformed in to their fetters. Then an epoch of social revolution is open. With the change in the economic foundation the whole vast superstructure is more or less rapidly transformed.[7] Marx conceded the possibility of peaceful evolution of bourgeois democracy into a proletarian democracy in some of the countries of west like US, U.K, etc.

Lenin accepted the view of Karl Marx that the transitional state between capitalism and communism can be only the revolutionary dictatorship of the proletariat. But he believed that democracy and capitalism were not compatible. Democracy in a capitalist society meant rule of a small rich class.[8] Lenin emphasized the revolutionary element in Marxism. He believed that it was possible to defeat the capitalist and the imperialist forces through a strong organization of the communist party. Lenin was a strategist and he show success to communist revolution in Russia. Lenin did not agree to karl Marx's idea of peaceful evolution of proletarian democracy. He instead believed that it was only through a strong revolution that proletarian democracy could be established.

The Nepalese Maoists had been highly influenced by the ideas of Mao-tse- Tung. They found Mao's ideas more suitable to the Nepali conditions. Maoism represented a variation of Marxism and Leninism that neither Marx nor Lenin could have fore seen. The Nepali Maoists were highly influenced by Mao's views on protracted war, new democracy, support of masses, permanency of revolution and the great proletarian cultural revolution.[9] Mao believed that the masses must be directly involved in the continuing process of revolution. Mao argued that the peasantry could be the most trusted segment of the society to fight against capitalist, imperialist and reactionary forces. Hence, countryside was most suitable to start a protracted guerrilla war. His strategy was to strike from rural areas and encircle the cities. Mao had very clearly said that none would give you power. Power has to be snatched. His famous saying was that power comes from the barrel of a gun. A strong party, an army and a united front were essential for launching a protracted guerrilla war. Mao said that violence and terrorism were the permanent features of political life. The people's war follows a long and widening road and on this road it encounters triumph and failure. In the end the people will triumph. He said that one has to fight and fail and fight again until you get the success at the end.

Mao also believed that even after the establishment of the dictatorship of the proletariat it was possible that reactionary elements would again try to surface by taking the advantage of the existing circumstances. Therefore, there was a need to eliminate such reactionary elements. For this purpose Mao declared great Cultural Revolution in China in the second half of 1960's.

The Communist Party of Nepal (Maoist) believed that the fundamental ideological postulates of Mao were suitable to the Nepali situation.[10] So they tried to follow the Maoist ideology in the form of their role model.

Agenda of the Maoist Movement

The Communist Party of Nepal (Maoist) gave sufficient thought to the main agenda of their movement. On the basis of their ideological notions they adopted the following agenda.

A - New Democracy

The Nepali Maoists drew the concept of new democracy (Naulo Janbad) from Chairman Mao. The establishment of new democracy was the ultimate goal of the Maoist revolution. But as an interim arrangement democratic republic of Nepal could be acceptable. Mao said that March along the path of people's war to smash the reactionary state, capture state power and establish new democracy. This was proletarian democracy that would come into existence after the destruction of feudalism and imperialism.[11]

The new democracy was much talked about by the prominent communist ideologues of Nepal during the early 1990's Madan Bhandari (UML) supported the concept of new democracy.[12] UML was of the view that they were supporting the multi party democracy in the country as they consider it a step towards new democracy. The party, however, differed on the question as to how to achieve this goal? It adopted the path of the multiparty democracy. The radical communists did not agree to this approach. They argued that the parliamentary democracy cannot fulfill the popular needs and aspirations. The new democracy was possible only by eliminating the feudal and the imperialist elements.

B - Restructuring the State

The restructuring of the Nepali state was viewed as an essential step towards the establishment of new democracy. The restructuring of state incorporated three aspects:

1. The Maoists strongly advocated for the withdrawal of political powers of monarchy and neutralizing him politically. They argued that monarchy represented feudalism and it was largely responsible for the failure of democracy in the country. Monarchy belonged to the class of oppressors. So the abolition of monarchy would be a major step towards establishment of the new democracy.
2. In place of the constitutional monarchy Maoists demanded to declare Nepal a republican state. They believed that the free and fair competitive democratic

politics could entre into Nepal only within a republican form of governance.

The second important aspect of the restructuring of the Nepali state was to declare Nepal a secular state. Nepal was declared a Hindu state ever since its foundation as a unified kingdom by the Shah rulers. This feature of the Nepali state continued even within the democratic form of governance. Although, Nepal was never a religious state in that way, declaring it a Hindu state was a strategy on the part of the king to place itself at the helm of political affairs. The institution of monarchy was closely identified with the Hindu philosophy of kingship, so declaring Nepal a Hindu state also served the interest of monarchy.

The Maoists argued that until Nepal would become a secular state it would not be able to head towards an inclusive democracy. Thus, abolition of monarchy, inclusive democracy, declaration of Nepal a republican and a secular state were three vital aspects of the Maoist agenda of restructuring the state.

C - Social Reform Agenda

The Maoists also emphasized upon the need for the transformation of the Nepali society. In a feudal society like Nepal it was not possible to sustain democracy for a long time. The Nepali society had been traditionally structured on the basis of a hierarchical social order.[13]

The power and status was granted to the people on the basis of his place in the social hierarchy. It led to the development of an exclusive socio-political order in the country that has been widely talked about as the 'Brahminic' social order[14]. The question of gender discrimination, ethnicity, dalits, regional identities, religious minorities, etc was not properly addressed. All these issues form vital aspects of the agenda for social transformation in Nepal. The Maoists emphasized the need to bring all these groups, communities and regions in the socio-political mainstream so as to ensure social parity, justice and integrity.

D - Economic Agenda

The Maoists raised a number of economic issues. Their basic thrust had been on restructuring the feudal order, which has been based on the exploitation of the poor people. Introduction of land reforms ascertaining redistribution of land-to-land less people, restructuring of wage structures, fulfilling basic needs of the people had been on the top of the Maoist economic agenda. Maoist would prefer a mixed, regulated and balanced economy in the long run.[15] The regional economic imbalances also need to be properly addressed. There has to be state control over major aspects of the economy.[16]

On the whole the Maoist agenda clearly shows that they aimed at restructuring the feudal based socio-economic and political order in the country.

ORGANIZATIONAL STRUCTURE

Mao fused the realities of Marxism and Leninism with the concrete practice of Chinese revolution. He strongly argued that it was not possible to launch a protracted guerrilla war and win the battle to install a new democratic order without solid organizational base of the revolutionaries. He talked about three magic instruments of revolution: the Communist Party, Army and the United Front (UF). The Maoists of Nepal adopted the formula prescribed by Mao.

The Party

The Communist Party of Nepal (Maoist) had come into existence before starting the revolution. CPN (M) was in fact the net result of the polarization of ultra left groups who had come into a sharp conflict with the Nepali government during the early nineties. It was obvious that the party emerged with a revolutionary image. It had strong disliking for the democratic parties like Nepali Congress for its 'leaning towards feudal and imperialist forces'; UML being a revisionist party and some of the other communist groups being neo-revisionist. The main task of the party was to formulate policies and spread the ideology of people's war. Pushpa Kamal Dahal (Prachanda) has been the president of CPN (M) since its inception. The party has a nationwide structure from grass root level to top, divided into cell committees, area committees, district committees, subregional bureaus, regional bureaus, divisional commands, central committee, politbureo and standing committee. The standing committee of the party is consisted of six top leaders of the party : Babu Ram Bhattarai, Mohan Vaidya, Ram Bahadur Thapa (Badal) Post Bahadur Bogati (Diwakar), Krishna Bahadur Mahar and Dev Gurung. The politburo is a bigger unit in comparison to the standing committee with 27 members, of whom 10 members are alternates. The central committee of the party is consisted of 100 members. The party also has a Central Advisory Committee.

The Party initially had three divisional commands: Western, Special Central and Eastern commands. The Special Central Command was dissolved in 2004 and Mid Central Command was constituted in its place. Each command has been allotted some administrative zones. Each command has its in-charge who is also an ex-officio member of the standing committee of the party.

Western Command	:	Mahakali, Seti, Karnali, Bheri
Mid Central	:	Gandaki, Lumbini, Rapti, Dhaulagiri
Eastern	:	Janakpur, Sagarmatha, Bagmati, Narayani, Kosi, Mechi

The party also has one international department to propagate its ideology and objectives outside the country and seek support from them.

The party has been the most powerful organization having full control over all other organizations. Prachanda has enjoyed full command and control over the party. His leadership has not been challenged so far from within the party. Another important point is that the party has not faced any split during the last more than a decade. However, there have been some problems at the regional level, particularly in relation to its regional organizations.[17] The party had suffered during insurgency due to arrest of party leaders, surrender to Royal Nepal Army (RNA), killings, etc.

The party has enjoyed a vide support base among various ethnic groups particularly the Mongolian communities; the Tarai ethnic groups and various caste groups; women; youth and student groups; labourers, peasantry, etc. The party has its major support base in the rural areas.[18]

The Army

Army constituted another important component of the Maoist organization. It was meant to attack on enemies, defend its position and bring areas under its control. Mao made it clear that it was not possible for the masses to fight a protracted war. It required a well-organized army trained in guerrilla warfare.

Mao said that armed struggle was a necessity in a violent revolution. It was not possible to attain the objectives of a revolution without a people's liberation army. Mao further emphasized that it was not sufficient to have trained guerrillas but there has to be a regular army.

A regular army was necessary in order to move from a stage of the strategic stalemate to the stage of the strategic offense. It is obvious in a way because once a stage of strategic stalemate is created retaliation by the state is quite likely and in that case it is not possible to survive without taking a position of strategic defense and strategic offense. Therefore, an army is required ultimately. Mao's concept of a people's liberation army was later on followed by other revolutionaries like Che Guevara in Chile General Giap in Vietnam, etc.

It might be true that the revolution had become a necessity for the Maoists;[19] so was an army. But initially Maoists lacked a well-structured army. They had a small organization in the name of army consisting of fighters, security men and volunteers. There were no dress and other codes for the army. They had small and ordinary types of arms. The Maoists had snatched most of these arms from the police custody and other places.

In the forth plenum of the party held in August 1998 it was decided to build up the military strength. The Maoists had given the slogan of creating the base areas, which was not possible without a strong army. The need for a strong army was also being realized due to the increasing government repression. The Maoists agreed that the development of people's military power was necessary to consolidate their strength.[20]

It was decided to establish military training camps. The formation of people's liberation army was announced at Kureli in Rolpa district in September 2001. The conflict between PLA and RNA between 2000-2001 at various places likes Dunai, Holari,

Salleri, Ghorahi, etc clearly indicated at the increasing military strength of the Maoists. In June 2002 it was decided to raise PLA to the brigade level. It gradually had a nation-wide network.[21]

In August 2004 PLA had three brigades namely Eastern Division (Barshman Pun: Anant), Central Division (Nand Kishore Pun: Pashang) and Western Division (Janardan Sharma: Prabhakar). Each brigade was divided into battalion, company, platoon, squad and militia. The militia contained untrained persons. The women also had a separate company. The women represented all cadres from trained guerrilla to militia. The Maoist army also had a Special Task Force. Prachanda was the supreme commander of the army. He had full control over each aspect of the army. Each division of the army had one Commander and one Political Commissar. Such a system was adopted with an objective to ensure full control of the party over the army.[22]

It is not clear as what was the actual strength of the army. In 2003 it was reported that the Maoists had 2 divisions, 7 brigades, 19 battalions and the militia.[23] According to one estimate Maoists had 4000 armed guerrillas, 5000 trained guerrillas, 20000 militia. and 20000 sympathizers.[24] According to International Crisis Group the Maoists had 5000-10000 guerrillas and 5000-25000 armed militia.[25] Some believed that the Maoist army consisted of 4000 armed guerrillas, 5000 militia and 20000 armed militia.[26] It is also said that the strength of the army was 9500 guerrillas and 25000 militia.[27] It can be safely said that the Maoists had on an average 5000 guerrilla trained men another 4000-5000 armed men and 20000-25000 militia. No doubt it was a big non-state military organization.[28] There have been reports that the Maoists at times followed policy of forced recruitment in the army. It is also alleged that children were also recruited.[29] There have been many stories regarding the army recruitment by the Maoists. It appears that initially there was no such crisis of recruitment in the army as there was lot of enthusiasm among youths and people were also, by and large, supportive. However, it was not that easy to sustain this enthusiasm after a certain period of time. There might have been realization among the rural people that it was going to be an endless fighting. The people were scared of large scale killing of the Maoist solders. They were also threatened by the strong repressive measures taken by RNA. It acted quite brutally at times.

So it was quite possible that the poor rural people became scared of joining the Maoist army. In these circumstances it was quite possible that the Maoists had to decide for taking up forceful measures in order to sustain the army.

The Maoist army was well trained in mountain guerrilla warfare. They sought training from external sources and ex-army men within the county. The Maoist arms and ammunition included ordinary rifles and local made fore arms, AK 47 rifles[30], M.16 rifles, 303 rifles, 81 mm mortars, SLR, INSAS rifles, rocket launchers, landmines, explosives, etc. The main sources of their arms and ammunition were purchase from black market, setting of factories to prepare certain kind of arms and ammunition, snatching arms from local security establishments etc.

The army was equipped with all kind of sophisticated communication facilities like satellite telephone, print media, internet, etc.

The United Front

Mao gave sufficient thinking to seek support from various sources within the country so as to consolidate support base of the communist party and to strengthen the revolution. The purpose of the United Front was thus to unite with all those forces that would be helpful in fighting the common cause.[31]

In September 2001 CPN (M) formed a United People's Revolutionary Council (UPRC) which was lead by Babu Ram Bhattarai as its convener and Krishna Bahadur Mahar as Assistant convener and Dev Gurung as Secretary. UPRC had 37 members. The people's government at village, district and regional level were constituted under UPRC. The Maoists tried to consolidate all those groups and forces that were dissatisfied with the state. That way they tried to provide adequate space to ethnic, dalit and regional identities in their framework of the United Front.[32]

The Maoists had following caste / ethnic based frontier organizations:[33]

	Organization		Leader
1.	Magarant National Liberation Front	:	Suresh Ali Magar
2.	Tamang National Liberation Front	:	Ganga Bahadur Tamang

3. Tamuwan National Liberation Front :	Mohan Tamu
4. Limbuwan National Liberation Front :	Bhakta Raj Kandangwa
5. Nepal Dalit Liberation Front :	Thaman Pariyar
6. Tharuwan National Liberation Front :	Ram Charan Chaudhary
7. Madhesi National Liberation Front :	Jai Krishna Goit
8. Karnali National Liberation Front :	Khadka Bahadur Bishwa Karma
9. Thami Liberation Front :	Chun Bahadur Thami
10. Majhi National Liberation Front :	Tul Bahadur Majhi
11. Newa Khola :	Dilip Maharjan

The Maoists also formed autonomous regions and appointed an in-charge of each region. Actually the ethnic groups had been demanding for autonomous regions along with these lines and the Maoists recognized them and formed their autonomous governments. There were 9 autonomous regions by 2004.[34]

1.	Kirat Autonomous Region	Hill areas of Mechi, Kosi and Sagarmatha	Gopal Khambu
2.	Tambasaling Autonomous Region	Hill areas of Bagmati (except Kathmandu) Narayani and Janakpur zones	Hit Bahadur Tamang
3.	Newar Autonomous Region	Kathmandu Valley	—
4.	Tamuwan Autonomous Region	Hill areas between Kali Gankaki to Budi Gandaki	Dev Gurung
5.	Magarat Autonomous Region	Hill areas from West of Kali Gandaki to Dhaulagiri, Rapti and Lumbini Zones	Santosh Magar
6.	Tharuwan Autonomous Region	Western Tarai areas from Rapti to Mahakali Zones	Ram Charan Choudhary
7.	Madeshi Autonomous Region	Tarai of Awadhi, Bhojpuri and Maithili Speaking areas	Matrika Yadav
8.	Bheri – Karnali Autonomous Region	Hill areas of Bheri – Karnali Zones	Khadga Bahadur Bishwakarma
9.	Seti – Mahakali Autonomous Region	Hill areas of Seti and Mahakali Zones	Lekh Raj Bhatt

Maoists expanded their support base to a large number of students and professional organizations. These were as following:

1. All Nepal National Free Students Union (Revolutionary)

2. Nepal Trade Union Federation (Rèvolutionary)
3. All Nepal Women's Association (Revolutionary)
4. All Nepal Janjati Federation
5. All Nepal Teachers Organization (Revolutionary)
6. Nepal National Intellectual's Organization
7. All Nepal People's Cultural Union
8. All Nepal People's Peasants Association
9. Nepal Trade Union Federation
10. All Nepal Transport Workers Union
11. All Nepal Construction Workers Union
12. All Nepal Hotel and Restaurant Workers Union
13. All Nepal Carpet Workers Union
14. All Nepal Construction Workers Union
15. All Nepal Meter Tempo Workers Union
16. All Nepal Press Workers Union
17. Himalayan Tracking Art Workers Union
18. Nepal Shop Workers Union
19. All Nepal Painters Union
20. Nepal Progressive News Paper Vendors Union

Maoist Strategy

The strategy adopted by the Maoists had different aspects. The basic objective of the Maoists as once stated by Babu Ram Bhattarai was to fight against the feudal state of Nepal. He said:

"We want to overthrow the present state and establish a new democratic republic, there will be no place for feudal, comprador, bureaucratic and capitalist forces, which are now flourishing under the protection and influence of foreign imperialist power."[35]

The Maoists had two broad things in mind while looking up at its strategies: To increase their organizational strength and resource capabilities, and to expand their area of control and influence in a gradual but offensive way.[36] They adopted several steps during the course of insurgency which included the following:

(I) Strategic defense,
(II) Strategic offense,
(III) control of areas they had captured,

(IV) Introducing their own rule and regulations and ignoring the government rules and ultimately overthrowing the government administration from the areas of their influence,

(V) Providing military training to the youth in the area of their influence and preparing them for guerrilla war,

(VI) Mobilizing peasantry, and

(VII) Capturing the countryside and encircling the cities through protracted war.

Protracted War

Protracted guerrilla war was the leading strategy of the Maoists. The Maoists of Nepal followed Mao's concept of mobilize and arm people in the countryside to seize political power through a protracted guerrilla warfare. The protracted war was a military – political strategy. Mobilization of rural people, drawing enemy into interior areas and guerrilla war were three basic ingredients of the protracted war. The radical communists had been advocating the concept of protracted war since 1991 and they made it their primary strategy in their struggle against the state. While conceptualizing the people's protracted war a Maoist leader said:

"People's war is a war waged by the oppressed people against their oppressors for liberation. The oppressor class has always been oppressing the majority through violence ever since class and the state power originated in the world. The oppressed class therefore, is forced to resort to counter – violence in order to create and maintain a new state power by pulling down the old one for the sake of its liberation. The people's war is a struggle of counter – violence waged by the people against the oppressor class and its state power. The people's war assumes a long-term character in any society in which the small property owners or peasants are in the majority. There is disparity in the pace of progress in different parts of the country, and the revolutionary class had to struggle against a powerful enemy force".[37]

The protracted war not only emphasized guerrilla armed insurrection but it also called for the continuity of the war by gradually expanding area of its operation from rural to urban till the state power is captured. The protracted war underlined the fact that for the Maoists the main form of struggle was guerrilla war and the primary organization was army.[38]

Strategic Defense and Strategic Offense

The Maoists adopted the strategy of taking a defensive position and an offensive position as and when it was required. They followed the approach that take a defensive position when the enemy was in a strong and better position. Strike on the enemy when it was weak or in a critical position. Thus the Maoists followed a strategy to take an offensive position when the conditions were favourable. They also followed the approach to move ahead gradually but steadily.

Strategic Balance

The Maoists also followed the strategy to reduce capacity and influence of the state. They considered it necessary to reduce state's access and control over its subjects in the countryside. They attacked police check posts, compelled the government officials to withdraw from the offices and the areas, attacked mainstream party leaders and workers, forced the local bodies officials to resign from their duties, destroyed the infrastructure like roads, bridges, air strips, communication channels, etc. so that the delivery system of the state was weakened. The Maoists also attempted to reduce the support basis of the state by mobilising various groups and organizations in an area through persuasion or forcefully.

Base Areas

The Maoists of Nepal also adopted the strategy to create its base areas. The base area strategy had dual objectives: to gain local popular support as well as to make its strong hold in different areas. Actually, for a prolonged protracted war three things were essential: mass support, sufficient economic resources and a suitable terrain for military action. A base area was a particular geographic region where Maoists had succeeded in exerting its control. The base areas were bordered by guerrilla areas. Beyond these areas were the areas under the control of the state. It is this area which was under the constant Maoist guerrilla attack according to the concept of base areas. This area was termed as Guerrilla Action Region.

Prachandapath

In 2001 Prachanda gave a new thrust to the Maoist insurgency in Nepal, which became popular as Prachandapath. Prachanda after reviewing the course of insurgency in Nepal for the last five years tried to conceptualize the protracted guerrilla war in the Nepali context. It was a set of ideas developed and synthesized on the basis of Marxist ideology and local conditions.[39] It was viewed as a Nepali contribution to the ideology of Marxism – Leninism and Maoism.[40]

Prachandapath was an exercise to decide about the appropriateness of the insurgency keeping in view the ultimate objectives and the Nepali conditions. Babu Ram Bhattarai opined rather more appropriately that Prachandapath was a school of thought that was more than a set of tactics but less than ideology.[41]

Actually after a certain period of time it was being realized that in a country like Nepal where political power was so much centralized it was not possible to win a war by letting the war confined to rural areas alone.[42] The Maoist strategists realized that there was a need to take the struggle directly to Kathmandu, the centre of state power. It was a necessity to create instability in the cities.

Prachanda advocated the necessity of infusing both protracted war and armed insurrection in their military strategy. Armed insurrection had been the characteristic of insurgency in the developed societies as Lenin did in Russia, while protracted war had been a characteristic of the third world societies, which have been poor, and rural peasantry based. It was viewed in Nepali conditions that it was necessary to take both the strategies in to consideration because of the existing realities of state structure and the inter linkages of the state with the globalized world in various ways. Thus Prachandapath connoted a fusion of the urban insurrection and protracted guerrilla war.[43]

Prachanda elaborated the necessary conditions for the success of people's war in Nepal. He said that:

(I) There was a need to follow a clear political and ideological line.

(II) Ensure involvement of the people.

(III) Involve more and more people in the war and make them conscious about the necessity of a people's war.

(IV) Attack on the enemy when it is appropriate and than disappear. This would require continuous monitoring of the enemy activities and find appropriate geographical and other conditions.

(V) Building base areas.

Prachanda advocated the approach of unite and struggle. He also emphasized to give priority to the rural areas but do not leave urban areas; give priority to illegal struggle but do not leave legal struggle too; give priority to areas of strategic importance but accord importance to mass movement as well. Prachandpath in a way emphasized the need to take the struggle to Kathmandu as it was not possible to win the war by capturing the rural areas alone.

Dialogue Strategy

The Maoists also used dialogue with the government as a strategy to rebuild its capacities. Cease-fire that Maoists declared were also an opportunity to balance the situation of armed movement. This was a strategy that Maoists had said to be learned from the Shining Path of Peru.[44]

Propaganda Strategy

The Maoists also adopted propaganda strategy both within and outside the country. The Maoist propaganda was aimed at gaining sympathy of the suppressed groups of the society as well as seeking support from different quarters. At the same time, it followed the tactics of confusing the government agencies. The propaganda strategy was adopted at times in order to build international opinion in their favour.

Summing Up

To conclude this discussion two things are important. The Nepali Maoists were highly influenced by the Marxist – Leninist – Maoist ideology. But they find Maoism more near to their conditions and they were very much attracted to the Mao's strategy of people's guerrilla war and new democracy. They tried to organize their movement along the line of the Chinese revolution lead by Mao. Three fundamental organizations of the Maoist movement: Party, Army and the United Front were based on the Maoist ideology. Thus, it is clear that broadly Marxism – Leninism – Maoism influenced the Maoists of Nepal, but specifically and strategically Maoism was their main politico-ideological basis.

The Maoists also gave due consideration to the appropriateness of Mao's strategy to the Nepali conditions in a changed and globalized world order. Therefore, they mixed up armed insurrection with the strategy of protracted guerrilla war. The Prachandapath gave a new direction to the Maoist insurgency in Nepal.

References

1. Peter B.Harris, *Foundations of Political Science,* Hutchinson of London, 1976: 328.
2. David C.Apter, *Introduction to Political Analysis,* Prentice Hall of India, New Delhi, 1978: 236.
3. Peter B.Harris, *n.1*: 310.
4. Stephan L.Wasby, *Political Science, The Discipline and its Dimensions,* Scientific Book Agency, Calcutta, 1970: 40.
5. Robert Lane, *Political Ideology: Why the American Common Man Believes What He Does,* New York, 1962: 15.
6. See, Martin Seliger, *Ideology and Politics,* The Free Press, New York, 1976.
7. William Ebenstin, *Great Political Thinkers,* Oxford and IBH, New Delhi, 1960: 677.
8. Lenin's most important work in this regard was *State and Revolution* (1918).
9. For studies on Maoism see, J.Gittings, *The Role of the Chinese Army,* Oxford University Press, Oxford, 1967; Robert L.Scalppino, *The Communist Revolution in Asia*, Prentice Hall, New Jersey, 1965; B.Schwartz, *Chinese Communism and the Rise of Mao*, Howard University Press Massachusetts, 1958.

10. Abi Narayan Chamalgai, "Maoist Insurgency: An ideological Diagnosis", in Lok Raj Baral (ed.), *Nepal: Facets of Insurgency*, Adroit, Delhi, 2006: 15.
11. See, Jacobes and Baerwald (eds.), *Chinese Communism, Selected Documents*, New York, 1963.
12. See, Madan Bhandari, "The Concept and Dynamics of People's Multi Party Democracy" (draft Paper), Kathmandu.
13. See, Prayag Raj Sharma, *The State and Society in Nepal*, Himal Books, Kathmandu, 2004, David N.Gellner, et.al. (eds.), *Nationalism and Ethnicity in a Himalayan Kingdom, The Politics of Culture in Contemporary Nepal*, Howard Academic Publication, Amsterdam, 1997.
14. Prayag Raj Sharma, *n.13*; Kamal Malla, "Bahunbad : Myth or Reality", *Himal* Vol. V, No.3, May-June, 1992 : 22-24, for detailed explanations see, Harka Gurung, *Nepal Social Demography and Expressions,* Kathmandu, 1998.
15. International Crisis Group, *Nepal's Maoists: Their Aims, Structure and Strategy*, Asia Report No. 104, 27 October 2005.
16. See for a detailed explanation of economic issues, Babu Ram Bhattarai, "Politico-Economic Rationale of the People's War in Nepal", www.http://insef.org.
17. In 2004 Maoist leader Jaya Krishna Goit separated from Madhese National Liberation Front. There were also some defections in Kirat National Liberation Front.
18. ICG, *n.15*: 16.
19. Arjun Karki and David Seddon, "The People's War in Historical Context", in Karki and Seddon (eds.), *The People's War in Nepal, Left Perspective.* Adroit, Delhi, 2003: 3-42.
20. Karki & Seddon, *n.19.*
21. Dhrub Kumar, "Military Dimensions of the Maoist Insurgency" in Lok Raj Baral (ed.), *Nepal Facets of Maoist Insurgency*, Adroit, Delhi, 2006 : 104.
22. See, Dinesh, "Janmukti Sena Ko Vikas ra Rajnitik Karya", *Janadesh*, August 10, 2004.
23. *Rajdhani* (Kathmanu), September 15, 2003.
24. Dhrub Kumar *n.21*: 102.
25. ICG, *n.15*: 8.
26. Ashok Mehta, *The Royal Nepal Army: Meeting the Maoist Challenges*, Rupa, New Delhi, 2005: 94.
27. *Kathmadnu Post*, May 21, 2005.
28. Dhrub Kumar, *n.21*: 102.

29. See, John Lancaster, "Concern Grows Over Nepal's Child Fighters", *The Washington Post*, June 14, 2005.
30. Sitaram Baral, "San AK-47 Ko", *Samay*, (Kathmandu), May 13, 2004.
31. Sudhir Shah, "The Moist Movement : An Evolutionary Perspective", in Deepak Thapa (ed.), *Understanding the Maoist Movement of Nepal,* Martin Chautari & CSDR, Kathmandu, 2003 : 362.
32. See, Uddhav P.Pyakurel, *Maoist Movement in Nepal*, Adroit, Delhi, 2007: 91.
33. Uddhav P.Pyakurel, *n.32*: 91.
34. *N.32* : 92.
35. *The Rising Nepal*, January 11, 1996.
36. B.C.Upreti, "The Maoist Insurgency in Nepal: Nature, Growth and Impact", *South Asian Survey,* 13:1, 2006:40.
37. *Saptahik Bimarsha* (Kathmandu), March 22, 1996.
38. See, *Selected Military Writings of Mao Tse-Tung*, Peking, 1967: 272. Also See, Che Guevara, *Guerrilla Warfare*, Penguin, London, 1967.
39. See, *Some Important Documents of Communist Party of Nepal (Maoist)*, Janadesh Publications, Kathmandu, 2004: 4 -5.
40. See Keshvraj Devkota, *Prachanda, Prachandpath ra Ganatantra,* Saogat Pustak Prakashan, Kathmandu, 2063: 118.
41. Babu Ram Bhattarai, "Dosro Rashtriya Sammenlan Ko Yugantari Mahatva", *Kantipur*, March, 2001.
42. IGC, *n.15*:18.
43. Uddhav P. Pyakurel, *n.32*: 17.
44. Abi Narayan Chamlagai, *n.10*: 18.

4

Maoist Support Bases, Factors and Forces

We have already discussed in the previous chapter that the political process in Nepal after the 1990 democratic movement had provided enough space for the rise of the Maoist movement in the country. It is a debatable issue whether democracy provides solution to various societal problems or it aggravates them. It can safely be said that if democracy remains in the form of certain political super structures and does not ensure promotion of social and economic democracy simultaneously, it is bound to give way to a grave social discontent. It is a fact that the democratic political leadership of Nepal failed in addressing itself to the issues of an inclusive democracy, with the result that the radical communists took advantage of the situation in raising an armed struggle against the state.

But it was not the political conditions alone that gave birth to an insurgency. In fact, there were a large number of domestic and external factors that proved supportive to the rise of the Maoist insurgency in Nepal. We intend to discuss some of these factors here in order to understand the support structure of the Maoists.

Geographical Conditions

In guerrilla war geographical situation plays a significant role. The Maoist strategy for a protracted guerrilla war was largely conditioned by a favourable geographical conditions. In fact, Nepal's topography suited the Maoist war strategy.

Nepal's geography is characterized by diversity. It provides example of a country where different sets of environments ranging between plain areas of the Tarai region to the high Himalayan mountains exist.[1] Three broad geographic regions of Nepal: The plains land called Tarai, the middle hills and the Snow-clad mountains- have affected settlement patterns, population concentration, resource bases, development network, population pressure over resources and so on. Situated along the Southern slopes of the Great Himalayan ranges, Nepal separates the Gangetic plains of India in the South to the Tibetan plateau in the North. Thus the country is located between two giant powers of Asia – India and China. Nepal is a landlocked country. India alone provides it a route to the sea. The nearest sea cost from Nepal border is 600 miles away.[2] Nepal is a smaller country in terms of size. It has an area of 145891 sq.km., with an average length of 800 km. East to West and a breadth of 175 km. North to South.[3] Thus, its length is more than four times of its width. The Western region is the broadest part of the kingdom with 150 km. width and the Eastern part is the narrowest.[4] Most of the high Himalayan ranges lies in Nepal including the Mount Everest.[5] The country is irregular and rectangular in shape.[6]

Nearly 83 per cent part of the country is hilly and mountainous and only 17 per cent is plains land. The country slopes Southward but the rise in the height from South to North is not straight and even.[7]

The Himalayas form extreme Northern part of the Kingdom covering 15 per cent of the total land area. The Himalayas also do not form a uniform topography. There are high peaks, big glaciers, lakes and deep passes. Most of the rivers of the country originate in this part. The climate is dry, harsh and unsuitable for human habitation. It is a resource scarce region. It is possible to move across the border through the passes during the summers.

The middle hills cover nearly 68 per cent of the total land area.[8] The Southern part of the hills is formed of low range hills called Shivalik Ranges (Churia Hills). There are big valleys in the hills like Kathmandu, Pokhara, etc. There is large scale population concentration in these valleys. The Hills are covered by dense forests. Agriculture is possible only in stair like small fields. In the valleys rich fertile land is available.

Tarai has an entirely different topography. It forms rich agriculture and industrial belt of the country. It is viewed as the economic backbone of the country. It is because of the rich resources and the availability of means of livelihood that there is larger concentration of population in Tarai. Nearly half of the population of the country is concentrated in Tarai. There has been a continuous process of migration to the Tarai form the hills and from across the border in the South. It has given a highly complex character to the socio – cultural milieu of Tarai.[9]

There are a number of regions in the hills that are quite inaccessible called the Remote Areas. These regions are cut off from the other areas by fast flowing rivers or mountains. There are dense forests in many parts where there is very low or nil human settlement. May parts of the country are still cut off from the outside world because of lack of means of transportation particularly in the Western region.[10] Some of the districts in the Far Western Hills and the Western Hills do not have roads even at the district head quarters. The only means of transportation have been small air strips which too function seasonally. These remote areas and dense forests have been an asset to Maoists as these areas are suitable for the operation of guerrilla war. In remote areas, since there is very little human settlement, it was easy for the Maoists to make their hideouts. The inaccessible areas lacked proper administrative and security mechanism. So it was easier for the Maoists to encircle the government officials and the establishments in these areas. Due to dense forests in the Western hills it was easier for the Maoists to attack on police posts and army and than run away into the deep forests.

In the South Nepal forms border with India on three sides : East-West and South. Indo – Nepal border is open and it is possible to move across the border easily. The open border provide an easy accessibility to the Maoists in the neighbouring Indian regions for the purpose of taking shelter, availing of the medical facilities for the wounded Maoist rebels, meetings, consultations, etc.

It is clear from this discussion that Nepal's topography was quite suitable for the guerrilla war. The Maoists took advantage of the geographic conditions for strengthening their movement

Western Region of Nepal: A Note

The Maoists selected the Western region of Nepal as their base area. The insurgency began from here. It appears that it was a well thought of plan to make the Western hills as the centre of their activities. Actually the geographical and socio – economic conditions of this region were quite suitable for launching a violent movement.

The Western region has been one of the most backward areas of Nepal. This region had been underdeveloped and poverty ridden since the beginning. The Central and Eastern development regions are the areas where most of the development activities in the country have been concentrated. The far Western region has been a bit advantageous as it forms border with India and it has been politically significant at times. But the Western and mid-Western regions have been neglected and disadvantageous in many respects.

The caste and class composition of the region is important. It has been a Magar dominated area. The Magars have been mostly working as peasant farmers, labourers and serving in the army. The community is poor. The high caste hill people have been dominating the agriculture and other resources of the region since the days of Shah and the Rana rule. There are big hill origin absentee landlords in the plains areas of the region. A number of NGO's have been involved in development works in Rolpa district. But these aid programmes have also not been helpful in transforming lives of the poor people of the region. The hill areas lack transport and the other basic facilities. Banke, Bardiya, Dang, etc. are food deficit areas. Large scale migration takes place from this region to Tarai or the nieghbouring Indian regions. Thus bulk of the population of the region is constituted of landless peasantry, poor labourers and Tribal. It is obvious that a larger section of the population is illiterate and lack basic amneties.

It is because of these conditions that the communists had been active in this region since the beginning. Some of the communist leaders selected this region for their activities, keeping in view the socio – economic landscape here. Mohan Bikram Singh, initially a member of the Nepali Congress party joined the Communist Party of Nepal in 1951 and became active in Peuthan. He along with communist leaders like Khagan Lal Gurung, Barman

Budha and Krishna Bahadur Mahara worked in the Western hills to cerate a strong base of the party.[11] In the first general elections of the country in 1959, CPN recorded its victory in Rolpa. After 1974 Mohan Bikram Singh organized its under ground activities in the Western region and crated a strong base for the radical lefts. In the 1980 referendum CPN (Fourth Convention) of Mohan Bikram Singh who had given a call for the bycott of the referendum replaced the photographs of king by Marx and Lenin at public places in Western Nepal. In 1991 general elections UPFN won three seats from this region. It clearly shows that the Western region of Nepal had been nurtured as a radical communist hub over the years. It was obvious for the Maoists to select Rolpa, Rukum, Peuthan as base areas for their activities.

Underdevelopment, Poverty and Discrimination

The economic factor has been basic to all kind of conflicts and insurgencies. In the third world societies state has been the primary agency to meet basic needs of masses and unleash development. In case of underdevelopment, non fulfillment of basic needs, poverty and discriminations in development, it is the state which becomes target of any conflict or revolution.

In Nepal also economic factor has been quite significant in the initiation of the Maoist insurgency. The Maoists characterized Nepali economy as feudal and semi – feudal.

Nepal inherited a backward, traditional and feudal economy when it stepped on the path of democracy in 1950. There was hardly any infrastructure and industrial base in the country. Nearly 94 per cent of the economy was based on agriculture.[12] After 1955, when Nepal moved on the path of modernization and development in a planned way, some headway was made towards structural development. However, it failed in bringing up any transformation in the economy. The traditional bases of land ownership continued to exist.[13] The same feudal class took over to import oriented business activities, industries and the other commercial activities. It is true that there took place an expansion of educational facilities, development of roads, health facilities but they were inadequate and marked by sharp regional imbalances.[14]

Nepal was characterized as one of the poorest country in the 1989 World Bank Report. It ranked 115 out of 120 countries. Nepal's GDP has not gone above 6.0 per cent for the last one decade. Nearly 42 per cent of the total population lived below poverty line. What is more striking is that its percentage of people below poverty line has not changed during the last three decades.[15] There have been vast income inequalities in the Nepali society. Nearly 37.7 per cent of the population had an income less than one US dollar a day. The poorest 10 per cent of the population consume 3.2 per cent resources, while the richest 10 per cent hold 29.8 per cent resources. The problem of employment and under employment has been severe in Nepal. Agriculture, which contributes nearly 40 per cent of GDP, alone, has the capacity to provide employment. But in the hill areas agriculture does not provide employment to all and for the whole year. The services sector is poor and the industrial sector is not well developed. This has resulted in large scale migrations particularly from the hill areas. The food deficiency is a big problem.

In the Western region particularly, a number of districts have been food deficit.[16] In the hills and mountains agriculture-land is insufficient. Another problem is that in Nepal roads are the primary means of transportation. But it is insufficient. Out of 75 districts 15 are still not connected by roads. In such circumstances people of these regions face difficulties in proper supply of food grains. Corruption has also been a serious problem. There have been a number of cases of corruption reported after 1990.

There were lot of expectations from the democratic government, particularly in terms of meeting basic needs of the people and introducing economic reforms. But the democratic governments failed in addressing to the problems of underdevelopment, poverty and unemployment. Unfortunately neither the government nor political parties gave any consideration to the socio – economic issues. It naturally generated widespread dissatisfaction.[17] It has rightly been pointed out that the formation and reformation of government proved to be a politics of power sharing and power grabbing. The functioning of the governments was marked by widespread corruption, favouritism and nepotism. Instead of strengthening the political process it lead to political decay and political disorientation.[18] It can be said that the economic issues became victim of political instability and disorder in Nepal. So a large chunck of the population was dissatisfied with the democratic governance.

On the whole the basic economic issues that had remain un addressed and therefore a cause of concern were: increasing population and high population growth rate, low economic growth rate, inadequate infrastructure, regional imbalances in development and regional inequalities and discriminations, resource gap, poverty, unemployment, income inequalities, problem of development in remote areas, food shortage, aid dependency, foreign debt burden, trade imbalance, rampant corruption and scarcity of essential commodities. The Nepali government did not give sufficient thought to recast its development priorities and programmes in order to resolve these problems and issues.

Support of Ethnic Groups

The ethnic groups have also been an important support bases of the Maoists. The ethnic people constituting nearly 37.3 per cent of the population have been dissatisfied with the Nepali state. Actually, in plural – societies mobilization of individuals and groups on the basis of ethnicity is an important feature. When various smaller groups and communities realize that they are being discriminated by the majority communities that also form the ruling elite, they begun to assert for their rights on the basis of their traditional identity. It leads to the ethnicisation of politics and the politicization of ethnicity. Ethnicity has been a source of tensions and conflicts in many societies; to the extent that the ethnic movements have given rise to separatist tendencies resulting into disintegration of the state. So, it is a fact that in plural societies social solidarity and stability can be maintained only by ensuring a balance between different ethnic groups in terms of distribution of resources and benefits.

In Nepal ethnicity has gradually become an important variable in the politics. In fact, the issues such as the formation of various organizations on ethnic lines, demand for regional and ethnic autonomy, political tensions arising due to unequal distribution of power among various communities and regions, etc. are becoming critical factors of Nepali politics. The long-standing domination of the Brahmin-Chettri-Newar trio has come under severe criticism by ethnic groups. The non-Hindu Tribal communities, which are undergoing fast social and political mobilization are challenging the traditional power base of the Nepali society and polity and also trying to assert for equitable redistribution of resources and goods. In fact, it can be said that as the political and economic structures of the country have become competitive and ethnic mobilization is taking place, various underprivileged ethnic groups have started demanding a greater share in politics and administration.

A brief look at the various ethnic groups will help us in understanding the plural nature of the Nepali society. Nepal has a multi-racial, multi-lingual and multi-cultural society. Its inhabitants can be classified into three main racial stocks: The Indo-Aryans, the Mongoloids and the Austro-Asiatic. Majority of the population of the country is Hindus followed by Buddhists, Muslims and Christians.[19]

The people speaking various languages and dialects of the Indian origin who had migrated from India to Nepal at different points of time are Indo-Aryans. They became part and parcel of the Nepali society in due course. They are settled in both the hill areas and the Tarai region. In the Tarai region a large number of people of the Indian origin migrated at a later stage are still awaiting citizenship of Nepal. The people of the Mongoloid origin such as Rai, Limbu, Tamang, Sunwar, Gurung, Magar, Kirati, Bhote, Sherpa, Chepang, Thakali, etc. are settled in the Himalayan and the hill regions. They are believed to have migrated to Nepal from the North. Their language, culture and life-style are quite similar to those of the people of Tibet. The people of Austro-Asiatic origin are Sutar, Dura, Dunwar, Rawate, Santhali, etc.

The People of the Tarai region that is constituted of the Indian migrants and the tribal groups have a regional identity. They include plains Brahmin, Rajputs, Banias, Bhumihar, Yadav, Kayastha, Kurmi, Rauniyar and the tribal like, Tharu, Sutar Rajbansi, Dhimal, Jhangad, etc. There are dalit groups in the hills and Tarai. The Newar mostly dwelling the Kathmandu valley have a separate cultural identity. There are Muslims and Christians as well. Muslims mostly dwell the Tarai region and Kathmandu.

The ethnic groups of the Mongolian origin were socially and politically marginalised with the establishment of the caste hierarchy and the Hindu hegemonies becoming as basic contours of Nepali society and polity. Founding the monarchy on the basis of Hindu philosophy of Kingship, declaration of Nepali (Gorkhali) as the state language, Nepal as a Hindu state and the Brahmin–Kshatriya domination on the state power further alienated the ethnic groups. The Nepali rulers initiated a process of Hinduaisation of non-Hindu caste groups, soon to crate a monolithic state. Such policies were detrimental to the cultural autonomy of the indigenous people.

The economic marginalization of the ethnic groups took place at two levels: Firstly, they were deprived of higher political and administrative positions as these were meant for Brahmins, Kshatriyas and Newars to some extent. Secondly, the traditional land occupied by the ethnic groups was confiscated from them and redistributed to Brahmins and Kshatriyas as Birta and as Jagir.[20] The traditional land ownership system known as Kipat was abolished and a new land tenure system Raikar was introduced. Under this system the traditional land and natural resources owned by the ethnic communities was reallocated to the high caste people who were the new settlers to the areas inhibited by the indigenous communities.[21]

Political change though took place in the country after 1950, the status and problems of the ethnic communities remained unchanged and unresolved. The constitutions were formulated, political system changed and governments came into operation one after the other but hardly any attempts were made to accommodate ethnic interests. The democratic elite also continued to rely upon the same traditional political and administrative elite. They had a vested interest in continuing with the traditional socio – economic structures and exclusive democracy.

There have been early instances of revolt by the Mongolian groups. The Limbu, Rai, Gurung and Magars tried to raise their voice during the early 1950's. There were also instances of revolt during the early seventies. There were indications of the rise of pan – tribal sentiments towards the end of the seventies. The people of the Mongolian origin had strong feelings against discrimination towards them. In September 1979, K.B.Gurung convened a conference of the people of Mongoloid origin. The conference demanded proportionate representation of the Mongoloids in the public sector. Gurung questioned the validity of declaring Nepal a Hindu state and demanded that Nepal should be declared a secular state.[22]

The 1979 movement for democracy and the consequent referendum of 1980 did evoke tribal sentiments but it seems that the Mongoloid people failed in mobilizing themselves on ethnic lines in an organized manner largely due to systemic prohibitions.

Various ethnic identities again started surfacing in the political arena of Nepal after the establishment of democracy in the country in 1990. It added a new dimension of ethno – politics in the country. It may be noted here that in three years time after 1990, nearly 44 ethnic associations had come to existence by the end of 1993.[23] It clearly reflects upon the mobilization of ethnic groups after the dawn of democracy in the country.

The resurgence of the Mongoloid ethnic groups indeed, took a new turn after 1990. With the beginning of the democratic process a number of tribal ethnic identities surfaced. These organizations began to assert for the promotion of their interests. On the eve of the 1991 general elections Nepal Rashtriya Jana Jati Party demanded division of Nepal into 12 autonomous regions such as Khasan, Jadan, Magarat, Tamuan, Tamba Saling, Nepal, Khmbuan, Limbuan, Kohila, Maithili, Bhojpuri and Awadhi.[24] Thus, demands for regional autonomy on ethno-linguistic lines began to surface. The issue of language also got complicated with the use of language other than Nepali in the parliament.

Following the use of Hindi language in the Nepali Parliament by the members of the, Sadbhavana Party, the parliamentarians of the hill ethnic groups also began to speak in their own languages. The ethnic groups have been highly critical of the Brahminic hold of politics.[25] The strong reactions of the ethnic Mongoloids against undermining their religio-cultural identity and their underprivileged position against the Brahmin-Chettri-Newar domination had reflected in the expressions of the Mongoloid leaders. Bir Nembang a Mongol leader raised voice for a separate self-ruled state in Limbuwan while Hark Raj Limbu formed a Limbuwan National Council-Rais on the other hand have demanded for a separate Khambuan.[26]

Ethnic groups have also expressed strong reactions against the discriminatory traditions of the Nepali society, by violating certain norms such as **Pani Ubau Andolan** (touch water movement) by untouchable castes and resentment against **Pani na calne-choi chito halnu naparne** and **Pani na clane choi chito halno parne** traditions. Some tribal groups started publishing news papers and other literature in their languages. The literature in indigenous languages was being provided to their community members free of cost. The educated people of the ethnic groups provided leadership in this regard. A neo-rich class began to emerge among the Mongoloid groups in the course of time, which was also providing leadership as well as resources to their ethnic based organizations. A number of teachers in the university and colleges belonging to a particular ethnic group provided leadership to it.

In nutshell the Mongolian ethnic groups had discontent over the following issues:

- Cultural hegemony of the Hindus.
- Nepal's continuation as a Hindu State.
- Deprivation of their land and other resources.
- Perpetuation of Bahunvad (Brahminism) and domination of Brahmins and Chettris in the political and administrative structures of the country.
- Inadequate political representation of the ethnic communities.
- Faulty census procedures and reports that had shown their reduced numerical strength.
- Question of distinct cultural identity.
- Social and economic inequalities and discrimination.
- Economic backwardness of the ethnic groups.

Since the formation of the political parties on religious and cultural basis was prohibited in the constitution of 1990, the various ethnic groups sought alignment with one or the other political parties. The later had tried to exploit the organized strength of these ethnic groups for their own purposes and also tried to patronize the ethnic leadership. In fact, the ethnic leadership was seeking support from their own ethnic organizations as well as the political party to which they had sought affiliation. However, political parties still did not appear to be too much concerned to the ethnic demands, particularly due to the prevailing structures of the political parties, which go largely in favour of Brahmin – Chettri cliques.

The Maoists expressed their serious concern towards the marginalization of the ethnic groups. The ethnic groups also realized that the Maoists had serious resentment against the state and the caste hierarchies. They believed that the Mongolian communities could be a potential source of support for the protracted war to be launched by them. The Mongolian youth were feeling oppressed and they were highly frustrated because of rampant unemployment and poverty. So they were easily attracted towards the Maoists.

The Maoists raised a number of issues that attracted the ethnic groups towards the insurgency. These were: proper representation to the ethnic communities in political bodies and the administration in terms of the strength of the ethnic groups; autonomy to the ethnic groups; equal opportunities to all languages including education in indigenous languages; declaring Nepal a secular state; abolition of caste based privileges and opportunities and inequalities based on traditional norms, beliefs and attitudes and cultural autonomy of the ethnic groups within a multicultural democratic order.

In fact, these were the issues for which ethnic groups were trying to mobilize themselves and assert. So they readily agreed to lend their support to the Maoists.

Women Support to Maoists

The women also constituted an important component of the Maoist support base. It was quite revealing that the women were mobilized in such a high spirit to not only support the Maoist insurgency but to take part in the guerrilla war. The women constituted a sizeable number of the Maoist guerrillas.[27] It was quite surprising that in a feudal and highly traditional society like Nepal, where not much steps have been taken towards empowerment of women, they became so much enthusiastic about the Maoist movement.[28] The answer to this question can be seen in the context of the deprivation and subjugation that the Nepali women have faced in the society and the failure of the democratic governance in Nepal in enforcing gender equity and status to the women.

The gender equality is an essential component of a democratic order. In fact, in modern times the project of democracy can not be completed unless the objective of gender equity is attained. It is now realized that the level of civilization of a country is best judged by the status that women are accorded in the society. It is generally assumed that most of the countries of the third world are in a transitional phase as far as the question of status of women is concerned. The women have been subject to discrimination, ill treatment and underdevelopment owing to social and religio-cultural traditions, attitudes and perception, male chauvinism, discriminatory developmental policies, etc. The issues involved in the empowerment of women are; social status and recognition, literacy, rights, health, adequate representation to women in service, politics and other walks of life and denouncing the social and religion based discriminations against women. The empowerment of women is thus equitable distribution of resources, power and status in political, social and economic realm.[29]

In Nepal the issue of empowerment of women has come up only in the last few decades. The conditions of women particularly in the rural hills are quite miserable. Nepal ranks 116 among the countries of the world in terms of the gender related index. Women constitute slightly more than half (50.05%) of the total population of the country. The female adult literacy rate is 26.4 per cent, which is quite low. In fact, Nepal has a lower status in terms of female literacy.[30] Women are largely engaged in agriculture. The women employment is mostly characterized by low skilled sectors, subsistence work orientation and low paid jobs.

The Nepali women are a most disadvantaged lot. In the social hierarchy the status of women is generally much lower. However, it has to be understood that there are sharp variations as well, in this regard among the Mongoloid communities and the other tribal people. In some communities women have an equitable or higher status as well. However, in general women lag far behind men in - access to education, resources and ownership rights. In nutshell it can be said that the women have been subject to many types of discriminations and ill behaviour in the society:

1. It is difficult for women to move to other sectors of employment than agriculture work due to low literacy and lack of training and skills.
2. It is difficult for women to raise their own capital because they cannot own land and also due to unfavourable property rights and inheritance laws.
3. Social customs, traditions, religious norms are still a binding force for women.
4. As the women are left to own all kinds of household responsibilities due to large scale out migration of men folks, their problems are multiplied.
5. There are serious problems of violence against women and trafficking in women and children.
6. Women are low paid for same kind of jobs.
7. The caste system disparages women in relation to men. She is subject to many social and family obligations and restrictions. She is a daughter before marriage and a mother after marriage.
8. Women are faced with the problem of early marriage, early pregnancy and multiple pregnancies.
9. Practices of debt slavery to women, voluntary sex and voluntary labour services have been in practice.
10. Women are faced with the practice of un touchability on days of masturbation and giving birth to a child.
11. The customs of Kumari, Jhuma and Deuki have exploited the women.
12. The schooling of a male child is always preferred against a girl child.
13. Nepal has high maternal mortality rate in the world at 875 per 100000 women.

14. The preference for a male child has been humiliating and tortures.

The Maoists called for equal rights to women in land and property. They also raised voice against economic exploitation of women and also pleaded for the cultural independence of women. They condemned untouchability to women.[31]

These actions and initiatives taken by the Maoists were enough to give support and sympathy of women who saw a new hope of their emancipation in the Maoist movement. The Nepalese Women's Association, All Nepalese Women's Association became active in mobilizing support to the Maoist movement. The women had helped the Maoist insurgency in several ways:

1. The women joined the Maoist army as trained guerrilla fighters. There were said to be 2 women in each guerrilla squad of 9-11 members.[32]
2. Where women were not directly recruited as guerrillas they worked as a supportive force.
3. Women helped the Maoist army in logistic services.[33]
4. Women were engaged in nursing and caring of the injured Maoist fighters.
5. They were also to arrange for cultural programmes in the Maoist army camps.

The Women attracted towards the Maoists because of two main reasons: The Maoist call for social reforms leading to gender equity. Secondly, the Maoist campaign against alcoholism, gambling of which women had become victims in the rural areas, drive against women exploitation and violence, etc. It may be noted here that in the beginning of their movement, the Maoists organized family courts to pass judgment against the cases of violence against women. They destroyed local distilleries, punished alcoholic villagers. They also imposed sanctions against polygamy in the areas of their influence. The Women formed mass organizations at village and district level to mobilize support for the Maoists. They played a significant role in the Maoist access to new areas.

Thus women constituted an important support base to the Maoist insurgency not only as guerrilla fighters but also in logistic and supply services.

The young women tired of household works and sufferings from traditional social bondage were attracted to the Maoist movement for freedom. There were also cases where women joined the Maoist forces to take a revenge from the state security forces. In certain cases they felt secure against the state forces by joining the Maoist army.

It is true that the women formed a viable support base of the Maoists but their joining the movement had a number of positive and negative dimensions. Some of them were as following:

1. The movement generated consciousness among women and enhanced their mobilization capacity.
2. It provided an opportunity to poor, illiterate or just literate girls to escape of a life of bondage.
3. It bought to the women a sense of revolt against the state machinery and the social bondage.
4. It is said that the family life of and activities of those women who joined the Maoists changed considerably.
5. The process of political mobilization of women increased.

But the Maoist movement also affected women in several ways:

1. It has been reported by some that there was an increase in violence and crime against women after the Maoist insurgency began.[34]
2. It was reported that the conflict had left 14000 women as widow.[35]
3. There were reports of forced recruitment of women in the army.[36]
4. The women became subject to double victim due to the Maoist insurgency. First, they became direct victims of the security forces and secondly, they had to meet the Maoist demand for food, shelter and sex.[37]
5. Women and children were assigned risky jobs by the Maoists. For instances they were to carry explosive material from one place to another. without having any idea about its dangers.[38]
6. There were problems of perception and attitude towards women within the Maoists as well.

7. Women were economically burdened as they were forced to make arrangement for food, etc to the Maoists in rural areas.
8. Women were over burdened in household responsibilities as the men were either killed or serving with the Maoists.

The women have been the weakest point in the family system and the society. It was therefore obvious that they faced the fallout of the Maoist insurgency. In the rural areas they faced widowhood, excessive family burden; sexual abuses and tortures, government retaliatory actions and hardship by the Maoists. It is not to say here that the men or the children were not the victims. They too suffered tortures and abuses of many kinds. The point is in an insurgency it is the weaker sections of the society, which become the first victims of the insurgents in many ways and that of the state apparatus in somewhat different ways. It destroys the individuals, the family, the economy and the women became the first recipient of these fallouts. But despite all that the women in the rural areas, particularly the tribal women supported the Maoist insurgency. Perhaps, they viewed the Maoist movement as a way towards their emancipation and freedom; a way-out to their poverty and hunger. What the 'women' had to pay for it is a different though relevant question.

Regional Support to Maoist Insurgency

The regional question also became an important supportive factor for the Maoists. It is a fact that the people of Tarai region have been discriminated in Nepal historically. The hill people and the ruling elite did not trust them ever. Hence, they had strong resentments against the state. After 1950 people of the Tarai region began to assert against the domination of the hill people. The major discontent of the Madhesis was against their under representation in the political super-structures, bureaucracy and army. During the fifties the people of Tarai also tried to assert their linguistic identity and demanded status and recognition to Hindi, which was lingu-franca among all the communities of the Tarai. A 'Save Hindi Movement' was launched in the Tarai during the fifties. But not only that the discrimination against people of Tarai continued, the citizenship rules were framed in a way to make it difficult for them to obtain Nepali citizenship.

After the introduction of the panchayat system in 1962, deliberate attempts were made to encourage Nepali language in the Tarai in place of Hindi, migration of hill people in the Tarai and the consolidation of citizenship rules. The people of the hill region migrating to Tarai were given surplus land by introducing land reforms. The surplus land was denied to the Tarai people who had been the tiller of the land for a long time. The people of the Tarai region viewed these steps as a deliberate denial of rights to them and a cultural invasion over them by the hill people. The Madhesis were considered as a second rate citizens. However, since organized political activities had been banned under the panchayat system, the discontent among the people of the Tarai region remained more or less latent.[39] The resentment of the people of the Tarai region has surfaced in a big way in the post 1990 Nepali politics. The Nepal Sadbhavana Party has come forward to protect the interest of the people of Tarai. It aimed at fighting against the discrimination towards the Tarai people and the policies of 'Nepalization' vis-à-vis Madhesis.[40]

It clearly indicates that the Tarai people are not only unhappy with their disproportionate representation in the power structure but also with the hill cultural hegemony.[41] During the May 1991 general elections Sadbhavana Party raised regional and ethnic issues and demanded regional autonomy for the Tarai, declaration of Hindi as an official language of Nepal, citizenship to all the people of Tarai and 50 percent reservation for the people of Tarai in army and administration.

The Maoists raised the issues of discontent among the people of Tarai against the hill dominated ruling class of Nepal. There was always an element of mistrust between the people of Tarai and the royalty. The Maoists realized that the Tarai people would support them in their quest for the restructuring of the state and inclusive democracy. Their support of autonomy also encouraged Tarai people to join the Maoist insurgent groups in a big way.

International Support Bases of Maoists

The Maoists were highly conscious about creating an international support structure ever since the time they thought of initiating a violent movement in Nepal. In fact, they were aware of the fact that without a widespread international support it was not possible to launch a protracted war. It was also important in the Nepali conditions due to the fact that Nepal had a strategic position in the Himalayas, a large number of countries and international agencies have been providing foreign and to Nepal and because of an open border with India, there were serious implications of any violent movement in Nepal. The Maoists had three broad objectives in mind while seeking international support:

(I) To seek logistic and other kind of support for the movement.

(II) To mobilize its support bases in as much countries as possible.

(III) To convince various countries and governments to not to support the Nepali state against the Maoists.

The Maoists tried to seek support from the following agencies:

(I) Communist parties, revolutionary organizations and communist countries, particularly the countries where revolutionary movements were going on or had taken place in the past.

(II) People, revolutionary organizations and governments in the neighbouring countries.

(III) Nepali Diaspora.

The Maoists accorded much significance to the mobilizations of international support.

Maoists discussed the issues relating to the launching of a revolutionary movement at many places such as in Peru, Philippines, Turkey, Iran, Bangladesh, India, Sri Lanka, etc.[42] It is believed that the Maoists had received international support at every stage in the movement since its inception.[43]

Revolutionary International Movement (RIM)

The Revolutionary International Movement (RIM) is a worldwide organization of the revolutionary parties. It believes in the ideology of Marxism – Leninism – Maoism and supports all kinds of revolution, insurgencies and protracted war against the state anywhere in the world. It provides a forum to the revolutionary parties to discuss issues, problems and challenges relating to launching a movement in their country. RIM provides possible guidelines and support to such parties and organizations.

RIM came into existence in March 1984 in London. It publishes a magazine called *A World to Win.* The CPN (Masal) was one of the founding members of RIM and Babu Ram Bhattarai is said to had been the person in contact with RIM. CPN (Maoist) became Member of RIM after it was constituted in 1995. CPN (Masal) was expelled from RIM in 1996. RIM helped CPN (Maoist) through its theoretical interactions with the Maoist leaders and also gave moral support to it. In a statement on February 1, 1998 to Central committee of CPN (Maoist) the committee of RIM said:

> "The participation of the Communist Party of Nepal (Maoist) in the RIM, the concern and assistance given by our party to the advance of the communist movement in the South Asia region and throughout the world, even at different movements in your struggle inspires us. The committee of RIM and the CPN (Maoist) will continue to march forward as in the past-united by our all powerful ideology – Marxism – Leninism – Maoism and determined to accelerate the development of the world proletarian revolution."[44]

The RIM has been coordinating and providing ideological support to all kind of extremist movements based on the ideology of Marxism – Leninism and Maoism. Two very significant founding members of the RIM have been the Communist Party of Peru (Shining Path) and the Revolutionary Communist Party of USA. Both the parties have been highly violent and using guerrilla tactics. The Revolutionary Communist Party had supported the Maoist movement. In a letter to CPN (M) in 1997 the party expressed the view thus:

"It is a great testimony to the strength of Marxism – Leninism – Maoism and is an important victory and source of inspiration not only for the CPN (Maoist) but for the RIM, of which we are proud to be a participant together with you and other comrades all over the world."

> "Comrades, the Revolutionary Communist Party fully supports you. The revolutionary warfare in your country is very day more a shining beacon for the oppressed masses in the United States and the world over, pointing to the path of people's war, which alone can bring about the defeat of imperialism and reactionaries and open the door to the bright new future of socialism and communism."[45]

Impact of Shining Path

The Maoists of Nepal viewed Peru as their role model for launching a revolutionary movement in the country. They were highly inspired by the Shining Path. It was thought that there were many similarities between Peru and Nepal. Both are mountainous countries having dense forests and isolated valleys. A large chunk of the population is rural based in both the countries. There are sharp socio – economic differentiation and inequalities in both the countries. The Communist Party of Peru (Shining Path) waged a violent movement against the Peruvian state in the 1980's. They followed the Maoist ideology of protracted guerrilla war. The Shining Path was formed in the late 1960's.

During the middle of 1980's Shining Path initiated a series of highly violent attacks in the rural arcas. In 1991 they began to attack metropolitan areas. Nearly 30,000 Peruvians were killed in these attacks. After the Shining Paths attacks in urban areas President Fujimori waged an aggressive drive against the Shining Path. The leader of the party Guzman was captured in September 1992, along with other leaders. A large number of Peruvians were convicted of terrorism related rages. The terror of Shining Path began to decline and it lost its strength and effectiveness by 1994.

It is true that the Shining Path had failed in its mission but there was a time when it was considered to be the most dreaded organization in Peru as well as outside. The Shining Path did set certain examples such as guerrilla war, establishing strong holds in remote forested areas, rural to urban insurrection and continuity of war instead of hit and run. These were important lessons for the Maoists. The Shining Path also gave this lesson that the movement has to be a violent one. The Shining Path also taught the lesson to deal with dissent ruthlessly.

Support From Indian Extremist Groups

The Maoists received support from a number of Indian political parties and extremist groups. There were two types of groups: those parties and groups that had ideological affinity with the Maoists. Secondly, those groups and organizations which were indulged in violent movement against the state or those who were agitating for autonomy. There were four main objectives behind closer linkages between the Nepali Maoists and the Indian extremists:

(I) Ideological and strategic consultations;
(II) Taking shelter across the border in India;
(III) Purchase of arms and ammunitions; and
(IV) Mutual benefits in terms of financial resources, training, communication, etc.

The Naxalites and People's War Group had close links with India. Other parties with whom the Maoists of Nepal were said to have links were RCC (M), CPI (ML) and PCC. The Maoists also said to have links with various insurgent groups of North – East India such as KLO, ULFA, NDFB, GLTF, NSCN-IM, etc.[46] It was easy for the Maoists to interact with the extremist groups in India because of an open border between the two countries.

International Support

The Maoists also received moral support from many organizations all over the world. LTTE of Sri Lanka, Worker's Party of Belgium, Worker's Communist Party of Norway, World People's Resistance Movement, Chinese Communist Party, etc. provided moral support to the Maoists.

Support from the Nepali Diaspora

The Maoists expected support from the Nepali living abroad. This support could be in terms of arranging financial resources and creating a public opinion in favour of the Maoist movement. Some of the Nepali organizations abroad that supported the Maoist movement were: Akhil Bharatiya Nepali Ekta Samaj, All India

Nepali Students Association, Nepali People's Progressive Forum, Belgium, etc.

Issue of South Asian Maoist Unity

CPN (Maoist) played a significant role in uniting the revolutionary parties of South Asia. On 1 July, 2001 CCOMPOSA (Coordinating Council of Maoist Parties of South Asia) was announced. The Marxist parties of South Asia such as; Purb Bangla Surbhara Party (CC), Purb Bangla Surbhara Party (Maoist Punargathan Kendra), Bangladesh Samyabadi Party (ML), Communist Party of Ceylon (Maoist), Communist Party of India (ML), (Naxalbari), Communist Party of India (ML(PW), Maoist Communist Centre, Revolutionary Communist Centre of India (MLM), Revolutionary Communist Centre of India (Maoist), Communist Party Nepal (Maoist) agreed to join it. The objective of this organization was to coordinate the activities of the Maoist parties of South Asia. It also aimed at building a compact revolutionary zone in the South Asian region.[47]

It seems that the Maoists wanted to strengthen their own movement by bringing the revolutionary parties of South Asia together. They wanted these parties against their governments so that the Maoist insurgency would not be singled out in the region.

Summing Up

It is clear that the Maoists had a wide support base that helped them in launching and sustaining the violent revolution. The topography of Nepal was quite suitable for launching a protracted guerrilla war. The Maoists took advantage of dense forests, isolated regions, caves and remote hill areas. It was not possible for the administration to take note of the Maoist activities in such areas. Some of these areas were totally un inhibited so there were no informers about the Maoist activities. The Maoists selected these areas to establish there training camps and hideouts.

The Maoists also took advantage of fragmented and hierarchical set up of the Nepali society. The ethnic groups of Mongolian origin, the Dalits, the people of Tarai and women had been facing discrimination and segregation for a longtime. The

Maoists attracted them by raising the slogans of people's democracy, equality and autonomy. It is also a fact that the democratic governments in the post 1990 period had failed both at political and economic fronts. As a result the people were dissatisfied. There were problems of basic needs. The questions of economic reforms had remained unattained. What is more important is that the popular expectations from the democratic governance were belied. In such circumstances people particularly the youth was attracted towards the Maoist movement.

The Maoists also enjoyed a strong regional and international support base. RIM provided the necessary ideological and strategic input to CPN (Maoist). Various revolutionary movements such as in Peru, Kampuchea, Philippines inspired the Maoists. The Indian extremist groups too were a source of inspiration and support. The Maoists took advantage of the open border between India and Nepal.

What makes a movement successful is the objective conditions in which it is initiated and the support base that it enjoys. In this respect it can be said that the Maoists enjoyed a large number of favourable conditions and a strong domestic, regional and international support base.

References

1. Pradyumna P.Karan & William M. Jankins, *Nepal, A Cultural and Physical Geography*, Lexington, 1960: 1.
2. Soorya Lal Amatya, *Economic Geography of Nepal*, Kathmandu, 1967: 2.
3. U.N.Malla, *A Brief Geography of Nepal*, Ministry of Information and Broadcasting, HMG, Kathmandu, 1967: 1.
4. Soorya Lal Amatya, *n.2* : 2.
5. S.H.Shrestha, *A Simple Geography of Nepal* (Nepali), Kathmandu, 1963: 8-9.
6. *n.5* : 8.
7. Harka Bahadur Gurung, "The Land", in Pashupati Shamsher JBR & Kamal P. Malla (eds.), *Nepal in Perspective*, Kathmandu, 1973 : 25.
8. S.H.Shrestha, *n.5*: 10-11.

9. See, Fredrick H.Gaige, *Regionalism and National Unity in Nepal*, University of California Press, 1975. P.Pant and S.C.Jain, *Regional Imbalance and Process of Regional Development in Nepal*, Berlin, 1980.
10. B.C.Upreti, *Nepal, Dilemmas of Development and Change in Far Western Hills*, Indus Publishing House, New Delhi, 2006.
11. See, Deepak Thapa & Bandita Sijapati, *A Kingdom Under Seige: Nepal's Maoist Insurgency*, The Printhouse, Kathmandu, 2003: 67-68.
12. See, Navin C. Joshi, *Readings in Nepalese Economy*, Chug Publications, Allahabad, 1978; Diwakar Chand, *Essays on Development of Nepal*, Chandini Publications, Kathmandu, 2003, B.P.Shrestha, *An Introduction to Nepalese Economy*, Ratna Pustak, Bhandar, Kathmandu, 1981.
13. Mahesh C.Regmi, *Land Ownership in Nepal*, California, 1975.
14. Mahendra P.Lama, "The Maoist Movement in Nepal: The Economic Implications", in Sridhar K.Khatri and Gert W. Kueck (eds.), *Terrorism in South Asia: Impact on Development and Democratic Process*, Shipra, Delhi, 2003: 87-88.
15. Diwakar Chand, *n.12*: 136.
16. B.C.Upreti, *n.10*.
17. Panchanan Maharjan, "The Maoist Insurgency and the Crisis of Governability in Nepal", in Dhrub Kumar (ed.), *Domestic Conflict and Crisis of Governability in Nepal*, CNAS, Kathmandu, 2000: 191-193.
18. Andrew R. Nickson, "Democratization and the Growth of Communism in Nepal: A Peruvian Scenario in the Making" *Journal of Commonwealth and Comparative Politics*, 30(3), November 1992: 258-86.
19. See, *Population Census 2001*, Tathyank Vibhag, HMG, Kathmandu, Nepal, 2002.
20. Mahesh C.Regmi, *A Study of Nepali Economic History*, 1972.
21. Lionel Caplan, *Land and Social Change in East Nepal*, Himal Books, Kathmandu, 2000.
22. Urmila Phadnis, *Ethnicity and National Building in South Asia*, SAGE Publications, New Delhi, 1990 : 123.
23. Dilli Ram Dahal, "Ethnic Calandron, Demography and Minority Politics: The Case of Nepal", in Dhgub Kumar (ed.), *State Leadership and Politics in Nepal*, CNAS, Kathmandu, 1995.
24. Krishan B.Bhattachan, "Ethno-Politics and Ethno-Development: An Emerging Paradigm in Nepal", Dhrub Kumar (ed.), *n.23*.

25. Prayag Raj Sharma, *The State and Society in Nepal, Historical Foundations and Contemporary Trends*, Himal Books, Kathmandu, 2004: 219.
26. *Nepali Patra* (Kathmandu), June 4, 1994.
27. See, Indira Adhikari, "Women in Conflict : The Gender Perspective in Maoist Insurgency", in Lok Raj Baral (ed.), *Nepal, Facets of Maoist Insurgency*, Adroit, Delhi, 2006 : 74-75, also see, Rita Manchanda, "Politics in Nepal : Women Now Swelling The Ranks of Maoist", http://www.chasque.net/ips-eng-notes.
28. Com. Parvati, "Women's Participation in the People's war", in Arjun Karki and David Seddon, *The People's War in Nepal, Left Perspective*, Adroit publishers, Delhi, 2003 : 166.
29. J.Rowlands, *Questioning Empowerment*, Oxford, 1997.
30. *Asian Development Outlook*, ADB, New York, 2001 : 121.
31. Mandira Sharma & Dinesh Prasain, "Gender Dimensions of the People's war", in Michael Hutt (ed.), *Himalayan People's War: Nepal's Maoist Rebellion*, Hurst & Co., London, 2004: 154-156.
32. Com. Parvati *n.28*: 171.
33. Ram Saran Mahat, *In Defence of Democracy: Dynamics and Fault Lines of Nepal's Political Economy*, Adroit, Delhi, 2005: 321.
34. Kamal Sarup, "Maoists Threat Nepali Women", April 5, 2006.
35. Kamal Sarup, "Recruitment of Women in the Army and peace", April 11, 2006.
36. Rita Manchanda, *n.27*.
37. See, Manjushree Thapa, *An Elegy for Democracy Forget Kathmandu*, PENGUIN, India, 2005.
38. Sujata Shakya, "The Maoist Movement in Nepal: An Analysis from the Women Perspective", in Arjun Karki, *n.28*: 389.
39. Ranakant & B.C.Upreti, "Regionalism in Nepal, A Case of Tarai", Ranakant (ed.), *Regionalism in South Asia*, Aalekh Publishers, Jaipur, 1984: 138 – 172.
40. *Saptahik Manch* (Kathmandu), June 28, 1991.
41. See, B.C.Upreti, "Regional Movements and Madhesi Politics in Nepal" *Nepali Jaournal of Contemporary Studies* (Kathmandu), Vol.VII, No.1, March 2007: 16-36.
42. See, "Inside The Revolution" interview of RW reporter Li Onesto with Prachanda in Arjun Kari, *n.28* : 88-89.
43. *n.42* : 89
44. Quoted from Steven C.Baker, "Nepal's Maoists Insurgency", *Front Page Magazine.Com*, July 25, 2003.
45. Steven C.Baker, *n.44*.

46. See, Sanjay K.Jha, "Maoist Linkages With North East Insurgents : Growing Concerns", 20 April 2004, Post 1374, http://www.saag.org. Also see, *Kathmandu Post*, April 13, 2004; *The Hindustan Times*, September 27,2004.
47. S.D. Muni, *Insurgency in Nepal, The Challenges and the Response*, Rupa, New Delhi, 2003: 22-23.

5
Growth of Maoist Movement

The understanding between the left parties and the Nepali Congress developed at the time of 1990 democratic movement broke out before the 1991 general elections. Actually both the left forces and the Nepali Congress wanted to enter into competitive politics independently. The radical leftist forces participated in the 1991 general elections but very soon they were frustrated with the working of the parliamentary democracy. They tend to take a different course. They realized that the existing political order that was bound to protect the interest of the feudal class would not succeed in establishing a truly democratic system. They also thought that it was not possible to attain the desired goals of democracy and socio – economic transformations without a revolution. Therefore, they began to talk of protracted war as early as 1992. Some of the writings around that period had indicated that the political situation in Nepal was leading the country towards an insurgency.[1] Not many people took note of these indications at that time. On the contrary, the state apparatus tried to contain them in terms of a law and order problem. The radical leftists finally got detached from the democratic political process in Nepal at the time of 1994 mid term elections. They gave up all hopes on the constitutional-democratic path and began to prepare for a revolution. They concentrated on building the party and their base areas and finally declared people's war on 13 February 1996.

Demand Charter

The Communist Party of Nepal (Maoists) submitted a demand

charter to the government in January 1996. It was a very comprehensive demand charter. Almost all the issues that the people of Nepal in general would be conscious of were included in the demand charter. It included issues relating to sovereignty and nationalism, people's welfare and basic needs, issues of foreign policy and relations with the neighbouring countries, development framework and soon. In fact, hardly any issue was left out. It was also made clear in the charter that if the government would not express any interest in the demand charter by 17 February 1996 a nationwide movement would be launched against the government from 18 February. The government that was faced with so many problems of its own was hardly expected to react to such a long demand charter of the Maoists in such a short time. It was not a question of giving assurance for the fulfillment of certain demands. There were serious policy issues involved in the Maoist demand charter. On the whole it appears that the Maoists were well convinced of the fact that it was not possible for the government to react to the demand charter in a positive way. They were perhaps already prepared for the retaliation in the form of protracted war. The demand charter was in fact, a pretext for the initiation of the people's war. The fact remains that the Maoists did not wait for the time limit given to the government and declared beginning of the people's war a week earlier on 13 February. So it is clear that they were not expecting any positive or favourable consideration by the government.

Popular Understanding About the Movement

Were the people of Nepal aware of possibilities of a violent movement is also an important question. It appears that, by and large, the people of Nepal were not aware of any such upcoming movement in the country. There were some scattered views regarding the Maoist movement but hardly any opinion about a protracted people's war seems to be there at that point of time. One reason could be that the activities and preparations of CPN (Maoists) were underground and they might have taken precautions to not to allow any news to come out before time. Another important aspect that has to be noted here is that the

Maoist preparations were taking place in the Western hills not in the cities, so there was a communications gap. Therefore, it seems that the common people hardly had any idea of the upcoming insurgency. There was no popular perception about the insurgency at the time it began. It was only after wards that the people began to opine about the Maoist insurgency.

Government's Perception

It has already been pointed out that the government considered the agitational politics of the radical communists as a law and order problem. They followed the same perception about the radical communists, which had been developed as early as 1992. It was not realized that the radical leftists were gradually heading towards insurgency. Therefore, they did not pay any extra attention to the activities of the Maoists. There were two problems: The government was more concerned about managing its own affairs. Secondly, there were many within the government who favoured a strong police action against the Maoists instead of entering into any dialogue with them. They wanted to crush the rebels.

The government response to the Maoist demand charter was one of ignorance and non concern. Prime Minister Deuba preferred to take a visit to India instead of dealing with the problem. There was also a confusion regarding the Maoist insurgency as such. Some believed that it was an ethnic uprising.[2] Actually the way ethnic groups were trying to assert for their demands, it gave an impression that an ethnic upsurge was in the offing. Some of the ethnic groups like Magars had demanded for autonomy. There was also an impression that the government wanted to ignore the Maoist problem deliberately so that they would not considered to be of any significance.

It may also be added here that one perennial problem of the democratic governments in the post 1990 period had been internal differences. The political parties had been faced with internal factionalism and groupism, and that also had its impact on the nature and working of the government. Some reports indicated that Prime Minister Deuba was of the opinion to discuss some issues with the Maoist leaders and find a solution of the problem.

But the then Home Minister Khum Bahadur Khadka wanted to take a strong action against the rebels.[3] Khadka belonged to the Maoist heartland of Western hills, so he looked at the problem from a different angle.[4]

So it seems that neither the people nor the government accorded any serious attention to the upçoming problem. There was an adhocism every where. It was only after the protracted war was launched that it was being realized that an insurgency was on its way in the country.

13 February 1996

The CPN Maoist declared its war against the state on this date, nearly a week earlier than the stipulated date of the starting of people's war. The Maoists distributed a leaflet that gave a call to the people of Nepal to join the people's war in order to smash the reactionary state and establish a new democratic state. CPN (M) selected six districts to launch people's war. These were: Rukum, Rolpa, Jajarkot, Salyan and Gorkha in Mid Western region and Sindhuli in Central region. Rukum, Rolpa, Jajarkot and Salyan formed the core areas of the Maoist activities.

The Maoist commandos attacked at several places on the first day of launching the people's war. In Chyangli VDC of Gorkha district office of the Small Farmer's Development Programme of the Agriculture Development Bank was ransacked. All documents of land and houses kept as collateral by the bank were seized and returned to the owners. The official records of the bank were also destroyed.[5] The Police posts were raided at Holari in Rolpa, Athabiskot in Rukkum and Sindhuli in Sindhuligarhi. The Maoists looted small arms and explosives from these police stations. The Maoists continued to attack the police posts, government offices, banks and the Nepali Congress activists. It was declared as the first phase of the Maoist insurgency. CPN (M) emphasized up on the following aspects:

(I) Publicity regarding the objectives and plan of the Maoists so as to popularize the protracted people's war.

(II) Attack on the government establishments in a phased manner so as to continue with their policy of destruction.

(III) Help those people in the rural areas who were considered to be victims of police atrocities, village money lenders, credit banks, etc.

(IV) Wage a war against social abuses like alcoholism, dowry and gender biased attitudes in the rural areas so as to take rural people and women in to confidence.

The second phase of the people's war began in March 1997 and continued till June 1997. The Maoists now concentrated in organizing the people's war. Efforts were also made to develop guerrilla war zones. The Maoists, however, continued with their strategy to attack on police stations and the enemies of the Maoist insurgency.

Government Instability and the Maoists

The beginning of the Maoist problem was marked by government disorder and instability. In fact, the period between 1996–98 was very critical for Nepal. There were weak and unstable governments that were more concerned about resolving their own crisis of stability and sustenance. It provided more space to the Maoists to popularize their strategies of protracted war and gain mass support.

The Sher Bahadur Deuba government was under stress due to a strong opposition from own party leaders as well as the opposition political parties. He had to quit in early 1997. Lokendra Bahadur Chand of Rashtriya Prajatantra Party (RPP) became the Prime Minister in March 1997 with the support of UML. But Lokendra Bahadur Chand government survived only for six months and had to quit in October 1997. The Nepali Congress succeeded in creating a split in RPP. Surya Bahadur Thapa another strong leader of the party became the Prime Minister with the support of the Nepali Congress. It however, withdrew its support to the government in April 1998. A new political party called CPN (ML) had emerged in December 1997 after a split in UML. Nepali Congress developed its understanding with CPN (ML) and formed a government in August 1998 under the leadership of G.P.Koirala.

The understanding between the Nepali Congress and the CPN (ML) was that the Prime Ministership will go to CPN (ML) in December 1998. Koirala backed out from this understating later on. In the meanwhile, the Nepali Congress went closer to UML and CPN (ML) was left out.

The third general elections were held in May 1999 in which Nepali Congress secured a majority. This time K.P. Bhattarai was assigned leadership of the government but it was not very late that Bhattarai began to face opposition from the Koirala camp. He was compelled to step down and G.P.Koirala took over as Prime Minster in March 2000. Yet another government change took place in July 2001 when G.P.Koirala had to give up the Premiership and Deuba once again took over the command of the government.

This is sufficient to make one understand that at a time when the country was suffered from a violent revolution political parties and leadership was busy in the making and remaking of governments. It was indeed a share power game no ideological commitment, no ethics and no norms of politics. The political parties were confined to promoting their interest of remaining in power in whatever manner it would be possible. The Maoists took advantage of this situation in exposing the governments and the problems of governance. The Maoists also tried to propagate how the governments of the day were ignorant to the sufferings and grievances of the people and that way tried to bring dissatisfaction of the people to surface, particularly in the countryside.

The government instability and disorder also gave opportunity to the Maoists to consolidate their position in the countryside.

Dilemma of the Moderate Communists

The moderate communists represented by CPN (UML) were in a dilemma. They were the followers of the constitutional and democratic path. They were not associated with the Maoists since the beginning. Their problem was as how to defend their position as a communist force that was supposed to be committed to socio-economic change in the country. Now CPN (Maoists) had taken up the task of bringing socio-economic and political transformation in the country. It had placed UML in an embarrassing situation. UML, however, argued that what the Maoists were doing was not a people's war. They were in fact, spreading violence in the name of people's war. In the 6th congress of the party held in July 1998, UML accused the Maoists for indulging in terrorist activities. The party maintained that the Maoists had failed in the post in political terms. Therefore, they were taking up a path of violence and terrorism.[6] It may be noted here that both the Nepali Congress and UML, two major political parties of the kingdom, ignored the Maoist problem for their own reasons. The Nepali Congress tried to overlook it potential as the government was not able to contain it. UML tried to ignore it by calling them terrorists as it was a challenge to their own survival as a communist party and a party representing the communist ideology in the country.

Maoist Threat to Local Elections

The Maoists threatened to sabotage the local bodies elections held in 1997 as a part of their strategy to create disorder and expose the incompetence of the government. The Maoists asked the people not to take part in the elections and not to vote. There were a number of Village Development Committees where voting could not take place. At several places candidates withdrew from the elections due to the fear of the Maoists. The polling could not be held in at least 87 Village Development Committees. These were the areas under the Maoist influence.

Dhami Commission

The constitution of Prem Singh Dhami Commission a UML parliamentarian from the Far Western Nepal, by Prime Minister Lokendra Bahadur Chand in April 1997 was the first major step taken by the government towards finding a solution to the Maoist problem.[7] Dhami submitted his report to the government in August 1997. It was a comprehensive report. The commission went deeply into the causes of the Maoist insurgency. It was admitted that there were a number of incidents of police atrocities against the Maoists. It suggested that there was a need to bring the Maoists into the political main-stream so that they withdrew the movement. The commission also suggested for introducing socio-economic reforms in the country. It appears that the Dhami Commission tried to focus upon the root causes of insurgency in the country. They also tried to emphasize that the police action was not the way to overcome the problem of insurgency in the county. There was a need to address the socio-economic issues that the Maoists had raised; and that there was also a need to bring the Maoists out of political isolation. Unfortunately, nothing could be done on the Dhami Commission report and it was put on self as the government changed in October 1997. No notice was taken of this report afterwards.

The Maoists, however, continued their attacks on police stations and government establishments in a planned way. They began to consolidate their position in the areas of their influence. They called these as liberated areas and people's power was to be established in these areas. The Maoists controlled 5 Village Development Councils in Rolpa in Western Nepal and established their administrative control.[8] The government was aware of the increase in the Maoist activities. They had established parallel administration in some areas in the Western hills. The government wanted to bring anti-terrorist bill but it could not be possible.

On 13th October 1998 the Maoists declared establishment of a Central Military Commission. It was an indication of the consolidation of the Maoist military power.

G.P.Koirala after taking over as Prime Minister in 1998 admitted the increased influence of the Maoists. While taking oath of the Prime Minister on 15 April 1998, he said that priority will be given to the resolution of the Maoist insurgency.

Operation Kilo Serra Two

Prime Minister G.P.Koirala announced operation Kilo Serra two against the Maoists in May 1998. It was said to be a strategy to crush the Maoist. But actually it appears that the government was worried about the increasing influence of the Maoists in the countryside. The way Maoists were receiving support from the rural youth and women was alarming. So not only that the Maoist movement was becoming more violent but it was gaining more popular support and sympathy. The government wanted to take a tough attitude. It was a security as well as political strategy. The sole effort of the government was to prevent the Maoists from gaining strength.[9] The Maoists and their supporters were attacked by the police in several districts of the Western region. The slogan of the Operation Kilo Serra Two was : search and kill. A large number of villagers were arrested and they were made subject to torture for their alleged support to the Maoists. It was reported that the police abused the women in villages and acted in a brutal manner.[10] Nearly 500 people were killed in the operation.[11] What was the outcome of the Kilo Serra Two? The fact remains that the operation Kilo Serra Two failed in containing the Maoist insurgency. On the contrary it exposed the police force for its brutality. The government though expressed its concern to the Maoist problem, it relied upon repressive measures. Unfortunately, the common people in the Maoist affected areas also became victim of the repressive measures taken by the government. Surprisingly the government took up the operation Kilo Serra Two in a situation where CPN (ML), a party which itself believed in mass mobilization and people's cause, was supporting the government from outside. None criticized the government for its act. On the other hand, the government actions aroused popular sympathy for the Maoists in the villages where the operation Kilo Serra Two had taken place.[12] Hence, it appears that the operation had failed in its mission and proved to be counter-productive in certain respect.

In response to the operation Kilo Serra Two Maoists announced its fourth plan on 27th October 1998. Not only that the Maoists attacks were increased but they gave much importance to the creation of base areas. The Maoists were looking forward for the consolidation of the movement. The CPN (Maoist) announced constitution of the Peoples Liberation Army (PLA) in February 1999.

The fifth Plan of the Maoist movement was announced in August 1999. The creation of base areas was again emphasized. The Maoists also increased their attacks in scale and space. The Maoist insurgency had entered into nearly 18 districts.[13] The most significant attack of the Maoists was in Gharligaun (Rolpa) in which 15 civilians and 15 policemen were killed. The Maoists attacked in a number of districts after CPN (Maoists) politburo member Suresh Wagle was killed by police in Gorkha district. In February 2000 Maoists claimed that only 9 districts were left out of their influence.[14] It clearly indicated at the increasing intensity of the Maoist insurgency.

The Deuba Committee

In the 1999 elections the Nepali Congress got majority and formed government under the leadership of K.P. Bhattarai. How to end the insurgency was a big challenge for the new government. Two earlier Prime Ministers of the Nepali Congress governments had failed in finding any solution to the Maoist problem. G.P. Koirala was known for his hard-line approach but that too had failed in resolving the crisis. It was a challenge for Bhattarai (as to how to control the Maoists) who had assumed the powers for the first time.

As a step towards that direction PM K.P. Bhattarai constituted a committee under the leadership of Sher Bahadur Deuba,[15] a person considered to be closer to Bhattarai camp. It was a high power committee and authorized to initiate talks with the Maoist leaders. The Maoists send a letter to the government through Durga Suvedi emphasizing upon three things: government should reveal whereabouts of the Maoist leaders who had disappeared; release the Maoist workers who had been arrested by the police and stop acts of state terrorism.

The Deuba committee submitted its report on 7 November 2000. It was a comprehensive report on the Maoists issue and its major recommendations were as following:

(I) The problem of Maoism had occurred not because of the failure of democracy in the country. There were problems with the structure of the Nepali state and the system of governance in the country. The frequent governmental changes and political instability had encouraged the Maoists to initiate an insurgency. The another dimension of the problem was poverty, discriminations, injustice and exclusion of groups and communities in the government structures.

(II) It was suggested that the problem could be resolved through peace talks with the Maoists, so as to find-out an immediate solution of the problem. From a long-term perspective it would be necessary to look into the root causes.

(III) The root causes of the insurgency were stated as faulty and discriminatory socio-economic structures of Nepal. The proper solution to the problem could be to restructure the society and economy.

But the report a became a victim of the factional politics of the Nepali Congress and no action was taken over it. In fact, the Koirala group of the party was critical of the approach of the Bhattarai government towards the Maoists. He was criticized for not handling the Maoist issue properly. Bhattarai had to resign and Koirala took over as Prime Minister of Nepal in March 2000. Koirala declared that his first priority would be maintenance of law and order, security of the people and good governance.[16] Obviously Koirala was hinting at tackling the Maoist problem. But it was not for the first time that Koirala was confronted with the Maoist problem. In fact, neither the Maoist problem was new to Koirala nor his attitude, and approach towards the Maoist.

The Maoists took several decisions to strengthen their organizational base. In April 2000 in a meeting of CPN (Maoist), it was decided to establish a United Revolutionary People's Council (URPC). It was also decided to dissolve UPFN and was finally dissolved in February 2001. The Maoists also declared formation of a number of its front organizations on ethno – regional basis. Similarly autonomous regions were also declared.[17] The whole idea was that the Maoists wanted to take into confidence the ethnic and regional identities. The creation of autonomous regions also indicated at the Maoist approach to the resolution of regional question. It was also aimed at expanding the Maoist support base.

Maoists announced the VI plan of the protracted war in July 2000. The slogan of this plan was; 'Raise to new hights the guerrilla war and the people's resistance struggle.'

The Maoist attack on Dunai in Rolpa district in September 2000 was a serious challenge to the Koirala government. Koirala wanted to send army to contain the Maoists but he could not do so. King who was also the supreme commander of the army did not agree to Koirala's proposal. However, the Royal Nepal Army (RNA) was deployed at 16 district headquarters. In October 2000, Deputy Prime Minister Ram Chandra Poudel initiated talks with the Maoist leaders. It was for the first time that the talks were held between the Maoists and a representative of the government. In November 2000 government released some high level Maoist leaders from jails.

Both the government and the Maoists were trying to play their cards. There was no proper understanding between the two and they lacked any short of mutual confidence. Therefore, there was mutual distrust. The Maoists, however, continued their attacks and the government relied upon deploying forces in their bid to contain the Maoist rebels. In January 2001 King extended its approval for the establishment of a new pera-military force, but the bill was not ratified by the parliament.

Prachand's New Directions

In the second national convention of CPN (Maoist) held in February 2001 at a secret location, which was the first mass meeting of the party since the initiation of the insurgency, the party Supremo Prachanda gave a new direction to the movement called 'Prachandapath'. Prachanda assumed the position of Chairman of the party. As pointed out in the earlier chapter, the Prachandapath combined the twin strategies of protracted war as propounded by Mao and general armed insurrection as followed by Lenin.[18] The new strategy of the Maoists as devised in the Prachandapath called for an increased emphasis on urban insurrection at the same time continuing with building bases in the countryside.[19] The strategy was to get hold of the rural areas and than surround the cities.

Why did a need to change the strategy occur? Actually, at the theoretical level it was perceived that it was not necessary to win a war on the basis of one single strategy. The local conditions were also significant in devising a strategy (s) of war. The Nepalese conditions had revealed that it was not possible to record victory against the state by concentrating on protracted war from the countryside. It was also necessary to make cities a target of their attack. So Prachanda underlined the necessity of complementing people's war in the rural areas by popular violent insurrection in the urban areas.[20]

It may be pointed out here that the significance of mass movement in urban areas can not be undermined in any prolonged insurgency. It is a widely known fact that in the third world societies the urban areas are repository of political power, wealth and resources. The rural areas only represent the peasantry and the poor masses. Hence, the ultimate success of a revolution would rest upon controlling the urban areas. What Prachanda was intended to do by way of Prachandapath were:

(I) To consolidate his supreme control over the party and the Maoist army.

(II) To give a new direction and thrust to the Maoist insurgency.

The Maoists criticized the royal massacre of June 2001 but it did not affect their movement much. They announced district people's governments in Rukum, Jajarkot and Salyan. The Maoists attacked in Holeri in a Massive way.

Prime Minister Koirala who was under pressure after the royal massacre, resigned on 19 July 2001 and Sher Bahadur Deuba took over as the Prime Minister of the country. Four important developments had taken place by this time:

(I) The Maoists had devised their strategy to attack on the urban areas along with protracted war in the countryside.

(II) The Maoists army had come up as a well knitted and well equipped organization.

(III) The Maoists had extended their influence in more than half of the total districts of the country.

(IV) They had established people's governments in some areas and the government administration had been almost wiped out in those areas.

These were highly significant developments and it was clear that the Maoists had succeeded in giving a momentum to the insurgency. But then it is also a fact that the Maoists were nowhere near to the attainment of their goals except in continuing the movement. The government on the other hand failed in containing the Maoists either by use of force that had been the main instrument of dealing with Maoists or some attempts towards negotiated settlement that had failed.

The successive governments in Nepal had failed in addressing to the issues of poverty, inequalities and exclusion.[21] On the contrary the repressive approach of the government in the form of operation Romeo and Kilo Serra Two did not help in tackling the problem of insurgency. Nepal's development approach did not help in bringing up the rural people.[22] One very significant and often raised contrast is that one of the severely Maoists infested regions had been Rapti Zone where Rapti Valley Development Project had been in operation for the last 15 years (1980-95) and the United States spent US$ 50 millions in this project.[23] But than what happened? The Maoist problem generated in this region it self. It only indicates that the government had ignored the existing realities and there were problems in its approach towards the socio-economic issues. The Maoists had taken advantage of this situation in expanding their influence in the rural areas.

The Maoists had continued and intensified their struggle against the state for the last five years. But they also realized the necessity to use other kind of instrumentality for conflict resolution, may be for their own tactical reasons. It may also be pointed out here that after the killing of King Birendra and his entire family the country was in a state of mourning. The people were strongly in favour of peace. The Maoists were also realizing the mounting pressure for peace. They were also concerned about the way royal massacre took place.

Ceasefire

The Maoists declared cease-fire on 23 July 2001, two days after Deuba became the Prime Minister of the country. Sher Bahadur Deuba had given his inclination for the cease-fire even before taking oath to the office. In fact, it is clear from the earlier discussion that even before this, Deuba had been involved in the efforts made for the resolution of the Maoist problem. He wanted to establish that he was capable of finding a political solution of the problem. Gyanendra the new monarch too was enthusiastic for holding peace talks for two reasons: He was in search of legitimacy as the new king. The Maoists had taken an aggressive posture after the demise of king Birendra. They opined that the traditional monarchic system had ended in Nepal with the murder of king Birendra. It meant that the new king was not acceptable to them. Hence, king Gyanendra was also looking to project his image as a person greatly concerned to the issues of peace and stability in the country.

It is clear that both the government and the Maoists favoured a cease-fire and enter into peace negotiations. But the point is that both the parties were looking for settling their own scores by way of holding peace talks.

Peace Talks

Three round of peace talks were held between August – November 2001. The government declared a peace negotiation team to talk with the Maoists on behalf of the government. It included:

Chiranjiv Wagle	Convener
Mahesh Acharya	Member
Narhari Acharya	Member
Bijay Gachhedar	Member
Chakra Bastola	Member

The Maoists also declared its negotiation team as:

Krishna Bahadur Mahara	Convener
Agni Sapkota	Member
Top Bahadur Raimajhi	Member

Daman Nath Dhungana and Padma Ratna Tuladhar were facilitators for peace talks from the side of the government and the Maoists respectively. P.M. Deuba hold an all party meeting before talks began and all the political parties supported Deuba for initiating a dialogue with the Maoists.

First Round of Peace Talks: The first round of peace talks began on 30 August 2001 at Godavari hill resorts, nearly 30 km.

outside Kathmandu. There was no specific agenda for the talks in this round. Both the teams introduced each other and developed familiarity with one another.

On 21 August 2001 Prachanda called a meeting of the left political parties at Siliguri in India. Probably, Prachanda wanted to apprise the like-minded parties regarding his own party's agenda for the peace talks. However, it appears that it was not convincing to the communist parties. Madhav Nepal, General Secretary of UML, the largest among the communist parties, informed in an emergency meeting of the central committee of the party that he had rejected Prachanda's proposal of constituting a Constituent Assembly.

Second Round of Talks: The second round of talks began on 13-14 September 2001 in Bardiya. The government proposed to release some of the arrested leaders and Matrika Yadav was released accordingly. The Maoists demanded that the condition of the prisoners who had disappeared from the police custody be clarified and return the armed police to barracks. They also demanded withdrawal of the security regulations and Integrated Security and Development Programme.[24]

The core issues raised by the Maoists were:

1. To start process of institutionalization of the republican system in Nepal.
2. Withdraw present constitution.
3. Preparations for a new constitution by the people. The government was not prepared to accept any of these demands.

Third Round of Talks: The Third round of talks was held on November 2001. The Maoists concentrated on the demand for the formation of a Constituent Assembly and preparation of a new constitution by it, and formation of an interim government. The Nepali Congress did not agree to it and as stated earlier UML had already expressed its disagreement to the issue of Constituent Assembly.

The Maoists withdrew from the peace talks on 21 November 2001. They arranged a massive rally in Kathmandu and again indulged in violent activities. The Maoists also declared formation of people's government in Dang, Syangja and Solukhumbu. They also attacked on the government establishments at these places.

The three-month cease-fire was over and the peace talks had failed. In fact between August – November 2001 there were opportunities for peaceful negotiations and reaching to some solution of the Maoist problem. But it did not happen and the negotiations failed. Both the parties were responsible for the failure of the peace talks. It was the responsibility of the government to see that the negotiations would be carried smoothly. But it appears that the government did not care much for it. There were allegations that the government was not well prepared for talks with the Maoists.[25] The Point that is there should not have been any reason behind the ill preparations of the government. Why talks were not taken seriously is a moot question. One argument extended in this regard has been that the negotiation team did not have any experience of peace negotiations so they could not handle the situation properly. It is also argued that they were not aware of diplomacy. These are not convincing arguments. The fact remains that the government initiated peace talks with certain preconceived notions. It was not prepared to consider any of the demands raised by the Maoists. The Nepali Congress and UML had already made it clear that they did not accept the proposal of the Constituent Assembly. The Maoists were also not much concerned about peace and stability in the country. They adopted a rigid attitude and were not prepared to accept any thing less than the demands that they had put forward.

It has also been argued that PM Deuba lacked internal support. His own party men wanted to see him a grand failure. He was opposed by his own party.[26] He could also not seek adequate support of the parliament not he got adequate support from other political parties.

The Maoists in a way operated tactfully and they were the gainers in some respect. They utilized the time of cease-fire in consolidating their military and organizational strength. They established themselves as a legitimate political power because the government agreed to negotiate with them. They also succeeded in getting some of their leaders released from jails.

The Maoists in a way publicized their main demands by placing them before the negotiation team.[27] It is true that they were neither accepted by the political parties nor by the government, but it received the public notice. Probably this was one the mission of the Maoists.

Declaration of Emergency

On 26 November 2001 government declared a state of emergency in the country. CPN (Maoist) and its sister organizations were declared as terrorists. The Terrorist and Disruptive Activities (Control and Punishment) Ordinance was promulgated. Article 12 clause 1, Article 13,15,16,17,22 and 23 of the constitution were suspended. Wide powers were assigned to the security forces and the Royal Nepal Army (RNA) was deployed to contain the Maoist problem. PM Dueba blamed the Maoists for the failure of peace talks and the subsequent developments and said that they had betrayed and they were to be wiped out.[28] The government also announced a surrender scheme for the Maoists. It was reported that 1989 Maoists surrendered by 19 December 2001.

International Support Against Maoist Insurgency

There are three important things regarding international support to the Nepali government in its efforts towards containing the Maoist problem. It was after the 11 September terrorist attack on the US that support to the Nepali government against the Maoist insurgency was considered to be significant by the international community. After the US President's declaration of war on terrorism anywhere in the world, the Nepali government also got moral support and their attitude became tougher in the context of the peace talks with the Maoists. With the failure of peace talks and the deployment of RNA against the Maoists international military assistance became an imperative need of the Nepali government.

It may be pointed out here that the western countries had shown their concern over the spreading of the Maoist violence in Nepal, after realizing the increased threat from the terrorist organizations all over the world. The United States of America expressed its concern to the increasing Maoist movement in Nepal because it also posed a threat to the American citizens there. The United States also believed that the increasing Maoist influence would bring it closer to China.[29] The US State Department's Patterns of Global Terrorism noted in 2002 thus:

"The Maoist insurgency poses a continuing threat to US citizens and property in Nepal. Repeated anti – US rhetoric and actions suggest that Maoists view Western support for Kathmandu as a key obstacle to their goal of establishing a doctrinaire communist dictatorship. Furthermore, the Maoists have forged cooperative links with extremist groups across South Asia. In 2002 Maoist claimed responsibility for assassinating two US embassy guards. In a press statement they threatened foreign mission, including the US embassy to discourage foreign governments from supporting the government of Nepal".[30]

The United States declared Maoists of Nepal a terrorist group and agreed to provide military assistance to Nepal government to combat the Maoists. The US officials and army officers visited Nepal from time to time. The United States Congress approved US$ 2 million to train the Nepali army. The US assistance included helicopters, 20,000 M-16 rifles, night vision equipment and training to the Royal Nepali Army through International Military Education and Training Programme. US also conducted joint military exercises with RNA in 2003. The United Kingdom provided helicopters, arms and military equipment. The Yudha Bhairav Battalion of RNA was trained and equipped by the United Kingdom and Israel. Denmark, Norway, the EU were the other countries and organizations that offered assistance to the Nepali government.

India donated Chetak helicopters, NSAS rifles, anti-landmine vehicles and training to the Nepali security forces.

The United States and the United Kingdom were interested in a strong military action against the Maoists. India though provided military equipment on the request of the Nepali government, was more interested in finding a peaceful solution of the Maoist problem. It being the closest neighbour, having an open border with Nepal was also seriously affected by the ongoing Maoists insurgency in Nepal. So India's problems were quite different from the European donors and the United States. The Maoists were using the open border to take a shelter in India. People from the rural pockets of Nepal were fleeing to India due tot the fear of the Maoists. There were people in Nepal who were expecting India to come in a big way for the help of Nepali government. Some also expected India to provide army assistance.[31] It was neither possible nor feasible for India to use these options. At the same time it was not possible for India to close the border or tighten the open border regime beyond a limit. So India's position was quite complex and the hard military solution to the Maoist problem was not feasible from the Indian point of view. Nevertheless, India did not make any efforts to influence the Nepali government towards finding a negotiated settlement of the problem. It followed the perception of the government of Nepal and extended its support accordingly.

Intensification of Maoist Attacks

The Maoists intensified their violent activities after their withdrawal from the peace talks despite the fact that the emergency had been declared in the country and RNA had been deployed against them. On 16 February 2002, 100 people were killed in a Maoist attack in Mangalsen in Far Western Nepal. The emergency was extended for three months on 21 February 2002. In March 62 Maoists were killed in a RNA operation. In April 48 policemen were killed in Dang. The government declared prize on live or dead of a number of Maoists.[32] It shows that the Maoists were posing a serious challenge to the Nepali armed forces as well. It was officially accepted in May 2002 that 25 per cent of the country had come under the Maoist influence.[33] In May 2002, the Maoists in Rolpa district killed 130 army men.

Prime Minister Deuba was being criticized for his failure in finding any solution to the insurgency, intensification of the Maoist attacks and the extension in the time period of emergency. In May 2002 the parliament was dissolved to hold fresh elections in near future.

In September 2002 the Maoists attacked in Sindhuli in a big way and killed a number of persons. On 4 October 2002 King Gyanendra deposed PM Sher Bahadur Deuba and the council of ministers and assumed all executive powers in his hand. On October 11 king Gyanendra appointed Lokendra Bahadur Chand as Prime Minister, a person who was closely identified with the panchayat system and a strong supporter of the monarchy. The Maoists criticized king's action and viewed it as an assertion of the feudal forces. However, king Gyanendra was desperately looking for acquiring political legitimacy after taking all powers in his hands. He was also looking for an opportunity to establish that he was interested in seeking peaceful negotiations with the Maoists. He also thought that if he would succeed in finding any solution of the Maoist problem it would enhance his political image. A letter was send to one of the underground Maoist leader indicating that the government was ready to enter into peace negotiations with the Maoists. Narain Singh Pun, Birendra Jhapali and Dhani Ram Lamichhine played an important role in this regard.[34] The Maoists gave a positive response to it.

Second Round of Peace Negotiations

The Maoists declared cease-fire on 29 January 2003. Both the parties formed its negotiation team as following:

Maoists :

Dr. Babu Ram Bhattarai	Convener
Ram Bahadur Thapa	Member
Krishan Bahadur Mahara	Member
Dev Gurung	Member
Matrika Yadav	Member

Government:

Badri Prasad Mandal	Convener
Narayan Singh Pun	Member
Upendra Devkota	Member
Ramesh Nath Pandey	Member
Anuradha Koirala	Member

After Surya Bahadur Thapa replaced PM Lokendra Bahadur Chand, Dr. Prakash C. Lohani and Kamal Thapa constituted the negotiation team from the government side.

The facilitators were Damannath Dhungana, Padma Ratna Tuladhar, Shailendra Kumar Upadhyaya and Karna Dhoj Adhikari. A Code Of Conduct (COC) was signed between the Maoists and the government on 13 March 2003. It was agreed that both parties will be abided by the cease-fire and cooperate with each other. A COC Monitoring Committee was also constituted. However, the committee was not functional.

Three rounds of talks were held between the two parties on 27 April, 9 May and 17-19 August 2003. The first round of talks was devoted to the handing over of the Maoist agenda of talks to the government.

The second round of talks was devoted to procedural issues. The government agreed to release three Maoist leaders from jail. It was also agreed that the movement of RNA would be limited within the radius of 5 kms. from its camp.[35] This became a bone of contention for the Chand government. The political parties criticized him. Demonstrations were held in Kathmandu on this issue. Chand had to resign on 30 May 2003. On 5 June 2003 Surya Bahadur Thapa another panchayat stalwart and a leader of National Democratic Party was appointed as the Prime Minister of Nepal.

In the third round of talks the Maoists insisted on their agenda and they remain confined to their demands of republican state and formation of the Constituent Assembly. The government was not prepared to accept any of these demands, so the peace negotiations failed. The cease-fire was breakdown on 29 August 2003.

The government was again not well prepared for the peace talks with the Maoists. In fact, from the beginning there were lingering suspicions. The cease-fire itself came as a big surprise to the political parties and the people of Nepal. No one expected a cease-fire so quickly, because king had assumed all executive powers in October 2002 and the Maoists too were critical of the king's action. The political parties suspected an understanding between king and the Maoists and they viewed the whole episode with doubts. It is true that the core issues were not touched during the three rounds of peace negotiations.[36] As a result, the failure of peace talks was certain. No one was prepared to compromise. The government team did not have a clear vision and it did not know what it had to do? If they did not have any perception about the republican state, the Constituent Assembly what for had they entered in to peace negotiations? It is said that the later team of the peace negotiations from the government side had done more homework and they showed more concern about the peace talks. But the point is what agenda they had? Were they in a position to persuade the Maoists to agree on some position? Were they clear about that position? It seems that both the parties lacked flexibility, mutual trust and concern for bringing peace in the country.[37] The Maoists had complaints regarding delays in the execution of the issues on which they had agreed during the second round of talks. The two sides lacked mutual trust and confidence.[38]

It has also been argued that there were no criteria adopted in selecting the convener and members of the negotiation team of the government. The political affiliations and personal loyalties of the individual members were taken into consideration instead of their diplomatic skills, negotiation abilities, etc. Equally important is the point that whether the negotiation team and the facilitators were free to offer anything to the Maoists? The fact remains that they were seriously constrained in this regards.

The Maoist contention was that they entered into the peace talks because people of Nepal wanted peace and stability.[39] They also agreed that their agenda was based on the restructuring of the state while the proposal submitted by the government insisted on the change of government only.[40] However, the Maoists too adopted a rigid attitude. They could get some of their leaders released from jails. The Maoists also succeeded in opening a debate among political groups and the civil society on the issues they had raised. It is also a fact that the Maoists had exhibited their political strength.

On 27th August the Maoists called for a one-day strike to denounce army's attack on their cadres in Ramechhap district on 17 August thereby killing 19 rebels and civilians. The Maoists had already given an ultimatum on 24th August that if the government would not include the demand of restructuring the state in the peace talks they would withdraw from the talks. On 29th August Maoists withdrew from talks. The Maoists demanded for overthrowing the monarchic rule. In a statement Prachanda said, "Since the old regime has put an end to the forward looking solution to all existing problems through the cease-fire and peace talks, we herein declare that the rationale behind cease-fire and peace process has ended."

After the withdrawal of the cease-fire the Maoists again took resort to violent activities. Fighting erupted between the Maoists and RNA and police forces in Khotang district on September 27, 2003, in Kalikot district on February 15, 2004 Bhimad in Makwanpur district on February 5, 2004, Yadukuwa and Jadukhola on 4 April 2004 and so on.

In the beginning of 2004 there was an upsurge of anti-monarchic demonstrations. The members of political parties, the civil society activists and many student organizations staged demonstrations against the king. He was alleged as an autocratic ruler and demands were raised for the immediate restoration of democracy. The five party alliances were also demanding restoration of democracy in the country. There was also international pressure on king Gyanendra for the restoration of democracy. As a result, king Gyanendra appointed Sher Bahadur Dueba as PM in June 2004. Deuba's appointment as PM was a strategy of king Gyanendra. He thought that Deuba's appointment would pacify the demand for the restoration of democracy.

Deuba wanted to constitute an all-party government but only UML agreed to support him, which had been a constituent of the Five Party Alliance. The four party alliance now decided to continue their protest for the restoration of democracy.

PM Deuba was once again assigned the task to negotiate with the Maoists for the restoration of peace and resolution of the conflict. Deuba set middle of January 2005 as a deadline for the Maoists for the truce. The Maoists did not accept his call. They on the contrary questioned the status of Deuba government, although earlier Maoists had agreed for peace negotiations with Chand and Thapa governments. The Maoists mounted a massive attack on security forces on December 15, 2004 in Argakhanchi district in which 20 security personnel were killed. On 16 December 16 Maoists were killed in a clash with the armed forces in Dailekh. On December 23, 2004 Maoists called for a blockade of Kathmandu.

Summing Up

It is a fact that none in Nepal or elsewhere had thought of Nepal facing a guerrilla war of such a high intensity. In 1996 when the Maoists began insurgency it was generally viewed a small movement. The government perception for a longtime was that it was a law and order problem. Even the popular perception was not that of an organized guerrilla war. But it seems that the Maoists succeeded in developing it into a war against the state. The local conditions supported it. The failure of the successive governments in addressing themselves to the issues of political stability and governance on the one hand and need for socio-economic reforms on the other proved to be a big factor in this regard. The international forces also supported the Maoists in various ways. What is more important about the Maoists is that they had a strong ideological backing. As far as their organizational strength is concerned they could easily insert their influence among ethnic and regional identities and depressed sections of the society. They could also make it easy to establish their control over isolated regions and poverty ridden rural pockets. The fact that the Maoists had influenced over 75 per cent area of the country is significant. The Maoists strategy and tactics also helped them in further developing protracted war. They took advantage of cease-fire in consolidating their positions. They also established the impression that they were ready for peaceful negotiations with the government but also did not compromise with their political objectives.

It is for these reasons that the Maoist insurgency could survive. But it is also a fact that the Maoists could not exert their influence over urban areas, particularly the Kathmandu valley, the centre of political power in Nepal, despite a change of strategy. As a result they failed in catching the nerve of the governmental establishment. Similarly they could also not affect the urban elite beyond a limit. It was the rural poor masses that were mostly affected by the insurgency. But they hardly had any say in the power structure of the country.

References

1. See, Nickson R.Andrew, "Democratization and the Growth of

Communism in Nepal: A Peruvian Scenario in the Making?", *Journal of Commonwealth and Comparative Politics*, Vol.30 No.3, November, 1992; Stephen L.Mikesell, "The Paradoxical Support of Nepal's Left for Comrade Gonzalo", *Himal* (Kathmandu), March – April, 1993; Krishna B.Bhattachan, "Possible Ethnic Revolution or Insurgency in a Predatory, Unitary Hindu State", in Dhrub Kumar (ed.), *Domestic Conflict and Crisis of Governability in Nepal*, CNAS, Kathmandu, 2000.

2. Deepak Thapa & Bandita Sijapati, *A Kingdom Under Seige, The Maoist Insurgency in Nepal*, Printhouse, Kathmandu, 2003: 86.
3. *Janabhawana*, February 26, 1999 cited in Deepak Thapa, *n.2* : 86:87.
4. Also see, Harka Bahadur Gurung, Anand Aditya, et.al. *An Overview of Recent Armed Conflict in Nepal*, NEW ERA, Kathmandu, 2001.
5. Govind Neupane, *Nepal Ko Jatiyo Prasna*, CDS, Kathmandu, 2000: 3.
6. See, for the declaration, http://www.cpnuml.org/documents/bthCongress.html.
7. The other members of the Dhami Commission were Yogesh Bhattarai, Pradeep Shumsher Rana (IG), Devi Ram Sharma (National Investigation Commission and Krishna Murari Sharma (Home) as Member Secretary.
8. See, *Kathmandu Post*, 14 May 1998.
9. Rishikesh Shaha, "Idea and Reality, Nepal and Rolpa", *Himal, South Asia*, July, 1996.
10. Deepak Thapa, *n.2*.
11. Deepak Thapa, *n.2*: 92.
12. Manjushree Thapa, *An Elegy to Democracy Forget Kathmandu*, PENGUIN, Delhi, 2005.
13. Arjun Karki & David Seddon (eds.), *The People's War in Nepal: The Left Perspective*, Adroit Publishers, Delhi, 2003: 26.
14. *n.13*
15. Other members of the Deuba Committee were: Ram Chandra Poudel, Sushil Koirala, Chirinjib Wagle, Purna Bahadur Khadka, Govind Raj Joshi, Chakra Bastola and Dr. Prakash Sharan Mahat as Member Secretary
16. *The Rising Nepal*, March 23, 2000.
17. See Chapter Third for details.
18. The basic tenets of the Prachandapath were explained in the Report: *Mahan Agragami Chhalang. Itihas Ko Apariharya Avashyakta*, Central Publication Division of the party, 2001.

19. International Crisis Group, *Nepal's Maoists: Their Arms, Structure and Strategy*, Asia Report No. 104, 27 October, 2005: 23.
20. Also see, Pradeep Gyawali, *Prachandapath: Vichar Ko Kendrikaran Ki Bhrastikaran*, Kathmandu, 2001.
21. See, Krishna Hachhethu, "Democracy and Nationalism, Interface Between State and Ethnicity in Nepal", *Contributions to Nepalese Studies*, 30: 2, July 2003.
22. Devendra Raj Pandey believed that the development approach of Nepal had failed See, his book *Nepal's Failed Development*, NSA, Kathmandu, 1999.
23. M.Mainali, "Development VS the Maovadi's", in Deepak Thapa (eds.), *Understanding The Maoist Movement in Nepal*, Kathmandu, 2003: 25-26.
24. It had been introduced in Gorkha district first and than extended to another 7 districts.
25. *Kathmandu Post*, April 29, 2002.
26. Bishnu Raj Upreti, *Armed Conflict and Peace Process in Nepal, The Maoist Insurgency, Past Negotiations and Opportunities for Conflict Transformation*, Adroit, Delhi, 2006: 123.
27. Bishnu Raj Upreti *n.26*: 123-124.
28. *The Indian Express*, December 2, 2001.
29. Arjun Kerki, *n.13*: 38.
30. Steven C.Baker, "Nepal's Maoists Insurgency", *Front Page Magazine.com*, July 25, 2003.
31. Nirupama Subramanian, "India and Nepal's Insurgency", *The Hindu*, August 9, 2004.
32. *Kathmandu Post*, April 12, 2002.
33. Arjun Karki, *n.13*: 43.
34. Sambhu Ram Simkhada and Fabio Oliva, *The Maoists Insurgency in Nepal, A Monogeaph*, Gevenva March, 2006: 181.
35. Bishnu Raj Upreti, *n.26*: 132.
36. Galtung, "Transformation of Conflict in Nepal: A Human Rights Perspective in Bipin Adhikari (ed.), *Conflicts : Human Rights & Peace Challenges Before Nepal*, NHRC, Kathmandu, 2004 : 122.
37. Sambhu Ram Simkhada, *n.34*: 182.
38. Bishnu Raj Upreti, *n.26*.
39. Babu Ram Bhattarai, *Yudha ra Barta*, Janadhwani Prakashan, Kathmandu, 2063: 78.
40. *N.39*: 73.

6
Maoist Movement and Human Rights Issues

The issues relating to the human rights are wide and complex. There is hardly any country in the world where the question of human rights has not come up. There are a large number of countries where the problem of human rights has persisted for a longtime. There has been a perception that the third world countries are more prone to human rights violation in comparison to the developed sates of the world. It is not always true because even in the highly developed states of the West human rights problem has occurred.[1] In a country like United States of America the attitude and treatment with the black people has been one significant aspect of human rights violation. Similarly, it is difficult to assert that human rights violation is a problem of the centralized – authoritarian states. In democratic societies as well, problem of human rights may occur. Nevertheless, one may agree with the view that the instances and intensity of the human rights problem is more in the authoritarian states. One positive aspect in the context of democratic systems is that there are several channels through which voices against the human rights containment can be raised and preventive steps can be taken up on a large scale. In fact, the democratic system provides a better awareness of human rights and more effective mechanism for their protection and promotion.

At the international level also, there exists an institutional mechanism for the protection of human rights. The United Nations Human Rights Commission has established its offices all over the world and it is through these organizations that UNHRC has been monitoring human rights in different countries. This apart there are a large number of general and specialized Non-Governmental Organizations (NGO) that have been active in monitoring and promoting the human rights in different countries.

To what extent all these domestic and international arrangements for the human rights protection have been effective in different countries having different political environment and dealing with different political situations is a significant issue.

Human Rights, Militancy and Insurgency

The human rights are at a stake as and when a society is faced with militancy, insurgency or social revolutions. More prolong is militancy or insurgency more is the severity of human rights violation. There are countries faced with prolonged insurgency and there the problem of human rights has been acute. There are counties in Latin America, Africa, Eastern Europe, South-East Asia, South Asia and West-Asia that have faced insurgencies of different types. There are countries that are continued with the problem of insurgency. Peru, Vietnam, Kampuchea, etc are some examples of strong insurgency amounting to large cases of human rights violation. Chechnya, Turkish Kurdistan, Bosnia, Kosovo, Afghanistan, Iraq, Haiti, are the recent examples of the areas where acute problems of human rights violation have occurred. The people of Tibet have been talking of human rights for long. At home in South Asia India, Pakistan, Sri Lanka and Nepal have faced insurgency and movements of different magnitudes. There are a number of human rights laws, conventions and protocols initiated by the United Nations and other international agencies. A large number of countries all over the world are signatories to these laws and agreements. Despite these and many other domestic arrangements in respect to human rights protection all the countries of the world have faced one or the other kind of problem of human rights violation at one point of time or the other.

There is a direct relationship between human rights violation and insurgency or militancy. Both the administrative machinery and the militants violate basic rights of the masses for their own purpose. It may also be pointed out here that it is the common men who largely become victims of human rights violation in a state of insurgency or militancy.

Human Rights Situation in Nepal

The problem of human rights violation had become highly significant in Nepal in the context of the Maoist insurgency. It was after the establishment of a democratic order in the country in 1990 that the question of protection and promotion of human rights received currency. During the era of panchayat rule there had been frequent cases of human rights violation but the issues remained contained due to the authoritarian nature of the state. The 1990 democratic constitution of Nepal provided for the fundamental rights of the people. The Human Rights Committee of the House of Representatives was assigned the responsibility to look after the human rights issues. A new environment for the promotion of human rights was being created in the country after 1990. The questions of women empowerment, rights of the weaker sections of the society, protection against child labour, education, basic amenities, etc were being raised. With the increasing awareness regarding human rights protection and promotion demands were being raised for the creation of a separate agency to look after the human rights issues. After 1990 a number of Non-Governmental Organizations (NGO) were established and many of them were concerned to the promotion of human rights of the different sections of the society. Some international agencies had also begun to take interest in Nepal. As a result the demand for a government agency became significant. In 1997 Nepal Human Rights Commission Act was passed. But due to political instability it could not be implemented immediately. In May 2000 Nepal Human Rights Commission came into existence. The NHRC was entrusted with the following Tasks.

(I) Promotion and protection of human rights.

(II) To Submit reports to the Nepalese government from time to time on human rights conditions in the country.

(III) Submitting special reports to the government on specific incidents of human rights violation.

(IV) To ensure harmonization of national laws relating to human rights protection with the international human rights declarations, agreements and protocols, their standardization and improvement.

(V) To Promote human rights education in the country.

(VI) Cooperation with the international human rights institutions and agencies as a representative institution of the country.

(VII) Appraising UN bodies and committees on human rights situation in the country.

NHRC is responsible for the projection of the human rights situation in the country and bring it to the notice of the government. It has to look into the cases of human rights violation and wage the government for their protection.[2]

The Nepal Human Rights Commission came into operation at a time when the country was faced with a serious problem of human rights violation. There are reports that indicate that during this period most of the cases of human rights violation were related to the Maoist insurgency in one way or the other.

Human Rights Issues and the Government

The government machinery has been largely responsible for the human rights abuses relating to the Maoist insurgency. Even before the Maoist problem had actually began cases of human rights abuses had occurred in Rolpa and Rukkum during the operation Romeo. The people were arrested without any charge and kept in jails. The innocent people who even did not know who the Maoist were, charged by the police in one pretext or the other. The members of Joint People's Front were particularly made target by the police forces. Barbara Adams made an interesting observation in this regard that:

"You do not have to go as far as Rukum or Rolpa to here of the terrorizing of innocent populations by political interest, backed by the palace. In Rolpa, it is mostly Magars who are suffering; in Kavre district, here close to home, mainly Tamangs. It is truly ironic and pitiable that the poorest and most marginalized indigenous populations are those which are suffering that most marginalized indigenous "people's war". It is ironic that thė often arrogant police elite, with caste and power, is tormenting them in a way their traditional rulers never could".[3]

The police and royal army in practice treated the supporters of the Maoists with an objective to teach them a lesson. There were a large number of aspects of human rights violation committed by the police and armed forces:

1. People were arrested without issuing any warrant on their names. They were either suspected as members of leftist extremist groups or sympathizers of the Maoists. A number of such persons were also arrested who were innocent and even did not know who the Maoists were. In many cases such persons were also arrested with whom they had personal rivalries or conflicts.
2. False charges were labeled against a number of people and then they were arrested under the Public Offences Act.
3. People organizing meetings or commemorating certain events were charged by the police forces.
4. Torture of various shorts and beatings had become a common feature. In this context Barbara Adams writes, "Our conclusion after a day in scenic, sunny Dhulikhel was that if the basic tenets of law and human rights would be so abused in accessible village like Dhulikhel, God help the poor innocent, uneducated villagers in more remote areas of the country like Rukum and Rolpa". It indicates that the situation was worst in the remote rural areas, where there was hardly any one to talk about the human rights.
5. The police arrested a large number of youths every time when strikes and blockades were organized. These arrested people were ill treated.
6. There was problem of forced disappearance.
7. In the rural areas people carrying their traditional household tools like Khukuri were charged as armed terrorists and treated by the police harshly for this reason.
8. Random killing of people in the name of suspected Maoist or Maoist sympathizers.

9. Youths and women were kept in jails without being charged. In many cases the court released them, as there were no substantial charges behind their detention.
10. In jails detainees were kept in highly in humane conditions. They were not provided even the basic facilities and treated like animals. The human rights activists were not allowed to meet them or observe their living conditions.

It was alleged that the government was violating the international human rights conventions, which Nepal had ratified. The Nepalese government was adhered to these conventions and regulations. For example the 1979 convention sets norms and standards for police behavior and action. But police treatment against detainees and prisoners was much against these regulations. It is interesting to note that at many times the police took signatures or thumb impressions on blank papers of those who were arrested by it. It was against the basic tenets of the human rights.

The problem of human rights violation became more serious after 2001 when emergency was declared in the country and army was deployed to contain the Maoist insurgency. The Royal Nepal Army tried to deal with the Maoists and the suspected Maoists much harshly. The cases of extra judicial executions, torture, arbitrary arrests, detentions, etc. increased after 2001.

In April 2002 the Nepalese government promulgated TADA. The situation of human rights further deteriorated in the country after the implementation of TADA.

It was indicated in a number of news paper reports that a large number of journalists and other media persons, teachers, advocates, civil society activists and trade unionists were detained in their home towns, house searched or tortured. They were suspected to be the Maoist sympathizers or they were writing in favour of the Maoist insurgency.

The government tried to contain the activities of the Maoists and those who were sympathizing the Maoists by mobilizing the rural people. Rural Volunteer Security Groups and Peace Committees were constituted in 2003. The committees were supposed to mobilize the village people towards maintaining peace and security. The village people were expected to join these groups and those who did not join them they were viewed as supporters of the Maoist insurgents.

The Nepalese government though acted with heavy hands on the Maoist insurgents and their sympathizers, it tried to blame the Maoists for all acts of human rights violation. It tried to explain that the Maoists were responsible for the law less ness and killings. Bhekh Bahadur Thapa leader of the Nepali delegation at the 60th session of the UN Commission on Human Rights said that, "Violence, intimidation, marring killing, summary executions, kidnapping and displacement of the thousands of innocent civilians have seriously undermined the efforts of HMG to ensure the employment of human rights by its people."

It was stated, "The security forces are working hard to guarantee a sense of confidence and security among the people at large, and to protect the rights to life and liberty of the citizens. Barring occasional individual aberrations the security forces are operating with maximum interest in their mission to provide security and to win the hearts and minds of the people while investigations have been initiated alleged violations actions have been taken against those found guilty of violations.[4]

However, in the 60th session of UNCHR at Geneva on 23 April 2004, the Amnesty International, the European Union and Switzerland urged the commission to establish, mandate and to monitor the human rights situation in Nepal and support a longtime and adequately backed observer presence in the country.

Human Rights Violations by Maoists

The Maoists were responsible for the violation of human rights for numerous actions and by its implications in several cases. The Maoists took a very harsh attitude towards their adversaries. The Maoists acted brutally against the police forces, army men and other government officials whom they suspected working against the Maoist insurgents. They were involved in arbitrary execution of the police and army men. A large number of police and solders were killed during the Maoist attacks. The Maoists followed a policy of revenge against the police and armed forces and adopted the tactic of killing against killing.

A large number of civilians were also killed during the Maoist attacks in different parts of the country. These killings involved those innocent people who became victims of the Maoist guerrilla war against the state forces. But the Maoists also victimized those people who were known to be the informers to the government.

Victimization of Women and Children

Trafficking in women and children has been a serious issue of human rights violation in Nepal. It is a continuous process not something particularly related to the Maoist insurgency. Nevertheless, the problem was aggravated due to violence, disorder and atrocities.

A large number of the Nepali women are brought to India every year for trafficking. It has indeed been a perennial problem in Nepal and the open border between India and Nepal make it easy for the Nepali women to spread all over the Indian metropolitan cities. Trafficking in women and children involves a deep-rooted process of gender discrimination. It is a curse upon them for generations who are involved in it. The problem of trafficking in women occurs due to lack of education among women, poverty, unemployment, social exclusion of women and discriminatory attitude of ignorance towards women and girls particularly in the rural areas, etc.

It has to be understood here that the trafficking in women is a continuous problem. However, the insurgency added to this problem in two ways. A large number of women were arrested and interrogated by the police forces for their alleged support or connections with the Maoists. It is also said that they were molested and sexually abused. They as a result, were forced to leave their places. The Maoist cadres also used women for the fulfillment of their sexual needs. They were at times forced to meet the food, shelter and logistic needs of the Maoist forces in the rural areas. Thus, women became victim of conflicts at both the ends: the administrative operations and the insurgents. Both the police and the Maoist insurgents forced them in this regard.

Children were also victimized and deprived of their rights. After a certain period of time when the Maoist army started facing short of combatants they began forced recruitment. In rural areas each family was asked to send at least one child to serve in the

Maoist army. It not only deprived these children from schooling and other facilities but also created terror among the rural people. Since the men had either gone out or serving else where such problems were faced by women there by adding to their hardship. In fact, it would not be wrong to state that in the rural areas it were women and children which suffered most form the insurgency.

Strikes and Blockades

One important dimension of the human rights violation was the strikes, bunds and blockades that the Maoist insurgents operated from time to time. The Maoists used all these tactics to pressurize the government as well as to create instability and disorder. This included general strikes and bunds, economic blockades, and so on. These strikes and blockades created problems for the people, disrupted their daily lives and deprived them of their daily needs and requirements. The longest nationwide strike ran for 10 days from 2 to 12 April 2005. In March 2006 also the Maoists had announced a five days economic blockade but it was later on withdrawn at the request of the Seven Party Alliance. These strikes and blockades were a violation of the human rights as it disrupted the routine works of the people and deprived them of their basic requirements.

Problem of Displacement

The Maoist conflict had resulted in large-scale displacement of population from the insurgency affected areas. According to one estimate 300000 people were displaced during the eleven-year-old Maoist insurgency. These people were particularly from the rural areas. In the western Nepal a large number of populations had migrated to Uttarakhand.[5] There were three basic factors:

1. Increased Maoist demands and atrocities on the villagers particularly during the later half of the insurgency.
2. The harassment by the police forces and the royal army and the movement of the armed forces in the rural areas, fear of killing resulted in people leaving their areas and migrating to the neighbouring Indian regions. There were several news reports regarding detention of the people

as they were being suspected as Maoists or the Maoist informers. At times such allegations were made due to personal reasons and politics in the rural areas.

3. The continuous instability and an atmosphere of fear and tension in the rural areas had created problems of employment, particularly to those people who were dependent on daily employment.

It may also be pointed out here that it were not only Nepalese people but a large number of Indian migrants in Tarai and other places had to return back to India due to the fear of the Maoists.

Problem of Forced Disappearance

The problem of forced disappearance of the people has been serious not only during the Maoist insurgency. Even after the withdrawal of the movement by the Maoists the problem of farced disappearance has persisted thereby seriously jeopardizing the human rights situation in the country. Asian Human Rights Commission in its report observed, "... from a human rights perspective much remains to be done. Violations continue to be committed by all sides, and this will remain the case until the culture of impurity that has accompanied the widespread abuses of the past, is removed. In order to ensure that impurity is dismantled, justice cannot be sacrificed on the altar of political expediency. Any and all allegations of human rights abuses committed by all sides need to be effectively investigated and prosecuted in line with Nepal's law and international obligations. Where laws are missing they must by created. To enable this to be most effective, the institutions of the rule of law must be strengthened to allow them to cope with this sizeable task. Investigations and prosecution need to be commenced without further delay, as these institutions can develop and they go, through practical experiences ......"[6]

The Nepal Human Rights Commission established a field office to look into the cases of forced disappearance. The judiciary took a serious note of the cases of forced disappearance.

The Supreme Court of Nepal in its decision on June 1, 2007 ordered the government of Nepal to immediately investigate upon the cases of forced disappearance. It was also ordered to establish an independent commission to conduct investigation and to enact comprehensive laws on enforced disappearance. The government had, however, failed in adhering to the order of the Supreme Court. The government of Nepal had instead decided to constitute the commission under the Enquiry Commission Act of Nepal that according to the Supreme Court was not in consistence with Nepal's international obligations pertaining to the human rights issues. Not only the judiciary but civil society organizations also rejected the government proposal on the problem of forced disappearance.

The Supreme Court of Nepal in its June 1, 2007 judgment on force disappearance ruled that the existing legal arrangements governing any probe commission enquires into cases of human rights violations, including forced disappearance were insufficient and the criminal legal apparatus of the country lacked necessary provisions to deal with these issues. It was thought that there was an imperative need to frame a separate law to deal with the cases of forced disappearance. The Supreme Court of Nepal had directed the government to constitute a commission on disappearance after having in acted a law that would govern the working of the commission. It was also remarked that it would be suggestive here to follow the UN convention on forced disappearance in this context. It may be pointed out here that these decisions of the Supreme Court were highly significant because the interim constitution of Nepal states that the decisions taken by the Supreme Court will be binding on the government.

But it appears that the interim government tried to overlook the directions of the Supreme Court and constituted a 'High Level Probe Commission on Disappeared Persons on 21 June, 2007, under the chairmanship of former Supreme Court justice Narendra Bahadur Neupane, The commission was to investigate upon the cases of disappearance of people during the Maoist insurgency and afterwards. It, however, remained, ineffective due to strong opposition by civil society and human rights organizations.

The Supreme Court of Nepal through its committees made special investigations regarding the disappeared people. In the case of Bhairabrath Barak case for instance 49 cases of forced disappearance were deduced. It shows that there were a large number of cases of disappearance. Most of the cases of forced disappearance were related to media persons, party activists, informers, etc.

NHRC and the Maoists

The Nepal Human Rights Commission has been much concerned about the Maoist insurgency in Nepal because it is a fact that the Maoist movement opened many dimensions of human rights violation in the country.

The Human Rights Commission desired the Maoists to return to peace and order. It believed that the Maoist insurgency had caused violence thereby posing serious challenge to human rights situation in the country. The commission also desired that the government and the civil society organizations needed to work for creating an environment in which all including the Maoist insurgents take cognigence of the international rules and regulations pertaining to human rights.

The Maoists, however, did not take much interest in the Human Rights Commission. They considered it an institution fovaouring the Nepalese government. However, they did not interfere much in the activities of the commission.

Role of UNCHR

The United Nations Commission for Human Rights began to take interest in Nepal after 1990 when a congenial atmosphere began to build up in the country for the promotion of human rights. The main objective of UNCHR was to create a strong environment for the protection and promotion of human rights. It followed a two-fold policy in this regards: to generate awareness among the Nepalese regarding the international rules, regulations and conventions. The UNCHR provided Nepali translation of these rules and regulations. It also provided technical and financial assistance to promote human rights through awareness building measures.

UNCHR became more concerned about the deteriorating human rights situation in Nepal due to the Maoist insurgency. It took interest in the activities of NHRC and offered its support to her. In November 2003 UNDP and UNCHR reached to an understanding to cooperate with NHRC in order to build up its capacity to monitor human rights in the country.

Role of NGO's

A large number of non-governmental organizations ranging between Amnesty International to local NGO's and human rights groups expressed their concern to the deteriorating human rights situation in the country. These organizations tried to surface the cases of human rights violation whether committed by the government security forces or the Maoist insurgents. It is alleged that these armed groups in exposing the cases of human rights violation threatened these organizations. There was lack of cooperation from the administration. The human rights activists were not allowed to meet prisoners in jails. Advocacy Forum, which was aimed at providing legal aids, was many times not allowed to meet prisoners or watch conditions in side the jails.

Human Rights Violation in Tarai

The situation of human rights has not been all that good in Nepal even after the withdrawal of the Maoist insurgency and the initiation of the peace process. There had been occasional incidents of violence and killings after mid 2006. However, the Tarai agitation has given a new twist to the problem of human rights violation in Nepal. Tarai has passed through a violent movement for the last one-year. The agitation in the Tarai has caused the same kind of situation of human rights violation, which had occurred in the country during the Maoist insurgency. The violence in the Tarai has taken lives of a number of people and there have been several instances of violation of human rights by the agitators as well as the government machinery.

The movement in Tarai has not only raised fresh challenges for the Nepali state but it has also made it clear that unless peace and stability is restored in the country through democratic inclusion of the regions and communities the problem of human rights violation will continue.[7]

The Madhesi Janadhikar Manch set the Tarai movement in motion. It turned quite violent in some districts of the region very soon. As in the case of the Maoist insurgency, the policy of the government was to suppress the movement. The Maoists had become part of the government by this time and it is quite surprising that those who were fighting against the state some times back were now suggesting for a strong action by the government against the agitators. There has been a breakdown of rule of law in Tarai over the past one year.

The Tarai uprising has been important in the context of the political dynamics of the country in the sense that this movement emerged with the support and initiation of those splinter groups of the Tarai region that had been earlier supporting the Maoist insurgency. So it was obvious that it changed the power balance in the Tarai and political support base of the Maoist weekend here to a certain extent. A number of groups have been involved in the Tarai agitation such as Janatantrik Tarai Mukti Morcha – Jwala group, Janatantrik Tarai Mukti Morcha – Goit group, Madhesi Janadhikar Manch, Magar Mukti Morcha, Tharuwan Mukti Morcha, Madhesi Tiger, Madhesi Yakta Kobra, Kirat Workers Party, Tarai Virus, Young Communist League and Madhesi Mukti Morcha. There has been widespread law less ness in the Tarai. There have been some incidents of Mass Killings in the Tarai region. On 21 March 2007 violence took place at Gaur in Rauthat district. The Maoists and Janatantrik Tarai Mukti Morcha indulged in conflict with each other. 29 persons were reportedly killed in Gaur incident. It indicated that the Tarai agitation was an offshoot of the Maoist movement. Another incident took place as Kapilbastu, where 15 persons were reportedly killed. A large number of people were displaced in such incidents. INSEC in a report on November 21, 2007 stated that:

" 234 persons were killed since 21 November last year of which 28 persons were killed by the government, 23 persons by Maoist and Young Communist League, 18 persons by JTMM – Goit, 27 persons by JTMM-Jwala and the rest were killed by armed groups in Tarai and unknown groups. Maoists and YCL were involved in the abduction of 495 persons while JTMM-Jwala abducted 107 persons and JTMM-Goit abducted 71 persons. It also reported that there were 122 incidents of property captured by the Maoists and YCL, 21 incidents of property captured by JTMM-Goit and 65 incidents by JTMM-Jwala". [8]

Summing Up

To sum up the discussion it is clear that the Maoist insurgency opened up a serious problem of human rights violation and abuses. It is a fact that all kinds of cases of human rights violations took place with the beginning of the Maoist movement in Nepal. Both the government machinery and the Maoist insurgents were equally responsible for this. The government approach to find a militarized solution to the problem of insurgency and its policy to contain all those individuals and groups who were sympathizing the Maoists in one way or the other, created problems of human rights violation. Once the Royal Nepal Army was deployed to contain the Maoists it created more problems as it acted in a manner to take revenge against the Maoists. The Maoists protracted guerrilla war on the other hand was based on violence. They also followed the same policy of harsh treatment against their adversaries.

The problem of human rights violation increased after 2001 and reached to its heights after the royal coup of early 2005. The withdrawal of the Maoist insurgency and the peace process also improved the human rights situation in the country. However, the imprints of the Maoists insurgency on human rights violation are still there. The problem of forced disappearance is still there as large number of cases of disappearance came up after the peace process began. The Tarai agitation has added a fresh dimension to human rights violation.

The protection and promotion of human rights is an issue that has to be taken up seriously in the process of rebuilding democracy in the country. There is a need to create a strong institutional foundation of human rights in Nepal. There is also a need to focus upon awareness building about human rights, particularly among the rural people of Nepal.

References

1. For a discussion of the issues relating to human rights see, Norem Sanajeoba, *Human Rights: Practices and Abuses*, Cosmos Publications, New Delhi, 1994; K.P. Saxena (ed.), *Human Rights: Perspective and Challenges*, Lancer Books, Delhi, 1994.

2. For details of the structure and functioning of the Nepal Human Rights Commission see, Bipin Adhikari, *Building Capacity of National Human Rights Institutions, The Case of Nepal*, Rights to Education Foundation, Kathmandu, 2004.
3. Berbara Adams, *Napal Crisis Unlimited, Reflections from the Crucial Years*, Adroit, New Delhi, 2006:131.
4. Quoted in Bipin Adhikari, *n.2*:
5. It was observed in some of the areas of Uttarakhand that the Nepalese from Western region of the country were staying in the villages and doing all kinds of works like agriculture, labour, house construction, etc. Earlier they were concentrated largely in the urban pockets, but now their strength had increased and they had spread all over the rural areas. The local people clearly mentioned that these Nepalese had come over there due to the fear of the Maoists.
6. *The State of Human Rights in Eleven Asian, Nations*, ATTRC, Hongkong, 2007: 151.
7. International Crisis Group Report on Tarai: *Nepal's Troubled Tarai Region*, Asia Report No. 136, July 9, 2007.
8. *INSEC Report*, (Kathmandu), November 21, 2007.

7

Taking a 'U' Turn: Maoists Joining The Political Mainstream

The politics of Nepal began to move fast and took a sharp turn since the beginning of the year 2005. The royal takeover of February 2005 was the height of the changing political dynamics of Nepal. It though came as a surprise to many political analysts yet it was not a overnight decision taken by the king. It was in fact, the final show of the political process that king Gyanendra had started in October 2002 by dethroning the elected Prime Minister and suspending the parliament. The royal takeover though ensured absolute powers to monarchy consequently it also opened avenues for the realignment of political forces that were opposed to the royal takeover.

Another significant development was the understanding between the Maoists and the democratic political parties to fight against the royal coup. This understanding and the subsequent developments paved a way for the Maoist's entry to the mainstream politics. What inspired the Maoists to follow a constitutional path for the restructuring of the Nepali state and society is a significant issue.

Interestingly, Maoists had joined the other political forces of Nepal in the 1990 democratic movement. They also participated in the 1991 general elections and emerged as the third major political party. But after the elections they gradually lost the track of constitutional democracy and began to indulge in violent tactics that ultimately culminated into a protracted war for almost a decade. The Maoists agreed to again follow the path of multiparty democracy towards the end of 2005. What prompted the Maoists to take this U turn? It was in fact not a small decision. Nevertheless, it opened a new avenues opened for peace, stability and democracy in the country. Whether or not the Maoists and the Seven Party Alliance (SPA) would succeed in their mission was an important issue. Will the Maoists path to multi party democracy remain a durable phenomenon? These are some significant issues in the context of the changed dynamics of Nepali politics.

In this chapter an attempt has been made to deal with these issues.

The Royal Coup

In a highly surprising way king Gyanendra dismissed the Sher Bahadur Deuba government on 1 February 2005 and declared a state of emergency in the country. It was a well thought of and planned decision taken by king Gyanendra.[1] In his announcement king Gyanendra said that he will himself assume all powers and rule the country directly as Chairman of the council of ministers for a period of three years.[2] The king took advantage of the constitutional provisions under article 19 which provided for emergency powers to him. However, Gyanendra's action was uncalled for as there was no such urgency for declaring emergency in the country. The kind of situation prevailed in the country had continued for last many years and there was nothing extra ordinary. Secondly, the way king acted was beyond the spirit of the constitution.[3] It was not clear as what was the justification behind announcing king's direct rule for three years? It was clear that the king was highly ambitious. He wanted to become a real player of politics. But no one would have thought of such a drastic and early action by king Gyanendra. The Royal Nepali Army assisted the king in implementing his political motives.[4] The civil rights provided in the 1990 constitution were suspended.

King Gyanendra's assumption of powers followed a series of actions against his political adversaries. The main political leaders were house arrested or detained or placed in jails. All kinds of communications such as media, radio and television were brought under control. The media persons, intellectuals and other persons of civil society who were considered to be the supporters of democracy were also arrested or they were compelled not to move outside their city or district. It is clear that king Gyanendra defied the 1990 constitution and democracy and imposed his personal despotism in the country. The king was desperately looking for a role in Nepali politics. He alleged that the political parties had failed in containing violence, controlling corruption in the country and improving economic situation. The political parties had not taken any serious steps to control the Maoists problem. So the king was not at all happy with the political parties.[5] Gyanendra also alleged that the government had failed in holding the general elections. It seems that the King was trying to justify his action by holding the political parties responsible for all the problems that the country was faced with.

King Gyanendra wanted to create a support base, which would strengthen his despotic rule and at the same time dawn the democratic forces. The royal army was already supporting him. What he now needed to create was a political support base. For this purpose he decided to take support of the old guards of the panchayat era. On 2 February king announced a 10 member council of ministers. On 14 February he appointed Tulsi Giri and Kirti Nidhi Bisht as Vice Chairmen of the Council of Ministers. Interestingly, king brought back those leaders of the panchayat era who had been out of active politics since long. But they had been strong supporters of the monarchy. Thus king tried to return to panchayat era.[6]

The council of ministers in its first meeting announced a 21-point programme. A Corruption Control Royal Commission was also formed to look in to the cases of corruption. It was an important instrument to take in to task all the political adversaries and opponents. In order to establish its control over the district administration the king appointed Zonal Commissioners in all the 14 administrative zones and development regions, as it was under the panchayat system. King tried to consolidate his powers with the help of royal army and the panchayat era political leadership. In the middle of the year he announced withdrawal of the emergency. But control over media, communication, etc continued. Actually, it was done just to satisfy the international community, which was pressurizing the king to return to multi-party democracy. The king continued with its absolute control over the state power.

King Gyanendra also tried to seek support from the international community in the name of controlling the Maoist insurgency. India, USA, UK and the other donor countries to Nepal though not happy with the action of king Gyanendra, continued to support him over the issue of armed action against the Maoists. Nepal also sought support from China, Pakistan, Russia, etc.

King and the Maoists

The Maoists also did not consider the royal takeover as a welcome development as it connoted reemergence and strengthening of the feudal forces. The government had began to consolidate RNA attacks on the Maoists after the royal takeover.[7] It seems to be a part of the strategy of the royal government because they thought that the Maoists would retaliate against the king's action. The Maoists in fact, retaliated in a big way and attacked in Sarlahi, Kavre, Bhojpur, Argakhanchi and Kalikot districts.

King Gyanendra wanted to give the impression that he was much concerned about the insurgency and wanted to find out a solution. He asked Maoists to surrender their arms and return to the mainstream politics. It was made clear that those who would follow this direction would be rewarded and those who do not would face military action. King said in a statement thus:

> "We call upon all those who have gone astray, taking up arms against the nation and the people, and those who are engaged in criminal activities against peace and democracy to return to the mainstream of national politics peacefully. Ensuring opportunities to freely express one's views with patriotism as the focal point, fulfilling one's aspirations and contributing with welfare of the nation and people are the inter alia features of multiparty democracy. We assure all those who avail of this

opportunity to join the national mainstream that the state will give them opportunities and rights equal to those enjoyed by our citizens without any discrimination whatsoever, neither the people nor the law will tolerate any terrorist activities against the state or its citizens."[8]

King Gyanendra though asked the Maoists to surrender and join the mainstream politics did not propose any negotiation with them. He was not prepared for any peaceful negotiation with the Maoists. It is also a fact that the Maoists were not in any illusion about the motives of king Gyanendra, therefore, they were not expecting any soft attitude from him. The Maoists called for a 3 days strike in February 2005 and than 11 days long strike in April 2005. The Maoists and the king were aware of each other's intentions and goals and hence, there was no possibility of any thaw between the two.

Seven Party Alliance

The king adopted a confrontationist attitude and was not prepared to negotiate with the political parties. He was critical of the political parties and blamed them for not taking the Maoist problem seriously. The King as stared earlier, also blamed them for mis -governance, corruption and weakening the process of national integration.

King's action against the leaders of the various political parties further pulled them apart. King's take over of political powers had already created a hiatus between the monarchy and the political parties. The disgusted political parties began to search for a united struggle against king's takeover. In May 2005 seven political parties including NC, UML, NC (D), Janmorcha Nepal, NWPP, ULF, NSP (Anandi Devi) and NSP (AD) agreed to form an alliance to fights against the despotic rule of the king. The Seven Party Alliance (SPA) agreed on a 6 point programme that included restoration of the House of Representatives and the 1990 constitution, management of conflict, progressive movement for the restoration of democracy on the basis of 1990 constitution, adherence to multi-party democracy and elections for a Constituent Assembly.[9]

SPA gave a call to do away with the autocratic rule of the monarchy. It accorded top priority to the restoration of the House of Representatives. It was however, doubtful if this would have resolved the crisis. SPA chalked out a weak agenda.[10] The more important issues were formation of Constituent Assembly and declaring Nepal a republican state. It was not clear if the restoration of the 1999 parliament would ultimately lead to the process of formation of the Constituent Assembly. Nevertheless, the Seven Party Alliance was the first major attempt of the political parties against the royal take over. It also paved a way for the polarization of democratic forces. It also gave a positive message to the civil society. On the whole it was a significant development and generated new hopes among the democratic forces.

International Response to King's Takeover

The international community though supporting the Nepali government against the Maoist insurgency did not like the royal coup. India, the United Kingdom and the United States of America expressed strong reactions over the king's takeover. The British government recalled its ambassador to Nepal. On 9 February 2005 the Indian ambassador to Nepal met King Gyanendra and urged him to return to multi party democracy. On 25 February 2005 India decided to suspend its military aid to Nepal till the country would return back to the democratic process. India's the than foreign minister Natwar Singh said in the parliament on 4th March 2005:

"The developments in Nepal constitute a serious set back to democracy and bring the monarchy and mainstream political parties in direct confrontation with each other. This can only benefit the forces that not only wish to undermine democracy in Nepal but the institution of democracy as well."[11]

The US Assistant Secretary in the Department of State Donald Camp visited Nepal from 26-28 June 2005. He said that the king's action was not acceptable to the United States. The United States welcomed the formation of the Seven Party Alliance. The United Nations Organization was also not happy with Nepal's return to authoritarian rule. UN General Secretary Kofi Annan during a meeting with king Gyanendra at Afro-Asian Conference on 22 April 2005, emphasized upon restoration of democracy in Nepal.

The various aid donors to Nepal like European Council, CIDA, DANIDA, FINIDA, DFID, GTZ, SBC, US AID, Norway, UNDP, etc, suspended their aid to Nepal.

Maoist Cease-fire

The royal takeover of February 2005 gradually induced a positive change in the attitude of the Maoists. They began to realize that the political dynamics of the country was quite complex and the methodologies that they were applying were becoming doubtful in terms of realization of their political objectives. Despite a strong protracted war against the state the monarchy had brought itself in the centre of politics. The political parties were most affected by king's action. The Maoists began to realize that it was an opportune time to wage a gap between the king and the political parties and on the other hand, themselves come near to the political parties. The king viewed both the political parties and the Maoists as major obstacles to his direct rule. He undermined the actions of both. Thus in king's perception both were his political enemies. The political parties realized that the return to the multi party democracy was not possible without a struggle against the monarchy. This prompted the major political parties to come closer to each other and also to look into the possibilities of joining hands with the Maoists.

The Maoists thought of providing a larger space to SPA for the consolidation of its struggle against king and declared a three-month unilateral cease-fire affected from September 2005. It was an important strategic move on the part of the Maoists because it created a difficult position for King. There was pressure on the government to respond to the Maoist cease-fire in a positive way. The government did not agree to do that. It argued that the Maoists were not serious about peace and that the declaration of the cease-fire was only a strategy to strengthen their activities and programmes and streamline their organizational base. The Maoists extended cease-fire for a month in December 2005. The Maoists succeeded in seeking popular sympathy as the cease-fire brought relief to them in many ways. People also began to think that the government was not interested in resolving the problem because it was not reciprocating to the Maoist declaration of cease-fire.

It may also be noted here that the Maoist cease-fire also gave a positive message to the international community because king Gyanendra was trying to play the terrorist card in order to seek international support against the Maoists. The Maoists gave the message that they were interested in peace and conflict resolution.

The Maoist cease-fire helped in building confidence among the political parties and the civil society.

Bridging the Gaps

Both the Maoists and the political parties were realizing that there was a need to fight jointly against the royal takeover. King Gyanendra had though lifted emergency and there was some moderation in his attitude, it was clear that he was neither prepared to accommodate the democratic forces nor there was any change in his attitude towards the Maoists or SPA. The Maoists had already shown their changing attitude by declaring a unilateral cease-fire. The Maoist leaders like Babu Ram Bhattarai and Krishna Bahadur Mahara were seriously thinking about a possible collaboration with SPA. They had discussed these issues in India with the Indian political leaders. G.P.Koirala, Bam Deo Gautam, Ramesh Nath Pandey, etc also visited India to discuss issues relating to the development of an understanding with the Maoists. In October 2005 SPA gave mandate to G.P.Koirala (NC) and Madhav Kumar Nepal (UML) to talk with the Maoists over the issue of a possible understanding. After a series of talks between SPA and the Maoist leaders consensus was reached on certain issues. The Maoists agreed to support SPA to launch a movement against the royal rule. SPA supported the Maoist cease-fire. CPN (Maoist) supreme, Prachanda also expressed his support to the political parties.[12]

G.P.Koirala, Gopal Man Shrestha (NCP.D), Bam Deo Gautam, Madhav Nepal and Khadga Oli visited India in November 2005 to discuss issues relating to the understanding with the Maoists. India not only encouraged for a polarization of the political forces for the restoration of multi party democracy but also provided space for informal consultations and meeting of the Maoists and SPA leaders.

It seems that both the groups wanted to utilize this opportunity. India's interest was obvious in peace and stability in Nepal. The continuation of the insurgency and political instability and authoritarianism was also not in India's larger interest.

SPA leaders were already in consultation with the Indian political leaders. There was also some change in the attitude of the Maoist leaders towards India. Till 2004 they viewed India as an expansionist and imperialist power. India was considered as their enemy. The Maoists had been demanding withdrawal of all 'unequal' treaties concluded with India. But the situation was gradually altering after the king Gyanendra's assertion to power. Now the king was being considered as the enemy number one. Leaders like Babu Ram Bhattarai were in favour of softening of the Maoist attitude towards India. Bhattarai though himself was facing a tough time within the party,[13] succeeded in reshaping and diluting the Maoist attitude towards India. It helped in bringing the Maoists and SPA together.

Maoists – SPA Understanding

In the middle of November 2005, leaders of the Seven Party Alliance finally started consultations for a collaboration with the Maoists.[14] These consultations proved to be important for an understanding between the Maoists and the Seven Party's Alliance. On 17 November the two groups agreed on a 12 point understanding. It emphasized re-structuring of the state for the establishment of an absolute democracy in the country. There was an understanding to do away with the constitutional monarchy. The 12 points agreed upon were as following:

1. To establish absolute democracy by abandoning autocratic monarchic rule, thereby creating an appropriate atmosphere for a long term peace and stability.
2. Restoration of the house of representatives, form an all party government and work towards holding elections for Constituent Assembly.
3. Bringing an end to armed conflict through a dialogue and seek international mediation for this purpose.
4. Expressing commitment to democratic norms, and values and complete faith on multi party democracy, civil

liberties, human rights, rule of law and the fundamental rights.

5. CPN (Maoist) expressed its commitment to create a congenial environment for the installation of democracy by allowing political activists of various political parties to return to their earlier positions, who had been displaced during insurgency.
6. CPN (Maoist) expressed its commitment not to repeat past mistakes.
7. The Seven Party Alliance expressed its commitment to not to repeat past mistakes, while in the government.
8. Respect to the norms and the values of human rights and press freedom and move ahead accordingly.
9. Boycott of the forthcoming municipal elections as the king with altrutive motives announced them.
10. Commitment to protect the independence, sovereignty, geographical integrity of the country and national unity. Maintenance of peaceful relations with all countries based on the principles of peaceful co-existence and good neighbourly relations with the neighbouring countries.
11. Call to civil society, professional organizations, diverse communities and regions, intellectuals and the media to participate in the peaceful movement to be launched on the basis of understanding between the political parties and the Maoists.
12. To settle any problem emerging between the two through peaceful dialogue at the concerned level or at the leadership level.

The Maoist-Seven Party Alliance understating was an important development and a much needed step to be taken by both. However, doubts were also raised regarding sincerity of the Maoists and the workability of the alliance. The U.S. Ambassador to Nepal J.F. Morierty warned the political parties not to enter into any collaboration with the Maoists.

Civic Polls

In October 2005 the Nepali government decided to hold elections for the 57 municipalities in February 2006. The Seven

Party Alliance strongly reacted against the decision as the elections would be held under an undemocratic environment. It also decided to boycott the municipal elections. The Maoists also declared to boycott the elections. However, the king was determined to hold the elections. It seems that the king was looking for gaining people's support and legitimacy. It was also an effort on his part to convey that the monarchy was much concerned about the representative governance. The elections would also act as a test case for the future course of action towards political liberalization. However, the civic polls turned in to a complete fiasco. It is true that neither the Maoists nor the political parties could prevent king Gyanendra to hold elections of the municipalities. But it also became clear that people did not trust the king. Out of 75 districts the elections were held in 28 districts. The voting turn out was only 21 per cent, which was lowest in the electoral history of Nepal. At most of the places the elections remained uncontested. King was badly exposed in these elections. It became clear that he lacked credibility. People did not trust the king that he was willing to restore the democracy. The United States termed these elections a hollow attempt by the king to legitimize power.[15] The lack of public support to the king encouraged the democratic forces.

Restoration of Democracy

In March 2006 it was decided to launch a movement for the restoration of democracy. The Maoists withdrew a 20 days economic and transport blockade scheduled from March 14, 2006 at the request of SPA. The movement that was finally initiated in April against the direct rule of the king received widespread support from all walks of the civil society. It was clear that the monarchy had lost popular faith. It was for the first time that the monarchy was denounced by the political parties and the people. The movement launched by the Seven Party Alliance had full backing of the Maoists. King tried his best to curb the movement. Curfew was imposed in Kathmandu. But it could not prevent the people from organizing wide spread demonstrations against the king. The crackdown over people by the government further agitated the people. King was abused and denounced like a common man.[16] On 21 April 2006 Kathmandu saw most wide spread and furious mass uprising in its history of last 237 years.[17] It appeared that the king was badly exposed and there was a strong internal pressure on him. King's policy of suppression was not fruit bearing. He also came under strong external pressure and had to concede to step down.

India's Mediation

At a time when a strong anti-king movement was brewing in Nepal, Government of India decided to send a senior political leader Karan Singh, to Nepal to pursue the king for a solution to the crisis. India's concern was that a peaceful political solution of the problem was an urgent requirement.[18] India's message for the king of Nepal was that "if he wishes to salvage the situation he should hand over power to a representative of SPA".[19] Karan Singh's visit to Kathmandu naturally aroused lot of excitement and speculations. He being a member of a royal family and having connections with the royalty in Nepal was interpreted in one way while his coming to Nepal at a time of deep political crisis as a representative of the Prime Minister of India was interpreted in many circles in different ways. Karan Singh met the king, leaders of political parties, members of civil society, etc. He made it clear that India would not like to involve in the internal affairs of Nepal; and that he was not there to advice the Nepalese but to articulate India's concern about the political developments in Nepal.[20] There is no doubt that Karan Singh prepared a strong ground for the restoration of democracy. The Communist leader Sita Ram Yechury followed his visit to Nepal. Yechury played a significant role in persuading the Maoists and also the other political groups in Nepal. India's foreign secretary, army chief and the other political leaders also played a role in this regard. India, no doubt, played a balancing act and helped bringing normalcy in Nepal.[21] But India's role, as usual, was not above controversy within the political circles in Nepal. There were two aspects: One is that many people and groups in Nepal and elsewhere has always misperceived India's mediation, role, etc. With whatever best intentions India would have acted, controversies are bound to erupt. Secondly, India did give such impressions which were interpreted as the Indian favour to monarchy. For instance Karan Singh's nomination for the mediation was bound to raise controversy due to his very identity as a member of a royal family. There was lack of clarity, as well, on the part of India. There were contradictory statements that created doubts and misgivings. It seems that India could not articulate its diplomatic postures the way it should have been. India also gave the impression as if it was favouring a role for the monarchy in the new set up.[22] India could have avoided these controversial issues

Why did India came forward to mediate? There have been diverse opinions in this regard. One opinion was that India wanted to save the monarchy because India had religious and emotional feelings towards the monarchy. Another opinion was that India thought that the Maoists would succeed in getting a political space. There was also an opinion that India thought that if she herself would not have come forward to mediate, others would have taken up that role. The political groups and leaders in Nepal were also looking for India's mediatory role.

It is true that India was concerned about the deteriorating political situation in Nepal, India's concerns were three:

(i) As a democratic and secular state India was concerned for the restoration of democracy in that country. India thought that the first step towards that direction could be handing over power to the democratic forces through the restoration of House of Representatives. The democratic forces and the Maoists could decide the future course of politics after that.

(ii) Because of a close neighbour, having strategically important, India was concerned about security and stability in the Himalayan region. Instability or unrest in Nepal had security risks for India as well. Due to the open border between the two counties, interactions between Nepali insurgents and extremists group in India, etc, security risks were high for India as well.

(iii) The large scale Nepali migration to the bordering region of India was an issue of vital concern. The continuation of violence, instability and royal despotism would have further increased cross border migration.

Restoration of the Parliament

King Gyanendra could not resist the pressure of democratic forces and after 18 day's agitation declared to restore the 1999 house of representative and hand over powers to the leader of the Seven Party's Alliance. In his announcement the king said:

> "....... The ideals of democracy can be realized only through the active participation of political parties. In keeping with the traditions of the Shah Dynasty to reign in accordance with the popular will in greater interest of the nation and the people and our unflinching commitment towards constitutional monarchy and multiparty democracy, we through this proclamation, affirm that the executive power of the kingdom of Nepal, which was in our safe keeping, shall from this day, be returned to the people and be exercised in accordance with Article 35 of the constitution of the kingdom of Nepal.........1990".[23]

What compelled the king to withdraw? King Gyanendra had tried to defuse the democratic forces and also to keep the political parties and the Maoists apart. But the two forces had come together. It was not possible to withstand their pressure for long. The king was also under pressure from the international community. India had already suggested the king to restore the parliament. There were clear indications that the monarchy was loosing its respect and importance and that the people were becoming highly critical of king Gyanendra's role. It is also said that the dissatisfaction was gradually brewing up among the armed forces, while king was dependent on the support of the armed forces.

The Seven Party Alliance welcomed king's declaration to restore the 1999 parliament. The Maoists did not appreciate it as they believed that it would delay Nepal's heading towards the goal of elections for the Constituent Assembly. They alleged that the Seven Party Alliance was betraying the people's movement.[24] The Maoists were in favour of an all party conference in place of the restoration of the parliament. They believed that they were by passed by SPA in this regard and that their support for the April movement was not fruit bearing to them.[25] They did not like revoking of the dissolved parliament. However, later on, they agreed to the situation. SPA elected G.P.Koirala of NC as its leader. Madhav Nepal leader of UML, declared that "the announcement of Constituent Assembly elections will be the main agenda of the reinstated parliament.[26]

The Parliament was reconvened on 28 April, 2006. The speaker of the house of representatives, Taranath Bhatt, was forced to resign for his controversial role during the king's rule.[27] The Deputy Speaker proposed on behalf of Prime Minister G.P.Koirala, who was ill, that "it is the people who have brought this change and we have to live up to their expectations".[28] It was proposed to have a cease-fire with the Maoists and arrange for elections to the Constituent Assembly. The issues that were important for the new government were Constituent Assembly, political stability and status of monarchy and peaceful resolution of armed conflict.

SPA – Maoist Agreement

The negotiations of the Seven Party Alliance with the Maoists finally reached to an eight point agreement along with a code of conduct. The agreement included framing an interim constitution, establishment of an interim government, which would take up the task to conduct elections for the Constituent Assembly, issues relating to disarming the Maoist forces, the future of the Maoists army and peace building. The code of conduct included the cessation of armed Maoist forces in rural areas, release of the Maoist prisoners by the government, disbandment of parallel government of the Maoists and return of the underground Maoists to overground.[29] This agreement was important as it formed a basis for the subsequent negotiations between the Maoists and SPA.

SPA formed a new government under the Prime Ministership of G.P.Koirala. The positions distributed to the constituents of SPA in the council of ministers were: CPN (UML) 6, NC-7, NC(D) – 4 and one each to ULF, NSP and Jana Morcha.

What Changed the Maoists?

The cease-fire of September – December 2005, the support to April 2006 movement for the restoration of democracy and the Maoists-SPA understanding for the restoration of multi-party democracy were three initial landmarks in the changing perception and attitude of the Maoists. The subsequent developments clearly showed that the Maoists had prepared themselves to give up the path of protracted guerrilla war and step on the path of multi – party democracy. The Maoists changed their strategy and reframe their objectives but did not give up the ultimate goals that they had fixed up in the beginning of the insurgency. Change in the Maoists strategy was a big surprise to many as it was not expected that the Maoists would agree to leave the path of insurgency so suddenly. Hence, the question arises what were the circumstances that prompted the Maoists to change their strategy? Before we discuss the post April 2006 developments it is desirable here to ponder upon these circumstances.

It may be noted here that the Maoists – SPA understanding gave a bi- angular direction to Nepali politics, instead of triangular as earlier. There were lot of speculations and excitement regarding the Maoists support to multi party democracy.[30]

Ideological Context

The Maoists had been talking of *Naulo Janbad* since 1991 as their ultimate goal which would be based on the principles of the dictatorship of the proletariat. In the later phase of their movement, they began to demand for a democratic republic as a transitional phase to new democracy. But since the April 2006 movement the Maoists agreed to join the multi party democracy. Similarly, the Maoists were initially concentrating on the protracted guerrilla war as a strategy to attain the goal of Naulo Janbad. In the middle stage of their revolution they began to realize that the Mao's strategy of rural insurrection was not sufficient enough to win a war. They perceived that the Nepali conditions were not appropriate to apply Mao's strategy. They fused Lenin's strategy with Mao's strategy and outlined a new strategy called Prachandapath. But than it was again realized that the revolutionary movement might not succeed in obtaining the ultimate goals. There are a large number of examples where armed revolution was started with much enthusiasm but got lost in between. Even the powerful movement like Shining Path failed in reaching to its goals. A number of insurgencies have continued for years in many parts of the world without any outcome.

It was also an important consideration for the Maoists as to why communist regime failed in the Soviet Union, Eastern European countries, etc. Perhaps there was a realization that the political competition was essential for political stability and it was possible in a multi party democratic set up only. The Maoists also appeared revisiting their opinion on many other issues which was indicative of the moderation of their perception and attitude. Perhaps, they appeared to be realizing the shortcomings of the communist revolution in a localized context and therefore looking for an alternative path to realize their goals in the context of the emerging political scenario in the country.

It many again be pointed out here that the Maoists of Nepal emerged as a revolutionary party and launched a 'people's war' with the objectives of restructuring the state and transformation of the society. They succeeded in bringing up these issues in the national agenda. But what can be considered as a tremendous achievement is the fact that the Maoists chose an alternative democratic path for this purpose along with the democratic forces of Nepal.[31] During the course of insurgency the Maoists gave an understanding of a violent revolutionary group that was looking for a complete change in Nepal through revolutionary means. They did talk of a republican state in Nepal but issues were not very clear in ideological terms. The ideological contents whether in the form of 'Prachandapath' or other issues were directed towards a revolutionary struggle to attain the goals set by them to bring a political change in the country. The Maoists leaders gradually tried to synthesize their ideology in favour of a democratic political order. They talked of incorporating the ideas of Mahatma Gandhi, Lord Buddha and Karl Marx in their policies and actions. It was an indication of liberalization or broadening of their ideas. It broadly meant that they now believed in a humanitarian, socialistic and democratic approach that would primarily focus upon the welfare of the people. The Maoist leader,

Pushp Kamal Dahal (Prachanda) in an interview in New Delhi said that "Gautam Buddha has given a call from here for the ideological synthesis of humanity, we now want to give a new ideological message for the New World."[32]

As pointed out earlier, the Maoists had been talking of a new democracy (Naulo Janbad) in Nepal. But it can be elaborated further. It appears that they would aspire for a communitarian democracy in which all the identities regions, groups and communities are associated in the national political process on an equalitarian basis. Their emphasis is that democracy should not remain a mere formality. It must work for bringing economic equality and social justice and change the lives of the people. Babu Ram Bhattarai in an interview said; "The Communists had tried out people's democracy in Russia and China we want to try out a new model which will incorporate the ideas of Gandhi, Marx, Lenin and be a synthesis of all."[33]

Prachanda during his visit to India also gave the impression that they should not be equated with the Naxalities and the other revolutionary groups in India. It seems that on the basis of this distinction they wanted to justify their ideology of democracy and the democratic governance as a means to social transformation. In fact, the Maoists joining the constitutional-democratic path indicated that their revolutionary path was more a strategy to open up possibilities for a political change rather than a social movement / revolution aimed at complete uprooting of the socio-political order. The Maoist leaders also tried to differentiate themselves from the other movements in South Asia. They believed that the major problem with the movement of LTTE in Sri Lanka was that it has been based on a narrow nationalist approach. It also lacked ideological and political context in its struggle against the Sri Lankan state. The fact remains that LTTE followed a separatist movement while the Maoists were a political movement aimed at restructuring the state.

The way the Maoist leaders had tried to look at the movement of LTTE showed that the Maoists would believe in a broad based nationalism, which would be secular and democratic in its approach and contents.

As pointed out earlier, the Maoists began to revise their attitude towards India. As late as October 2004, the Maoists talked of confronting the Indian expansionism. However, this issue had been quite complex. The Maoists used the Indian Territory for their meetings, hide outs, treatment, etc. They maintained contacts with the India political leaders. But as a part of their strategy they had hardly left any opportunity to criticize the Indian government like many other sets of political actors in Nepal. But after king's takeover the Maoists softened their attitude towards India this helped taking them nearer to SPA. It appears it was also a part of their strategy to normalize their attitude towards India in order to build an understanding with the democratic forces.

The Maoist leaders themselves had some short of difference of opinion regarding their attitude towards India, centralized leadership, possibilities of winning the targets through protracted war, etc. Babu Ram Bhattarai was of the opinion that the party need not to adopt a confronting attitude towards India. He believed that the king was number one enemy instead of India. Bhattarai not only urged to take a new line and tried to outline the shortcomings of international communist movement, he also stressed that the support to the demand of the Constituent Assembly could open a new way to their movement.[34] Bhattarai's difference of opinion was considered to be a breach of the party discipline. He faced suspension from all party positions. Disciplinary action was also taken against Hasila Yami and Dinanath Sharma who were closer to Bhattarai. After the royal takeover as the political situation changed in Nepal and it became apparent that there was a need for forging new alignments at domestic and regional level, suspension of Babu Ram Bhattarai was withdrawn. He was also assigned, with the responsibility to talk with the Indian leaders on the upcoming political issues in Nepal. There were some leaders within the party like Rabindra Shrestha, Mani Dhwaj Thapa who were not happy with the rehabilitation of Bhattarai in the party positions. They tried to raise a voice against it but they were expelled from the party.[35] Prachanda very tactfully saved the party and his political supremacy in the party remained intact. The party tends to follow the Bhattarai line afterwards. In October 2005, in the politburo meeting of the party in Rukkum it was accepted that it was possible to forge an alliance with the capitalist political parties against the feudal monarchy.[36]

Initially, when the Maoist declared protracted war a weak, ill-equipped and un trained police forces were in front of them. The Maoists established that they were better equipped and well trained in guerrilla war. RNA too was not well trained in guerrilla war so it was easier for the Maoists to challenge the army. But RNA received international support beyond expectations of the Maoists. It was not only granted arms and ammunition but also got training in guerrilla warfare. The Maoists gradually began to realize that it was not that easy to defeat RNA. There were all possibilities that their attempts to intensify the war could result in more external military aid to Nepal. The Nepali government had already increased its defense budget and that she was also trying to consolidate its defense and military strategies against the Maoists. The Maoists on the other hand were gradually loosing popular interest in joining their army. The initial enthusiasm was receding. People in general in the rural areas, were terrified by the war. They were indeed becoming victims of both the agitating groups. So they were no more interested in serving the Maoist army as they use to be in the beginning of the insurgency. Lot of killings was a problem for the Maoists. There are many news paper reports to indicate recruitment of younger people in the army. All these factors were not good indications for the continuation of war.

Another significant aspect that has to be noted here is that the Maoists envisaged a new strategy in 2001 in the form of Prachandapath. But the Maoists could not register much success in getting hold in the urban areas. In Nepal the centre of power is exclusively Kathmandu but the Maoists hardly had any support base in the capital city. So the ideological input which was much propagated as the contribution of the Maoists appeared to be loosing its practical significance.

It is also believed that the Maoists were not finding comfortable in the context of international communist movement.[37] Initially Revolutionary International Movement formed their main support base. But some of the Maoist leaders in Nepal began to point out shortcomings of the international communist movement. It was being argued that it was not possible to attain their goals by the classical Maoist strategy and tactics.

A number of Human Rights reports had focused on the killings in the insurgency.[38] Many Human Rights organizations had become active in Nepal. It was also building a short of pressure on the Maoists. The Nepali civil society was also gradually becoming active in finding a solution to the political problems of Nepal. Some members of the civil society became active in persuading the political parties and the Maoist leaders. This also played a positive role.

In view of the changing domestic and international situation the Maoists changed their strategy and conceded the path of democratic republican state through an elected Constituent Assembly as their political objective.

The Maoist Road Map

The Maoists had already extended their cooperation to SPA. They were not happy with the restoration of the parliament because they were not a gainer in this context. They also believed that the restoration of parliament could delay the political process leading to the formation of Constituent Assembly. In a special meeting of the Central Committee of CPN (Maoist) held in Punjab in India in May 2006, the Maoists decided about its road map to achieve its goals. It decided about a 10 point road map for peace talks with SPA. It emphasized the following aspects:

(I) declaration of ceasefire,
(II) adoption of code of conduct,
(III) formation of a dialogue team,
(IV) release of all political prisoners,
(V) initiation of dialogue,
(VI) dissolution of old parliament,
(VII) constitution of government,
(VIII) adoption of an interim constitution and formation of interim government through an all party conference,
(IX) demarcation of new electoral constituencies,

(X) Constituent Assembly elections supervised by a reliable third party and,

(XI) Restructuring of PLA and RNA as per the popular mandate expressed through elections.

Maoist Arms Management

The question of the Maoist arms management was important in taking the peace process further due to many reasons. There was a general impression that the peace process would not proceed further unless the issue of arms possessed by the Maoists and their armed forces was properly settled. It is true that the Maoists and SPA had undergone an understanding to work together for the restoration of peace and democracy in Nepal. But both the groups were clear that the understanding was quite sensitive and fragile. There were mutual suspicions towards each other. Any breakdown of the understanding between the two could take the Maoists back to arms. The Maoists were also suspicious about the role of RNA. It was also essential to put RNA under control as a step towards confidence building. The questions of sustaining the Maoist army and the rehabilitation of the young army men were also important.

Both the Maoists and SPA had agreed for the management of the Maoist arms and armed forces, along with RNA. It was also agreed to approach the United Nations Organization for its mediation in the peace process and the arms management. The understanding on this issue was crucial because many other political issues were suppose to rest on the management of the Maoist arms. It was agreed that both the Maoists and SPA leaders would write a letter to the UN Secretary General. On 02 July 2006 G.P.Koirala wrote a letter to the UN Secretary General without consulting the Maoist leaders. The understanding between the Maoists and SPA was only regarding arms management. The Maoists condemned Koirala for this. They viewed it as a breach of faith. Prachanda wrote a separate letter to the UN General Secretary on 24 July 2006 protesting against the letter send by PM G.P.Koirala. It created a deadlock between the Maoists and SPA. Koirala was accused for not being interested in the peace process. But this deadlock was resolved soon and it was agreed to write a joint letter to UN. The letter jointly written subsequently requested the UN for its supervision in managing the Maoist arms.

G.P.Koirala and Prachanda agreed that there was a need to call a summit meeting to discuss pending issues. It may be noted here that the question of republican state, interim constitution and the elections for the Constituent Assembly had been conflicting issues. SPA had often expressed contradictory views on these issues and also regarding the status of monarchy. It was quite frustrating to the Maoists who were not in favour of any short of delay. They were apprehensive about the elections of CA and also believed that the delay in settling the issues could frustrate the Maoist cadres. The Maoists were also conscious of the fact that there were internal destabilizing factors and they would take advantage of the situation of indecisiveness.

The summit talks again took place between Prachanda and G.P. Koirala on 8 October 2006. It was agreed that CA elections would be held in June 2007. The issues relating to arms management, etc were also discussed. UML objected to these talks. Koirala made it clear to UML that if it did not cooperate they would move ahead on their own. SPA constituents later unanimously agreed to the six point agreement signed with the Maoists.

Six Point Agreement

The six point agreement concluded between SPA and the Maoists on 7 November, 2006 reaffirmed their commitment to peace, stability and democracy in Nepal. It was also agreed that all the agreements concluded earlier would be implemented. The charges leveled against the Maoist leaders were withdrawn and it was agreed to release all the political prisoners. The Maoists and SPA also agreed for the management of army and arms, finalization of the interim constitution, interim legislature, interim government the future of monarchy and other issues.[39] It was a comprehensive agreement the understanding relating to the Maoist army, interim constitution and elections for CA were important as they had been the cause of concern for both since June 2006. UML though one of the signatories to the agreement added its note of dissent stating that the fate of monarchy should be decided by a referendum along with the elections of CA and that proportional system should be adopted for the elections of CA.

Verification of Arms

In pursuance of the letter send by the Maoists and SPA and the agreement signed by the two, the United Nations send a Technical Assessment Mission to Nepal. The mission aimed at the following:

a. To monitor cease-fire arrangements.
b. Provide technical support for the planning, preparations and conduct of CA elections and
c. To monitor the management of arms and armed personnel and provide necessary assistance and guidance to the two groups in the implementation of their agreement.

The first phase of arms management began in December 2006 and completed in February 2007. A nine member Joint Monitoring Coordination Committee was constituted to took after the issues relating to the arms management. The Maoist army personnel were cantoned with their weapons at Kailali, Surkhet, Rolpa, Sindhuli, Ilam, Navalparasi and Chitwan camps. The arms were kept under single lock system. It was also decided that RNA would reciprocate by restructuring its activities and keep a similar number of arms locked under a parallel system. Funds were provided by the government to each cantonment and a Cantonment Coordination Office was established at each cantonment.

30852 Maoist fighters were registered with the commission.[40] The criteria for registration was age and year of entry in service registered by the solder to the Maoists army. 3428 weapons were registered to the commission.[41] These were kept in 7 camps and 21-satellite camps.[42]

The second phase of verification of arms was to commence on May 1, 2007 but it could not be possible due to political instability. The issues of elections to CA and the republican state were still unsettled and there were apprehensions and the deferring opinions in this regard. The Maoist leaders had also complained about the lack of facilities in the cantonments. The Maoists also raised the issue of remuneration of the registered Maoist solders by the government. They were also concerned about the future of their solders. It has to be mentioned here that the placement of these combatants in the cantonments was a temporary provision. Ultimately they were to be rehabilitated.

The second round began on June 14, 2007. In total 31152 Maoist combatants were registered. The issue of management of the Maoist arms was by and large settled. But there were suspicions. It was a general impression in Nepal that some discrepancy was there in the actual number of arms possessed by the Maoists and the arms registered by them.[43] The Maoist supremo Prachanda said in a statement in mid 2007 that the Maoists can take arms again if need be.[44] Does it mean that all arms had not come over ground? It is true that bringing up hidden arms over ground in the process of disarmament is a difficult job and it might not be fool proof hundred percent. But there has to be transparency if political stakes of the country rest on the disarmament. Nevertheless, it can be said that it had been an important achievement and UN did a commendable job.

Comprehensive Peace Accord

The Maoists and the government of Nepal concluded a historical peace agreement on 21 November 2006. The agreement conveyed full commitment of the Maoists and the government of Nepal to build peace, democracy and stability in the country. It was considered to be an attempt of the Maoists and the government of Nepal to transform cease-fire between the two into sustainable peace.[45]

The two sides expressed their commitment towards political and socio-economic transformation of the country. It stated that no authority relating to governance will rest with the king. All property possessed by late king Birendra and his family will be nationalized and placed under a trust. It stated that all property of king Gyanendra received by him in the capacity of the king of Nepal will be nationalized.

Both the parties agreed to strengthen multi-party competitive democracy and resolve the issues relating to gender, ethnic, dalit and regional identities. It also mentioned about management of the Maoist arms and armed forces as per earlier agreement concluded. Both sides agreed to abandon all kind of activities that would create a war like situation and expressed their determination for peace in the country.

It was significant that the agreement declared an end to the armed conflict. Adherence to human rights, fundamental rights of the people of Nepal and humanitarian laws was also expressed. It also added to economic and social rights along with political rights of the people.

One significant aspect of the accord was that: "Both sides agree to become responsible and accountable in a personal and collective way and not to repeat in future mistakes committed in the past and also to correct these mistakes on a gradual basis."

The agreement appealed to the civil society, the professional groups, the class organizations, the media, the intellectual community and all the Nepali people to actively participate in building a new Nepal and establishing lasting peace through the elections to the Constituent Assembly by ending the armed conflict.

The peace accord was significant as it paved a way for the settlement of the pending political issues. It also gave a message to the Nepali masses that serious efforts were being made towards peace and stability in the country. It was a confirmation on the part of the Maoists that they were prepared to end armed conflict and join the multi party democracy along with the other political parties.

Disarming the King

One important dimension of the post April 2006 politics of Nepal has been to withdraw powers of the king and make the monarchy ineffective in the politics of the country. It has not been viewed sufficient to disarm king Gyanendra politically. There has been a strong opinion that king Gyanendra and his associates had done lot of atrocities on people during his direct rule. The interim government took a number of decisions to be size the king. His status as head of the state and chief of the army was abolished. The Raj Parishad was abolished. The reinstated parliament curtailed the king's privileges. It ended the concept of king in parliament. The need for royal assent to the bills was abolished. King's assets were brought under the review of taxation. The Nepali Congress was though still toeing with the idea of a ceremonial monarchy[46], the Maoists were not prepared to make any compromise with regard to the monarchy.

The Nepali Government constituted a commission under the Chairmanship of justice Krishna Jung Raimajhi to recommend action against 202 people including king Gyanendra. Justice Krishna Jung Raimajhi submitted its report to the government on 20 November 2006. The commission held king Gyanendra responsible for the atrocities on the people at the time of April 2006 pro-democracy movement. It was also recommended that action be taken against king Gyanendra not in his capacity as the king but as the then head of the state. The chairman of the Committee said, "We have decided to recommend the parliament to take necessary steps against the king as we found him guilty"[47] It was also clarified that though king Gyanendra did not respond to the questions send by the commission it does not mean to say that he did no wrong. It is for the first time that a commission was constituted against the king of Nepal.

The Government decided to form a five-member committee to recommend action against the king. The fate of the monarchy would ultimately be decided after the CA elections. But if the current developments are any indication, the institution of monarchy has lost its credibility and the way to its come back is extremely difficult. As far king Gyanendra is concerned there are still people in Nepal who would look for a minimum status to the monarchy in the new political set up, but it is difficult to state whether they would be able to reverse the trends. It can be said that the role played by king Gyanendra has proved to be detrimental to the institution of monarchy in Nepal. It seems that king Gyanendra in his capacity as the head of the state is likely to pay for all that happened during his direct rule. Not only that his powers have been withdrawn but the facilities provided to him have either been withdrawn or seriously curtailed. His personal property is under scrutiny, the monarchy of Nepal has lost power and popularity. The Maoists seem to be quite desperate to see an end to the monarchy as early as possible. It was also decided that the monarchy would be abolished if the king was found conspiring against elections to CA.[48] The king and members of the royal family were also asked to declare their property and provide details about their personal accounts in banks in Nepal and abroad.[49] In the budget for the year 2007-2008 it was decided not to provide any allowance to king and the members of the royal family.[50] Earlier there was a provision of an allowance of Rs. 18.7 million for the king and the royal family.

Interim Constitution

The Maoists and SPA agreed in June 2006 to frame an interim constitution. An Interim Constitution Redrafting Committee was constituted for this purpose, under the chairmanship of Laxman Prasad Aryal. It was not an easy task to frame the interim constitution. There were many conflicting issues.[51] The draft of the interim constitution was submitted on 15 December 2006. It was promulgated on 15 January 2007.

The interim constitution has 169 articles. It will remain in effect till a new constitution framed by the Constituent Assembly is promulgated. It declared Nepal a multi cultural state in place of a Hindu state as earlier.

The interim constitution provides for a 330 member interim legislature called legislature – parliament. The Maoists insisted for naming it as legislature and SPA as parliament. Both the denominations were retained. Out of 330 seats in the interim legislature NC received 75 seats UML and CPN (Maoists) 73 each, NC (Democratic) 42 and the remaining 48 seats were to be filled from the other constituent parties of SPA, marginalised groups and various professional groups.

The interim constitution had also provided for the constitution of a 425 member Constituent Assembly as following:

1. 205 members of the Constituent Assembly to be elected directly from the existing parliamentary constituencies on the basis of first – past the post election system.
2. The political parties will nominate 204 members in proportion to the votes they score in the election to the Constituent Assembly.
3. 16 members will be nominated by the council of ministers.

Every Nepali who has attended 18 years age has right to vote in the election to CA. The time accorded to CA for the framing of the constitution is 2 years from the time of its constitution. However, the election dated scheduled for June 2007 were postponed to 22 November 2007 and now it has again been postponed indefinitely.[52] The Constituent Assembly will perform dual functions as a constitution making body and as a legislature for the interim period.

One important feature of the interim constitution is that the Prime Minister will be the head of the state as well as the head of the government. The king is stripped of all positions in the government. He will no more be ceremonial head even. This constituted the 6th statute of Nepal, first being the statute of 1948 declared by the Rana Prime Minister, Padma Shumsher JBR, to affirm up total rule by his clan and the 5th in 1990 to lift ban on political parties. The PM will use all powers hitherto exercised by the king. The constitution has provide various rights to the people of Nepal such as right to education, employment, health, untouchability, torture, right to information, etc. It also provides for the directive principles of state policy. The interim constitution can be amended by a two-third majority of the home.

There will be a constitutional council that will recommend appointments to various constitutional bodies. A six member Security Council has been constituted to look after the Royal Army. It will be headed by the Prime Minister.

The interim constitution was amended for the first time on March 9, 2007 to accommodate the demands of the people of Tarai. It was decided to grant proportional representation in all state organs to Madhesis, Dalits, ethnic groups and backward castes.[53] A Constituency Delimitation Commission was also constituted later on. The second amendment to the interim constitution was introduced in April 2007. It was concerning the abolition of the monarchy by two third majority of the interim parliament if he would be found indulging in sabotaging the elections to CA.[54]

During the drafting of the interim constitution differences had erupt between the Maoists and SPA that delayed the process for some time. But these differences were resolved. The interim constitution reflected up on the desire of the Maoists and SPA to restructure the Nepali state. It also indicated towards the possible course of political change in Nepal.

Maoists Joining the Interim Government

The peace process in Nepal covered one major landmark with CPN (Maoists) joining the interim government on April 1, 2007. Actually the Maoists were expected to join the government for some time but due to the unsettled political issues there was an over all delay in all aspects of political life in Kathmandu. It was, however, a positive development that despite delay the Maoists were persuaded to join the interim government.

G.P.Koirala resigned as Prime Minister and the interim parliament again appointed him as Prime Minister of the interim government. The speaker of the house Subhash Kumar Newang read the proposal on behalf of the eight parties (SPA and CPN (Maoist) to reappoint Koirala as Prime Minister.[55] Koirala became Prime Minster of Nepal for the 6th time. Two significant aspects of the cabinet formation were that for the first time the king did not administer the oath of office to the member of the cabinet. Similarly, for the first time oath was taken in the parliament in stead of the Narainhity royal palace as earlier.

The interim government consisted of 21 members including 16 cabinet ministers and 5 ministers of state. The Nepali Congress received 4 cabinet positions namely, defense, home, finance and peace and reconstruction; CPN (Maoist) got 5 including information and communication, local development, physical planning and works, forest and women. UML got 5 cabinet ranks and state minister and Nepali Congress (D) three cabinet ranks and one minister of state.[56] The Maoists joining the interim government included Hisila Yami (Comrade Parvati) wife of Maoist leader Babu Ram Bhattarai and President of All Nepal Women's Association (Revolutionary). Hisila Yami had been closely associated with the Maoist protracted war.

The newly formed interim cabinet outlined its main objectives as holding elections to the Constituent Assembly, establishing law and order in the country and promoting economic development. The formation of the interim government was highly praised by the political leaders. Prakash Man Singh, Vice President of NC (D) said "The Constituent Assembly would now draft the political future of the country". The Maoist supremo Prachanda also said: "Once we entered mainstream politics following the cease-fire, we were prepared to form a new Nepal. So we have come prepared to shoulder responsibilities for the sake of the nation".[57]

The international community also welcomed the Maoists joining the interim government. In fact, it was a significant development for many reasons:

1. The Maoist entry in the government put an end to the speculations of those forces that were still looking for the possibilities of a breakdown in the peace process. Many of the supporters of the royalist camp were still hoping that the Maoists would not join the government.
2. It was believed since the Maoists had now become a part of the governance they would now not blame the government for obstacles and delays in the peace process.
3. There was also an impression that the Maoists would exert pressure from inside the government to settle the pending political issues.
4. The joining of the Maoists to the government strengthened the democratic forces and it also encouraged the civil society in Nepal, which has been desperately looking for the strengthening of the peace process.

The Maoists joining the interim government was looked at with suspension in certain political circles in and around Nepal. There was an impression in Nepal among some that the Maoists would dominate the government and dictate their terms to the government. In India there was an impression among some of the political leaders that the joining of the Maoists to the interim government could boost the morale of the Naxalities in India.[58] The Maoists, however, did not agree to it and refuted any kind of relations with Maoists in India, particularly the Naxalites. Dinanath Sharma a senior Maoist leader said: "We don't think our party joining the interim government will boost the Indian Maoists, as our party has no links with the Indian Maoists other than ideological one". He further explained that, "There has not been any cooperation or joint action between the two groups, except ideological relationship".

Trouble in Tarai and the Maoists

The agitation in Tarai region beginning towards the end of 2006 brought a yet fresh jolt to the peace process in the country. Tarai has been a neglected region since the early days. The Kathmandu based ruling elite never trusted the people of Tarai called Madhesis. Hence, they were marginalised politically and economically.[59] Despite the fact that Tarai constituted economic backbone of the country, the royal authority of Nepal tried to bring the resources of Tarai under the possession of the hill people through various measures during the panchayat rule. It was done due to their distrust on the people of Tarai most of whom had migrated there from the neighbouring Indian regions. The question of rights over land and other resources, citizenship, linguistic identity, adequate political representation and share of Tarai people in administration and army agitated the people of Tarai.

Some concern had been shown towards the problems of Tarai after 1990 and some attempts were made to accommodate interest of the Tarai people. But they were inadequate. The Tarai people were still looking for a broad based approach to their problems that was indeed lacking in the governmental deliberations.

When the Maoists called for an insurgency the people of Tarai were largely attracted to the Maoists call because they had raised the question of ethnic and regional identities. The Maoists talked of a federal state in Nepal that suited to the interest of the Maoist insurgency and joined the Maoist army in considerable number. The Maoists formed a number of regional organizations in Tarai to raise their support base.

Three important things happened after the Maoists withdrew the war against the Nepali state.

(i) The Maoists focused primarily on the issue of republican state and elections to CA. They believed that the ethnic and regional issues could be left for the consideration of CA. The people of Tarai wanted to keep the issue of federal state alive. They felt neglected and realized that nothing was going to happen to their grievances immediately. It was indeed frustrating to those who had joined the Maoists with lot of enthusiasm and high hopes.

(ii) The Maoists lacked a strong base in the Tarai region. Therefore, they relied much on their regional organizations in Tarai for support. Some of the Maoist leaders of Tarai like Goit, Jwala Singh developed differences with the Maoist central leadership and began to work independently towards the end of 2004. Janatantrik Tarai Mukti Morcha was a splinter group of the Maoists. They began to advocate autonomous Tarai region as their central demand.

(iii) The people of Tarai were already dissatisfied with the Nepali government. The Maoist insurgency helped in promoting a militant mood in Tarai.[60]

It led to the emergence of a violent situation in Tarai. A number of groups became active in this region such as The Jantantrik Tarai Mukti Morcha, The Madhesi Janadhikar Forum, The Madhesi Mukti Tigers, The Tarai Cobra, The Chure Bhawar Ekta Samaj, etc. The demands raised by the Madhesis are formation of the Madhesi autonomous region, right to self determination, proportional representation in CA, declaration of feudal set up, etc. The Maoists came in clash with agitators at may places in Tarai.[61] The problem with the Maoists seem to be that though they themselves supported the Madhesi question, the way splinter groups in Tarai were coming up was not liked by them. The Maoists were in favour of controlling the agitation politics in Tarai. The Maoists might also be worried as it could encourage dissensions within the Maoist camp. Laxman Tharu of MJRF said in a statement that; "If they continue to follow the reformist line by disrupting the revolution we will pull out the people's liberation army along with the arms".[62] It shows that the Maoist's fears were genuine and they would have obviously preferred to bring the violence in Tarai under control as early as possible. The agitation in Tarai caused panic among hill people working in the region.[63]

The agitating groups of Tarai were not satisfied with the first amendment in the constitution as stated earlier. Another problem is that there is not a unified agitation in Tarai. The different groups are suppose to be dealt with separately by the government.

The issues raised by Madhesis are important and in the new political set up of Nepal these issues have to be dealt with carefully. The question of federal structure is not so easy. It has to be understood that even Tarai does not have a cohesive social group culturally and linguistically. The ethnic issue is equally important. The Maoist used all these groups in the insurgency. It is not possible to overlook these issues now. These groups are highly mobilized now and they have to be accommodated and satisfied.

The Muslim community of Nepal is also raising their voice for adequate representations of their community in the power structure. The intellectual Muslim Association of Nepal demanded 10 per cent reservation in CA.[64] They have also alleged that the Muslim community has been traditionally marginalised.

The various ethnic groups of Mongolian origin also aspire for a federal state in Nepal. They had joined the Maoist insurgency with the hope that they would seek proper representation in the new political set up and that they would also be granted autonomy. They are still hopeful that the question of autonomy would be resolved to their satisfaction. Therefore, the questions of federation and ethno – regional autonomy was important. The Maoists need to keep these issues very much within the track.

Political Uncertainty and Desperate Maoists

The Maoist's joining the interim government was initially viewed as a major breakthrough in moving towards attaining the goal of building a new Nepal. But the progress was very slow to the frustration of the Maoist leaders. The Maoist view has been to resolve the questions relating to republican state, CA and monarchy as early as possible. They thought that delay would generate more complexities. The Maoists had problems for a number of reasons. They alleged that the government did not consult them while making various appointments. They were not happy with king Gyanendra's defending his earlier actions on the democracy day of Nepal and the king's birthday bash.[65] The Maoists were also suspicious about Koirala's stand on the future of monarchy. He had in fact, created confusion by taking different stands at different points of time. The Maoists also had the fear that the royalist forces can play a disruptive role and create problems in smooth conduct of CA elections.

In June when elections to CA were postponed for November 2007, the Maoists began to demand for declaring Nepal a republican state before the elections. The Nepali Congress stand was that it could be done by CA only. The Maoists threatened to start yet another movement. The Maoists were also worried about the non-response of the demand of the adjustment of the Maoist combatants in security forces. They also threatened that if this issue along with the problem of adequate facilities in the Maoists army camps were not resolved they would not cooperate with the second round of arms verification.

The Maoists submitted a 22 point demand charter to the government, which included abolition of monarchy, declaring Nepal a republican state before holding elections to CA and proportional representation election method for all the seats of CA. It may be recalled here that it had already been decided in the interim constitution that half of the seats of CA would be elected on the basis of proportional representation. Why Maoists wanted a change in the electoral system is an important issue. It is a fact that the Maoists, both as a revolutionary group engaged in protracted guerrilla war and as a partner with SPA involved in peace process, have established the fact that they are a political force to be reckoned with. Now they seem to be worried about their political future within the democratic political set up of the country.

There have been speculations about the 'left unity' in the context of delays in dealing with a number of political issues. But in the over all context the possibilities of a united left front with the Maoists are bleak. CPN (UML) largest among left parties, does not appear in any mood to align with the Maoists. There have been differences between the two. CPN (UML) being the second largest political party has its own political aspirations. So the party seems to be more conscious about her own prospects in the elections. The other smaller communist factions hardly Bee any bright political future in aligning with the Maoists. The Nepali Congress has been strengthened with the rejoining of its splinter group NC (D) with the party.[66] It may also be recalled here that the splinter groups of the Maoists in Tarai are in an agitational mood. They are critical of the Maoists for leaving the revolutionary path. The Maoists have been apprehending of their cadres joining these splinter groups. In fact, it was due to such fears that the Maoists were always in favour of taking early decisions about republication state and elections to CA. The already fragile base of the Maoists in the Tarai is further weakened. These development add to the worries of the Maoists regarding their future political dynamics.

Maoists Quit Interim Government

The Maoists declared on 18 September 2007 to quite the interim government as the government did not agree to their demands. A Maoists leader said, "We have pulled out from the government on September 18 as the talks failed to reach an understanding on the immediate abolition of monarchy and a proportional electoral system".[67] It is a serious blow to the peace process in Nepal. However, the Maoist leader Mahara made it clear in a statement that "Now we will focus on peaceful protests to meet our demands".[68]

The decision taken by the Maoists have seriously added to the political uncertainties in Nepal. They have clearly said that they would not join the government again unless their demands are met with. The Maoists have also talked of waging a nationwide movement for creating momentum for federal democratic republic.[69] 87 members of the parliament led by the Maoists registered an application at the PM office to call a special session of the parliament to amend the constitution to change the election system of CA.[70]

Yet another set back to the peace process was the decision of the government on October 5 to postpone the elections of CA indefinitily.[71] This decision of the government was not unexpected in the context of their differences with the Maoists. The Maoists could boycott the elections if they were to be held on the scheduled date. But what is unfortunate is that it has not been possible to hold elections to CA for a year now.

CPN (UML) and two other left parties registered their note of dissent over the issue of postponing CA elections. The civil society in Nepal was also not happy with the decision of the government. The international community also expressed its displeasure over the decision of the Nepali government. The Indian view point was that it affects the credibility of the government and also disturbs the process of democratic transformation and legitimization in the country.[72] The United States of America and Britain also expressed their displeasure over the decision of the Nepali government.[73] Similarly China also expressed its concern over the postponement of CA elections. The chief of UNMIN, Ian Martin called upon the Maoist leaders and urged them to be soft on their demands. It shows that the international community is also concerned over the postponement of the elections. The general impression is that the postponement of CA elections for a longer time period would be counter productive.[74]

Efforts have been made to reach to some understanding with the Maoists. However, the Maoists are so far strict to their demands of proportional representation and republican state.[75] If the stalemate is not revolved Maoists may adopt other pressure tactics such as resigning from the parliament thereby further worsening the political situation in the country.

The demands raised by the Maoists were discussed in the parliament in November 2007. There was by and large a consensus on the issue of republican state. But the government made it clear that it can only be done by the Constituent Assembly. The peace process was derailed between October – December 2007. But both the Maoists and the government have shown enough resilience. Both the Maoists and SPA were continuously engaged in negotiations[76]. It appears that the political groups in Nepal are learning from the circumstances. The civil society has become much more active.

Back on the Track

With the signing of the 23-point peace agreement between the Maoists and the SPA on 23 December 2007, the peace process is once again on the track. One would like to add a happy note here that the political parties and the Maoist leaders have shown enough maturity. In fact at no stage efforts were left aside to bring back the peace process. The Nepali Congress leadership agreed to the Maoist concern about the republican state. The new amendment to the interim constitution agrees that Nepal will be declared a federal republican state. But it will be ratified and formally declared in the first meeting of the newly constituted Constituent Assembly. It means that the monarchy has to go ultimately. The fresh date for the election to CA has been fixed as 10 April. With this the Maoists agreed to rejoin the government[77].

Summing Up

The Nepali politics again reached to a critical phase. The question that will Maoists go back to the same position from where they took a U turn a year and half back had become important. Fortunately they do not appear to be in a mood to take resort to violent movement again. But nothing can be said in a definite way. The Maoists adopted a strategy to lay pressure on the government as much as possible to declare Nepal a republican state. In fact, they have been demanding to declare Nepal a republican state before elections to CA since June 2007, when elections were postponed for the first time. But the demand of proportional representation on all seats of CA is an after thought. It appears that the Maoists are highly conscious about the future dynamics of Nepali politics. They are also conscious about their own status and role in the up coming politics.

The Maoists and SPA seems to have reached to some understanding now. One may say that what has happened in Nepal for last two years is remarkable in many respects. The Maoists joining the democratic political parties for a peaceful political transformation in the country is a highly significant development. There can not be any doubt that it has contributed to peace in Nepal, it ended violence and war, it has accorded a political status to the Maoists. It also enhanced the image of the Maoists among civil society in Nepal and the international community. It is also a fact that the Maoists cease-fire also accorded strength and courage to SPA and above all it gave a new dynamics to the Nepali politics in the way to political transformation. Therefore, there is lot that the Maoists have added to the Nepali politics in a short period of time. But what appears to be wrong with the Maoists is that they are too impatient to reach up to the ultimate political goals. They have tried to reach to agreements with SPA quickly seemingly, without giving a serious thought to its pros and cons and the wider perspectives of the Nepali politics. As a result they tend to change their strategy after some time and raise new demands. Earlier they agreed to first-past the post for half of the seats of CA but now they want proportional representation in all seats. The demand for dual representation system and increase in seats of CA to 601 was agreed later on.

The problem with SPA seems to be that they want to move ahead with their own speed. They have not learned much form the political history of Nepal in the immediate past years. The political parties some time appear to be following a policy of one step forward to step back word. The political leadership lack self confidence and determination. As a result the misunderstanding erupts between the Maoists and SPA thereby hindering the peace process again and again. Nevertheless, there is resilience and a determination towards democratization.

References

1. Bishnu Raj Upreti, *Armed Conflict and Peace Process in Nepal*, Adroit Publishers, Delhi, 2006: 325.
2. For text of the speech see, *The Kathmandu Post*, February 2, 2005.
3. Manjushree Thapa, "Nepal's Troubled Kingdom" *The Hindu*, April 23, 2006.
4. Michael Hutt, *"Nepal and Bhutan in 2005, Monarch and Democracy, Can they Coexist? Asian Survey*, Vol.XLVI, No.1, January-February 2006: 120.
5. *The Kathmandu Post*, February 2, 2005.
6. Michael Hutt, *n.4*: 121.
7. Uddhav P.Pyakurel, *Maoist Movement in Nepal: A Sociological Perspective*, Adroit, Delhi, 2007: 118.
8. Bishnu Raj Upreti, *n.1* : 342.
9. *The Kathmandu Post*, May 9, 2005.
10. Bishnu Raj Upreti, *n.1*: 348.
11. Bishnu Raj Upreti, *n.1*.

12. *N.1*: 359.
13. This point has been discussed in detail in the next pages in this chapter.
14. *Nepal Weekly*, Vol.6, No.15, November 20, 2005.
15. *The Hindustan Times*, February 9, 2006.
16. *The Hindustan Times*, April 24, 2006.
17. Manjushree Thapa, *n.3*.
18. *The Hindustan Times*, April 19, 2006.
19. *n.18*.
20. *The Hindustan Times*, April 21, 2006.
21. Nilobia Roy Choudhary, "The Great Indian Balancing Act", *The Hindustan Times*, April 23, 2006.
22. *The Hindustan Times*, April 24, 2006.
23. *The Hindu*, April 22, 2006.
24. *The Hindu*, April 26, 2006.
25. International Crisis Group, *Nepal's Peace Agreement: Making it Work, Asia Report*, No. 126, 15 December d, 2006: 3.
26. *The Hindustan Times*, April 26, 2006.
27. *The Hindustan Times*, April 29, 2006.
28. *n.27*.
29. Sita Ram Yechuri, "Learning from Experience, an Analysis of Approaches of Maoists in Nepal and India", *Economic and Political Weekly*, July 22, 2006: 3170-71.
30. Babu Ram Bhattarai, "*Rajtantra ra Loktantrik Ganatantra*, Janadhwani Prakashan, 2063: 48.
31. *Economic & Political Weekly*, November 18, 2006, Editorial, 4711.
32. *The Hindustan Times*, November 20, 2006.
33. *n.32*.
34. See, Babu Ram Bhattarai, "Royal Regression and the Question of a Democratic Republic in Nepal", *Economic and Political Weekly*, 9April, 2005.
35. See, *http://www.moowadi.worldpress.com*
36. *n.35*.
37. International Crisis Group, *Nepal's Maoists: Purists or Pragmatists*, Asia Repot No. 132, 18 May 2007: 3-4.
38. See, for example, Bhumika Ghimre, *Human Rights Report on Nepal*, US State Department, March 31, 2006.
39. See, Appendix IX for details.
40. *ANI* February 17, 2007. *Reuters* February 18, 2007, *The Assocrated Press*, February 23, 2007.
41. *n.40*.

42. The arms registered were 91 mortars, 61 machine guns, 2403 rifles, 61 automatic rifles, 114 side arms, 212 shotguns, 233 home made arms, 203 others.
43. Nihar Nayak, "Arms Management in Nepal", *World Focus*, July 2007: 263.
44. *N.43*: 263.
45. See, appendix x for details.
46. See, Amit Dhakal, "Koirala Advocates Ceremonial Monarchy", *The Hindu*, June 15, 2006.
47. *The Hindu*, June 15, 2006.
48. *The Hindustan Times*, April 3, 2007.
49. *Statesman*, March 13, 2007.
50. *The Hindustan Times*, July 12, 2007.
51. ICG, *Nepal's Constitutional Process, Asia Report* No. 128, 26 February 2007: 5-7.
52. *The Hindustan Times*, October 3, 2007.
53. *The Hindu*, March 10, 2007.
54. *The Hindu*, April 11, 2007.
55. *The Hindustan Times*, April 2, 2007.
56. *The Hindu*, April 2, 2007.
57. *The Hindustan Times*, April 2, 2007.
58. *The Hindustan Times*, April 2, 2007.
59. See, B.C.Upreti, "Regional Movement and Madhesi Politics in Nepal", *Nepali Journal of Contemporary Studies*, Vol. VII, No. 1, March, 2007 : 16-36.
60. ICG, *Nepal's Troubled Tarai Region, Asia Report*, No.136, July 9, 2007.
61. See, *The Times of India*, January 29, 2007, *Asian Age*, February 25, 2007.
62. *The Hindustan Times*, August 6, 2007.
63. *The Hindustan Times*, July 28, 2007.
64. *The Hindustan Times*, June 30, 2007.
65. *The Hindustan Times*, July 13, 2007.
66. *The Kathmandu Post*, September 9, 2007.
67. *Asian News Digest*, October 6-12, 2007 : 6492.
68. *n.67* : 69492.
69. www.nepalnews.com.np/archive/2007/sept.
70. *The Kathmandu Post*, September 29, 2007.
71. *Asian News Digest*, October 20-26, 2007 : 6554.
72. www.nepalnews.com.np/archive/october
73. *The Himalayan Times*, October 6, 2007.
74. *The Himalayan Times*, October 7, 2007.

75. *The Hindustan Times*, October 24, 2007, *Kathmandu Post*, October 25, 2007.
76. *The Hindustan Times*, December 23, 2007.
77. *The Times of India,* December 25, 2007;*The Hindu* December 25, 2007.

8

Issues, Challenges and Prospects

The Maoists of Nepal have passed through different phases in the last more than a decade. In the first phase, which ran almost for a decade, the Maoists were quite enthusiastic about attaining the goals of social and political transformation in Nepal through a protracted guerrilla war. It is true that the Maoists had launched a massive revolution but they realized that in the Nepali conditions it would not necessarily be possible to achieve the desired political results through a war. Nepal's return to the authoritarian rule in early 2005 and inability of the political parties in fighting against the king's direct rule was considered to be an opportune time by the Maoists change the course of their struggle. This led to the beginning of the second phase of the Maoist movement which is peaceful and democratic and steadily moving towards attaining the desired goals.

The Maoists have truly given up the insurgency but it had existed for a decade. So it has left its impact on Nepali society and politics. Therefore, one primary issue is what has been the cost of the Maoist movement to Nepali people and society. Than the Maoist gave dynamism to a number of social and political issues. They have not been addressed so far. To what extent these issues are going to be settled? The Maoists withdrawal from the interim government has left a situation of uncertainty. It has naturally delayed the peace process. What are the prospects of socio political transformation, peace and democracy in Nepal has become a highly significant question at the movement.

The Maoist insurgency has thrown up a number of questions some of which still remain unanswered. The prevailing socio – economic and political conditions gave girth to an insurgency in Nepal.

No movement is fought without certain aims of the people or the organization involved in the movement. The Maoists believed that it would be possible to establish a new democracy in the country based on the principles of the 'dictatorship of the proletariat'. It was after a decade of protracted war that the Maoists realized that it was not possible to attain the objective of new democracy through a war. Hence, they compromised with two things: constitutional and democratic path in place of protracted war and multiparty democracy in place of new democracy as a preliminary arrangement. This shift in the Maoist strategy raises a number of questions. The Maoist's was a socio-political movement. They did talk of socio-economic transformation in the country through a large number of reforms. But their ultimate aim rest in the political sphere.

Is the path that Maoists have chosen in the form of second phase of their struggle is sufficient enough to take the Maoists up to their ultimate political goal? Does the option to take recourse to insurgency is still open to the Maoists? In the second phase the Maoists are not that independent actors as they were earlier in the first phase. The democratic forces and the Maoists are partners now and a closer understanding between the two is a must. There is a broad understanding between them as far as the question of CA is concerned. What shall be the formation of CA and how it is going to proceed over the issues of monarchy, secular and republican state is a vital issue but none seems to have given thought over it. There has been a highly fragile balance between the Maoists and SPA so far. Some times it appears that the basic factor is that enemy's enemy is a friend. But is it possible to attain the ultimate political objectives of rebuilding state in Nepal with this approach is a moot question. The understanding between SPA and the Maoists is suppose to be up to the elections to CA. What is going to happen afterwards is equally important. What are the possibilities of SPA-Maoists understanding in the elections of CA and beyond? If we look back to the past than the things are not encouraging. In 1950 when Nepali Congress declared its struggle against the Rana rule, the Communist Party of Nepal though supported it, did not join the Nepali Congress to fight against the autocratic rulers. In the 1980 referendum the Nepali Congress chief B.P. Koirala refused to participate in the referendum jointly with the communists. In 1990 the movement for democracy was fought united, but all the political forces acted independently afterwards. Now also the same situation is likely to occur. In that case is the Maoist agenda of restructuring that state and society is acceptable to all the political forces? The communist and the Nepali Congress are two main actors in this regard along with NDP and NSP as supportive groups.

The Maoists are not the sole representative of the Nepali proletariats. There are a number of political parties that have been active, and form constituents of SPA. There are communists outside SPA. UML an important segment of SPA, is the second largest political party of the kingdom. These political parties despite being the believers of the communist ideology did not subscribe to the Maoist movement. UML remained critical to it. What are the possibilities of the left unity in the present context? It is a significant issue because a united left would be more assertive in the up coming political context. But is such an unity possible is a moot question.

II

The history of the emergency of the communist forces in Nepal is closely linked with the foundation of the political parties of Nepal. The Communist Party of Nepal closely followed the foundation of the Nepali Congress Party. As the leadership of the Nepali Congress and the party itself owes its socialization and foundation of the party in India so does the Communist Party of Nepal. The communist leaders of Nepal took interest in the national movement in India and maintained closer links with the Communist Party of India. The Communist Party of Nepal shifted to the Nepali soil only after the anti – Rana movement began in Nepal. The communist party took up aggressive postures against the Nepali government since the beginning. They raised the fundamental issue of framing of the constitution by a Constituent Assembly. The issue of framing of the constitution by a Constituent Assembly was never accepted by the Nepali monarchy and interestingly it has come to the political fore front after the end of a decade old Maoist insurgency in the country.

There have been three important dimensions of the communist movement in Nepal: Firstly, the growth of the communist movement in Nepal has been characterized by continuous fragmentation and dissensions, along with the disintegration of the communist forces at the international level. Secondly, the divisions within the communist groups of Nepal have not only been based on the ideological terms but also on the political loyalties, power dynamics and personal preferences. For instance, the communist leaders and groups have also been strong supporters of the royalty. Thirdly, the majority of the communist forces have been struggling against the royal authority and have supported the democratic process. Even the hardcore communists which later on got converted into the Maoist insurgents supported the 1990 democratic movement and joined the subsequent democratic political process.

How to understand the hardcore communists joining the 1990 democratic movement, taking part in the electoral process and thereafter gradually turning into a rebel group ? There can be two explanations: One is that the hard core communists which had disassociated themselves from the moderate communist groups by now realized that it was not possible for them to enter into the power dynamics of the country through a constitutional – democratic path. Therefore they adopted a revolutionary path. Another explanation is that the hardcore communists were expecting a socio – economic and political transformation in Nepal after the establishment of democracy in the country but the democratic government could neither streamline the democratic process nor it could properly address to the socio – economic issues and problems. Therefore, the Maoists began to prepare themselves to fight for the establishment of a new democracy which would ensure both restructuring of state and transformation of the society.

The Maoists had perhaps linked these two broad objectives. They thought of establishing a new democracy in Nepal which would ensure social transformation and also their prospects for entering into the power structure. Thus, the Maoists had a political agenda and wanted to get their political goals realized. But they also knew that for the realization of the goals of a new democracy socio – economic transformation of a feudal society like Nepal was a necessity. Therefore, the Maoist movement was a social and political movement.

But than what prompted the Maoists to choose a revolutionary path? There was not one factor responsible for it. Instead it was a cumulative effect of so many factors. The Maoists were frustrated with the working of the parliamentary democracy. The government took up negative postures towards the radical communists. After 1991 elections they realized that their prospects to entre into the power structure were very bleak. The right wing political parties as well as the moderate communists too were not in their favour. It was also frustrating to them that the democratic government was neither addressing itself to the socio – economic issues, nor it was doing anything to change the power configuration of the country. The feudal elements and the traditional bases of political and administrative power were still important. They believed that these conditions would not change through constitutional or democratic methods. The non – responsive attitude of the government to popular aspirations and the issues of socio – economic reforms also encouraged the Maoists to raise these issues in an assertive manner.

The Maoist insurgency was not a sudden development. After 1991 the hardcore communists were gradually heading towards that direction. The attitude of the government towards them and the political situation in the country helped them in proceeding towards that direction. The Maoists received support from the like minded international and regional organizations and groups in ideological, organizational and logistic terms. The local geographical conditions were suitable for launching a protracted guerrilla war. The dense forests, isolated regions in the Western hills were quite suitable for the Maoists to build their hide outs. The extreme poverty conditions in rural areas, exploitative nature of the society, problems of unemployment, frustration among ethnic groups and youth, dalits, Madhesis and gender discriminations helped the Maoists in seeking support from diverse sections of the society. The open Indo-Nepal border also proved to be an asset for the Maoists for their unabated visits to India, taking shelter and for availing medical and other facilities in that country. The Maoists had a strong leadership that, by and large, remained unchallenged. The top leaders of CPN (Maoists) were proved to be powerful political leaders, top strategists, ideologue, planners and intellectuals.

The Maoists tried to give enough dynamism to its revolution: **socially** by raising a struggle against social abuses, ill practices and exploitation; **economically** by fighting against feudal practices; **ideologically** in the form of Prachandapath, **politically** by entering into peace negotiations with the government and **strategically** by moving from rural to urban insurrections.

The Maoists sustained its protracted war against the Nepali state for a decade. But they realized that in Nepali conditions it might not be possible to attain the desired political goals through a violent war. They took advantage of the emerging political situation in Nepal after the royal coup of 2005, and ultimately joined the democratic forces to initiate a process of rebuilding state and society in Nepal through a constitutional – democratic process.

How about the protracted war then? The Maoists took a turn after 2005 true, but it was the decade old protracted war that brought them to this position. The protracted war in fact converted the Maoists into a political force to be reckoned with. The insurgency loosened the nod of feudal cliques in Nepal. It is a fact that the issues of republican state, secularism, inclusive democracy, federal state, etc are getting a wider political recognition because of the Maoists insurgency. No one listened to the demand of Constituent Assembly in 1950 but today this issue has become unavoidable. Similar is the case of monarchy, Hindu state, etc. In fact, these are the issues that the Maoists have been fighting for. Therefore, one would agree that the Maoists insurgency gave a new dynamism to Nepali society and polity. One may say that there have been wide spread socio – economic consequences of the insurgency. A war is bound to cause hazards of various shorts. It is more important if the socio – political goals that have been set are realized.

III

Let us now briefly look back at the imprints of the Maoists movement. Can a backward and poor country like Nepal afford an insurgency is a central issue here. The Nepali economy has suffered most due to the Maoist insurgency. The major economic activities in the country were badly affected and became dysfunctional. The impact on the Nepali economy was in two ways. A number of regular economic activities either came to a standstill or reduced to minimal due to the diversification of funds towards fighting against the Maoists insurgents. Secondly the economy was severely disrupted by the Maoist insurgency. The major effects on the economy may be stated as following:

1. The over all economic growth rate was adversely affected due to the Maoist insurgency. There was a general decline of

GDP over the years and the lowest growth rate (0.8%) was recorded during 2001-2002.

2. There was a tremendous increase in defense budget ranging between 20 to 30 per cent of the annual budget.
3. The development expenditure was obviously reduced as priority was given to combating the insurgency. It affected a large number of development or humanitarian programmes.
4. Tourism, one of the major aspects of modern day's Nepali economy, was badly affected due to insecure conditions within the country.
5. The industrial sector was adversely affected. Production of tobacco, textile, beverage, etc fell down.
6. The lowering down of production in industries like carpet, garments, etc. reduced the volume of Nepali exports.
7. Agriculture production was badly hampered because of adverse conditions in the countryside. The food production went down consequently.
8. There was a sharp reduction in the foreign assistance and grants received by Nepal.

These points clearly indicate that the Nepali economy was badly affected by the insurgency. This apart, there was a loss of infrastructure in many parts of the country. The telecommunication towers, roads, air strips, bridges, government buildings, bank offices, police stations, school buildings, power plants, etc. were damaged by the Maoists. It had cost $ 250 million till 2002. The harassment to businessman, industrialists and local shopkeepers adversely affected trade and commerce. Not only the industrialists and businessmen but the big investors were also hesitant in making investments in Nepal. A number of NGO's abandoned their activities due to insecurity to their staff members, particularly those who were working in the rural areas.

The Maoist movement cost lives of more than 15000 people including the Maoists, the government security personnel and civilians. The Maoist insurgency disrupted the smooth functioning of the society. There was a fear of insecurity, particularly in the villages. It is true that initially there was lot of enthusiasm and support for the Maoists in the rural areas. But as the movement became more and more violent and the Maoists became more aggressive in their attitude people were afraid of the Maoists. The forced closer of schools and markets, destruction of government offices etc., caused problems for the common man.

In the rural areas the poor people were over burdened economically, as they were constrained to meet demands raised by the Maoists like food, shelter, etc. It was a big burden to those who were already economically marginalized. Initially the people were enthusiastic about joining the Maoist army. But later on it became a burden for them. They lost the interest as the insurgency prolonged, the movement became more violent and there was a strong retaliation from RNA.

There was a disruption of social life in the Maoist influenced areas. No body was allowed to entre the villages without permission from the Maoists. On the other hand there was a close watch on the activities of the villagers by the security forces. Both the Maoists and the security forces suspected village people for their activities against the either. The Maoists insurgency induced the instinct of violence in the society. The violence, terror, etc was used by people to fulfill their narrow interest in the name of Maoist insurgency. Thus Maoists contributed to the factors and forces of social destruction and disturbances. The Maoist movement also became a burden for the rural women.

A large number of people evacuated the villages and moved else where due to the fear of the Maoists. Migration to the neighbouring districts of India had increased considerably.

A large number of cases of human rights violation and abuses by the Maoists and the government agencies were reported by Nepal Human Rights Commission, Amnesty International, etc. Torturing, Killing, bombing, kidnapping, child labour, trafficking in women, detentions, in human punishments, etc became common features.

The Maoists insurgency contributed much to governmental instability and disfunctioning. The governments of the day failed in finding any peaceful solution to the Maoist problem. It also failed in reaching to a military solution of the problem, although all out efforts were made to fight against the insurgency. The Maoist insurgency also became a pretext for the change of government. Interestingly, the failure of the government in containing the Maoist insurgency became a major factor for the rise of authoritarian powers. On the whole it can be said that the Maoist movement was a set back to political stability and good governance in Nepal.

IV

It is true that the Maoist movement adversely affected the socio – economic and political dynamics but there were certain positive dimensions of the movement. It were the Maoists who for the first time raised voice against orthodox social behaviour and customs, money lending or indebtedness, alcoholism, practices of bounded labour, etc. In a highly traditional and back-word society like Nepal it was not easy to raise voice against these practices. Since the Maoists was an organized and aggressive movement so they could do it. It is true that these aspects of the Maoists movement could not be sustained for a longer period but it had its impact on the rural people. The Maoists for the first time raised voice against feudalism, authoritarianism and the institution of monarchy as a protractor of these tendencies in an organized way. There had been movements in Nepal against authoritarianism or the establishment of democracy but the feudal orientation of the society and the monarchic state could never be challenged. They always prevailed over all political changes and political reforms. The Maoist insurgency was a real challenge to such practices and forces.

One reason why democracy could not be sustained in Nepal was the continuation of the dominance of feudal forces. The democratic governments always followed a reconciliatory attitude towards the feudal forces, and thus tried to sustain their continuation in sharing power. The democratic political leaderships in Nepal whether belonging to Nepali Congress, UML or NDP, etc always looked towards monarchy with a compromising attitude. The king was seen as the ultimate protector of political interest of individual leaders, parties, groups and so on. As a result, monarchy remained a powerful institution within the democratic systems as well. Consequently, the democratic institutions and leadership remained weak and fragile.

The Maoists put forth the agenda of state restructuring and social transformation. There is some success in that direction. There are obstacles and the goals are yet to be realized fully. But one can say that the Maoists succeeded in making them as the major contours of political change in Nepal at the moment.

The Maoists had thrown the ball in the courts of SPA by joining the political mainstream and during the last one year it has given a significant dynamism to the Nepali politics although with all shorts of ifs and buts. The Nepali politics is at crossroads today. Seemingly there would be no going back to old norms and practices of politics and there would be a stepping towards building a new state and democracy in near future. But the task is still hazardous.

V

But having said all that one would like to ponder upon what issues are left in the context of efforts made by SPA and the Maoists towards building a new state and democracy? Interestingly, the core issues relating to the restructuring of state and social transformation are still to be realized.

The issue of declaring Nepal a republic state is significant and fundamental. The Maoists raised the question of a republican state. SPA agreed to it when it entered into an understanding with the Maoists. It was agreed that the Constituent Assembly would decide about the republican state. But with the delay in the elections of the Constituent Assembly and inconsistent attitude of SPA over this issue, the Maoists were prompted to demand for the declaration of Nepal a republican state before elections of the Constituent Assembly. It became a bone of contention and caused a political deadlock in the country. The Maoist withdrew from the interim government as the government was not prepared to accept it. The Maoists know that their political future rests on the realization of the demand of a republican state. The Maoists have also demanded for total proportional representation system for elections to CA. They are perhaps working to their own prospects in elections to CA. It is likely that the Maoists would agree to hold elections in early 2008. There is also a general consensus that the issue of the republican state will be settled by CA.

Why SPA is not prepared to accept the Maoist demands? The interim Constitution has already laid that CA will settle the issue of republican state. This is one thing but more than that is it that the political parties are still not prepared to take such a drastic decision? This is perhaps the problem of a country where political leadership is finding constrained to take a forward looking political decisions but are not sure about the mood of the society. Does political parties apprehend that a decision of declaring Nepal a republic could go against them in elections to CA? Are they faced with the god father problem? Are the political parties still not prepared to come out of the bondages of traditional bases of politics and power in Nepal? The Maoists are also suspicious about the role of monarchy. They apprehend that the monarchy might play a destructive role in CA elections. Hence, they want declaration of republican state before elections.

The question of future of monarchy is associated with the issue of a republican state. The institution of monarchy will be politically dysfunctional automatically. Monarchy represents feudal class of the Nepali society. The abolition of monarchy would also defuse this feudal class. The Maoists have been consistently demanding abolition of the monarchic system. SPA though agreed to political neutralization of monarchy has not been so consistent as the Maoists have in this case. They have been talking of minimum role to monarchy, ceremonial monarchy, etc. It has created doubts in the minds of the Maoists.

The issue of elections of CA has become crucial at the moment. It is for the second time that the elections to CA have been postponed. Actually the future political process in Nepal rests on the elections of CA. So delaying of the elections means delaying the future political process and the whole agenda of rebuilding the Nepali.

The issue of transformation of the society is a long process. But the process has to begun at some point of time. Till now the political issues have been accorded prominence and the question of socio – economic reforms has not received adequate attention. The issues relating to social transformation also need to be taken up later or sooner.

There are a number of groups, communities and regions that are desperately looking for their inclusion in the political framework of the country. Both the Maoists and SPA have been talking about establishment of an inclusive democracy. But these issues have been left for CA to settle. However, these groups and the regions are becoming impatient. The agitation in Tarai is a result of this. Actually a number of groups and communities were excluded in the politico – administrative framework of the country in the past. Even before the rise of the Maoist movement the Mongolian ethnic groups had begun to demand for autonomy on the basis of their ethnic identity. The Maoists streamlined their aspirations and took advantage of their grief against monarchy and the Hindu identity of state. The Maoists raised the issue of accommodating various ethnic and regional identities within the framework of a federal state. It is now certain that the ethnic and regional identities can only be satisfied within the framework of a federal state. However, the issue of federal state is not less complex. The viability in the Nepali context is an important point. Moreover, one has also to be conscious of the fact that the accommodation of ethnic and regional identities within a federal state also opens doors for ethnic and regional tensions and political mobilization.

The minority issue is also coming up. The Muslims have already started demanding their adequate politico – administrative representation. The Christians also constitute a small minority groups they are not yet mobilized like Muslims. The minority issues have also to be dealt with in the new political dynamics of the country.

The issues relating to the depressed sections of the society are also important and need to be addressed properly. The women and dalits constitute depressed sections of the society. There is a need to change perception towards them and envisage ways and means for their upliftment and empowerment.

All these issues are bound to come up and if not addressed properly they would give rise to socio – political conflicts both horizontally and vertically. The Maoists have a moral obligation to see that the issues relating to ethno – regional and weaker sections of the society are properly addressed.

VI

The Maoists gave relief to the people of Nepal when they decided to join the mainstream politics and cooperate with SPA in order to realize their political goals which have been broadly acceptable by SPA as well. The management of the Maoist arms and armed forces, promulgation of the interim constitution and the inclusion of the Maoist in the interim parliament and the interim government has been the major landmarks towards building peace and stability in the country. The agenda of restructuring the state and transformation of the society is yet to be taken up. The first and foremost step in that direction is elections to CA. The process has been delayed and the elections are postponed twice. Certainly they can not be postponed for a longer time period. Actually, the parties in the government are looking at the elections to CA from their own point of view. They will have to rise above individual party interest and take the National interest into consideration. It is true that all the actors in the present political process in Nepal have their individual political stakes and interests. But they have a common agenda which is supreme and it is only through the realization of this supreme agenda that the individual interest of various political groups can be met with. Therefore, the agenda of building a new democratic Nepal has to be taken up seriously.

Appendix – I

Major Landmarks in Communist Movement in Nepal

1949 Formation of the Communist Party of Nepal (CPN) in India.

1950 The party was shifted to Nepal.

1952 The Communist Party of Nepal banned by the government.

1954 Man Mohan Adhikari selected as General Secretary of the Party.

1956 Ban on CPN lifted.

1957 Keshar Jung Raiamajhi selected as General Secretary of the party by the 2nd Congress of CPN.

1959 CPN won 4 of 47 seats it contested for 109-seated parliament in the first general election.

1960 CPN was banned along with all other political parties.

1961 Durbhunga Plenum of CPN was held.

1962 CPN was divided along the line of USSR and China, where Keshar Jung Raimajhi was representing Russian line and Tulsi Lal Amatya was representing Chinese line.

1968 Conflict between Puspa Lal and Tulsi Lal mounted and the party was split in to two factions.

1971 *Jhapa Andolon* (movement) in eastern Nepal launched by young communists, influenced by Naxelite movement in India.

1974 Formation of CPN (Fourth Congress) by Mohan Bikram Singh and Nirmal Lama.

1978 CPN (Marxist Leninist) established by the young communists.

1983 CPN (Fourth Congress) split into CPN (fourth Congress) and CPN (Mashal).

1985 CPN (Mashal) Split into CPN (Masal) and CPN (Mashal).

1987 Communist factions led by Puspa Lal and Man Mohan Adhikari united to from CPN (Marxist).

1989 Pushp Kamal Dahal (Prachanda) took over as General Secretary of the CPN (Mashal).

1989 Various communist parties formed a united front: ULF and participated in the 1990 democratic movement with Nepali Congress.

1990 CPN (Forth Congress) and CPN (Mashal) formed CPN (Unity Centre) under the leadership of Prachanda.

1991 CPN (United Marxist – Leninist) was formed.

1991 CPN (Masal) boycotted the general election. But Babu Ram Bhattarai did not agree and led a breakaway faction to join the CPN (Unity Centre).

CPN (Unity Centre) created a political wing called United People's Front of Nepal (UPFN) to participate in the general elections and won 9 out of 205 seats in the parliament.

1994 CPN (Unity Centre) and United People's Front split into two factions led by Prachanda and Nirmal Lama. Babu Ram Bhattarai led the pro-Prachanda United People's Front.

1995 CPN (Maoists) was formed.

Appendix – II

Major Landmarks in Maoist Movement in Nepal

1996

- **February 13** Initiation of the people's war by the Communist Party of Nepal (Maoist)
  - Kathmandu: A soft-drink bottling factory owned by a multi-national company was attacked and a portion of the building torched
  - Gorkha District:
    - A liquor factory was 'blasted'.
    - Office of the Small Farmer's Development Programme of the state-owned Agricultural Development Bank in Chyangli (Village Development Committee) (VDC) in Gorkha was ransacked.
  - Kavre district: A usurer's house was raided at night, property and cash reportedly worth 1.3 million rupees were seized, and loan documents worth several million rupees reportedly destroyed.
  - Rolpa, Rukum and Sindhuli districts: One police outpost raided in each district. The outpost at Holari (Rolpa) had its store seized, including a "substantial amount of high explosives". Athbishkot-rari, (Rukum) was also raided. The Sindhuligarhi post in Sindhuli was reportedly raided without resistance.

December 1999 K.P. Bhattarai Government instituted High Level Commission under the leadership of Sher Bahadur Deuba to suggest solution to the Maoist problem.

25 September 2000 Maoists heavily attacked Dunai headquarters of the Dolpa district.

27 October 2000 Government and Maoist established informal contact (Deputy Prime Minister R.C.Poudel met Maoist Central Committee leader Rabindra Shrestha in Kathmandu.

2001

- January: The government created the Armed Police Force to fight the insurgents.
- May 28: Chairman Prachanda gave an interview with the journal A World to Win (RIM).
- August 3: The first round of peace talks began.
- November 23: Peace talks collapsed when the Maoists withdrew and attacked police and army posts in 42 districts.
- November 26: The monarchy declared a nationwide state of emergency and employed the Royal Nepal Army to start attacking the Maoists.

2002

- The United States Congress approved US$ 12 million to provide training to Royal Nepal Army officers and supply 5,000 M-16 rifles.
- May: Peace talks collapsed.
- May 11: a photograph Discovered by Nepal government soldiers in western Nepal, the photograph depicted Nepal's Maoist rebel leaders Babu Ram Bhattarai, Hishila Yami, Ram Bhahadur Thapa (alias Badal), and Pushp Kamal Dahal (alias Prachanda).
- May: Prime Minister Deuba, at King Gyandendra's word, dissolved parliament due to opposition to the state of emergency and the issue of fresh new elections.
- October 4: King Gyanendra deposed Prime Minister Deuba and the entire Council of Ministers, assumed executive powers, and cancel the elections for the dissolved House of Representative, which had been scheduled for November 11, 2002.
- October 11: King Gyanedra appointed Lokendra Bahadur Chand as Prime Minister.

2003

- January: The United States of America held exercises with the Nepali army.
- January: Maoist insurgents killed the Inspector General of Police, his wife and his bodyguard while on their morning walk.
- January 29: A second ceasefire was established and peace talks began.
- May 13: Code of conduct jointly declared by the government and the Communist Party of Nepal (Maoist) for the mutually agreed period of cease-fire.
- August 17: Killing of '19 rebels and civilians' in the Ramechhap district of central Nepal.
- August 24: The Maoists threatened to withdraw from the cease-fire if the government would not agree to include discussion of their participation in the Constituent Assembly within 48 hours.
- August 26: Maoist ultimatum expired.
- August 27:
    - The rebels called for an one-day strike to denounce the army's attacks on rebel cadres.
    - The rebels unilaterally withdrew from the January 29th cease-fire. Prachanda's statement revived the rebels' demand for an end to monarchic rule in favour of a people's republic.
    - September 27: Twelve Maoists were killed in a gun battle with security forces at Chhita Pokhara in the Khotang District, 340 kilometers east of Kathmandu.
- October 13: At least 37 people were killed when an estimated 1,000 Maoists attempted to storm a police-training centre in Bhaluwang.
- October 27: Lieutenant Colonel Adrian Griffith and six Nepali nationals were freed 42 hours after being taken captive in Beglung, 300 km west of Kathmandu, while on a drive to recruit young Gurkha soldiers to serve in the British army. Party Chief Prachanda said, "We are sorry for the incident that took place against the policy of the party".

- November 11: The government defense ministry accused the rebels of abducting twenty-one 9th and 10th grade students from Riva Secondary School in Mugu District, Western Nepal.

2004

- February 5: 14 suspected Maoist activists and two civilian were reportedly killed in a government raid in village Bhimad of Makwanpur district. Amnesty International later wrote a letter to Prime Minister Surya Bahadur Thapa and Colonel Nilendra Aryal, Head of the Royal Nepal Army (RNA) Human Rights Cell demanding an immediate inquiry.
- February 10: Two central committee members of Communist Party of Nepal (Maoist) Matrika Yadav and Suresh Ali Magar were reported to have been handed over by India to Nepal. They were reportedly arrested in Lucknow after Nepal provided information in this regard.
- February 13: Ganesh Chilwal led an anti-Maoist protest on this day, the ninth anniversary of the commencement of the revolution.
- February 15: two men shot Ganesh Chilwal dead in his Kathmandu office.
- February 15: Fighting erupted at a Maoist base in Kalikot District, 360km West of Kathmandu. The base was said to hold 1000 Maoist troops.
- February 17: A security official said a private helicopter flying troops to Kalikot was hit by Maoist fire but it returned safely to Kathmandu.
- February 18: 65 Maoists were reportedly killed.
- February 15 and 16: State radio reported 13 rebels were killed in seven separate small clashes across the kingdom.
- February 18: Khem Narayan Faujdar, a member of the parliament dissolved by King Gyanendra in 2002, was shot dead by two suspected Maoists riding a motorcycle in the Nawalparasi District, 200 km southwest of the capital, according to police.

- April 2(?): The largest rallies since 1990 begin in Kathmandu. They were variously labeled "pro-democracy" and "anti-monarch".
- April 3: More than 12 trucks were burnt while waiting at a Western Nepal border post to pick up petrol from India. India condemned the attacks.
- April 4: "Some 150 demonstrators were struck during a police baton charge" during demonstrations in Kathmandu.
- April 4: Maoist rebels attacked a police post in Yadukuwa, Jadukhola killing at least nine police men, 35 police were reportedly missing, 9 dead, and 7 wounded. 8 to 9 rebels were reported dead.
- April 4: In west Nepal three Indian traders were shot and injured and had their vehicles burned.
- April 5: A three day national strike began, called by CPN (M) and opposed by an "alliance of five political parties" who were protesting in Kathmandu against the monarchy.
- April 5: In the morning, 3 soldiers were killed and 7 injured by a CPN (M) landmine activated by their vehicle at Dhalkhola, 50km East of Kathmandu.
- April 5: At least 140 people were injured in clashes in Kathmandu as "about 50,000" demonstrators confronted police. Demonstrators tried to break through a police barricade close to the royal palace. Police responded with tear gas and police batons reportedly injured protesters. Both sides threw rocks and bricks. Demonstrations also occurred in Lalitpur and Bhaktapur. King Gyanendra had reportedly been away touring villages in Western Nepal.
- August 16: The Soaltee Hotel, a popular luxury hotel in Kathmandu, was bombed for refusing a rebel demand that the hotel be closed.
- August 18: A bomb exploded in a market place in Southern Nepal. The blast killed a 12-year-old boy and wounded six others, including three policemen. Also, Maoist rebels demanding the release of captured guerrillas stopped all road traffic near Kathmandu by threatening to attack vehicles.

- September 10: A bomb exploded at the United States Information Service office in Kathmandu.
- September 13: U.S. Peace Corps suspended operations and non-essential U.S. Embassy personnel were evacuated from Nepal.
- September 15: Twenty government security personnel were killed in the Western district of Arghakhanchi when the rebels mounted a surprise attack.
- December 16: Sixteen Maoist rebels were killed in clashes with Nepalese security forces in the Western district of Dailekh.
- December 23: Maoist forces launched blockade of Kathmandu
- December 26: Over 15,000 hold peace rally in Kathmandu.
- January 4: Three government security personnel and twenty-four Maoist rebels killed in fighting.
- January 8: Maoists detained and later released 300 passengers from six buses that defied their blockade of Kathmandu.
- January 10: Prime Minister Deuba said he would increase defense spending to fight the Maoists unless they come forward for talks with the government.
- January 11: Protests and blockades over government fuel price increase between 10% to 25%.
- January 15: Maoists allegedly detained 14 Indian Gurkhas from Chuha village in Kailali.
- February 1: King Gyanendra dissolved parliament and banned all news reports. Army began arresting senior political leaders, journalists, trade unionists, human rights activists and civil society leaders. All telephone and internet connections were cut.
- June 6: Some 37 civilian killed and over 70 injured after a packed passenger bus run over a rebel landmine in Chitwan district.
- August 9: Maoist rebels killed 40 security men in Mid Western Nepal.

- September 3: The rebels declared a three–month unilateral ceasefire to woo opposition political parties.
- November 19: After negotiations, the Maoist rebels agreed to work with opposition politicians in a common front against the rule of king Gyanendra of Nepal.

2006

- January 2: Rebels decided not to extend a four month ceasefire saying that the government had broken the ceasefire with numerous attacks on Maoist villages.
- March 14: The Maoist rebels extended road blockade; nationwide strike called for April 3.
- April 5: General Strike began, with Maoist forces promising to refrain from violence.
- April 6,7: Protesters clashed with police, hundreds arrested and, dozens injured.
- April 8: A curfew was imposed in Kathmandu from 10 a.m. to 9 p.m. The king ordered protesters violating the curfew to be "shot on sight".
- April 9 General strike. Government extended curfew, BBC reported three dead on two days of unrest, as thousands of demonstrators defied curfew.

Appendix – III

14 Point Maoist Demand Charter

The Unity Centre submitted a demand charter to the Prime Minster of Nepal, G.P. Koirala on 5 March 1992. Nirmal Lama took it to the Prime Minister's office on behalf of the party. It included the following demands:

1. Control prices of fertilizer, electricity, water, telephone and goods of daily necessity. Stop black marketeering, smuggling and corruption.
2. End congressisation of the administration, education, communications and other fields.
3. End government terror, killing, firing, suppression and hooliganism.
4. Abrogate unequal treaties, agreements and understandings, including the 1950 Treaty [with India], and cancel the understanding that hands over rivers to India.
5. Provide settlement to squatters and stop displacing them without providing alternate areas of settlement.
6. End the expulsion and suspension of employees. Re-appoint employees who were sacked during the last agitation.
7. Determine the wages of industrial and agricultural laborers. Make arrangements to provide work and food for the poor people.
8. End injustice and exploitation of farmers. Fix a reasonable market price for agricultural products.

9. End commercialization of the education sector and provide education and study materials at a reasonable price.
10. End discrimination against oppressed people and the Dalits. Provide equal opportunity in the media, including radio and TV for all languages.
11. End all kinds of discrimination against women, including their sale in the market. End discrimination in the distribution of citizenship papers. Ensure that daughters have equal rights of property.
12. End discrimination towards people living in the Tarai and remote areas.
13. Take action against the corrupt people of the Panchayat regime.
14. End the conspiracy between the king and reactionary forces, helped by the Congress government, in ending the gains of the People's Movement of 1990.

Appendix – IV

40-Point Demand Charter of Maoists

1. All unequal stipulations and agreements regarding the 1950 Treaty between India and Nepal should be removed.
2. HMG should admit that the anti-nationalist Tanakpur agreement was wrong, and the Mahakali Treaty, incorporating it, should be nullified.
3. The entire Nepal-India border should be controlled and systematized. Vehicles with Indian number plates, playing the roads on Nepal, should not be allowed.
4. Gorkha recruiting centres should be closed and decent jobs should be arranged for the recruits.
5. Where foreign technicians are given precedence over Nepali technicians for certain local jobs, in several areas of Nepal, a system of Work Permit should be instituted for the foreigners.
6. The monopoly of foreign capital in Nepal's industry, trade and economic sector should be stopped.
7. Sufficient income should be generated form custom duties for the country's economic development.
8. The cultural pollution of imperialists and expansionists should be stopped. Hindi video, cinema, and all kinds of such newspapers and magazines should be completely stopped. Inside Nepal, import and distribution of vulgar Hindi films, videocassettes and magazines should be stopped.
9. Bribing by imperialists and expansionists in the name of NGO's should be stopped.
10. A new Constitution be drafted by the people's elected representatives.

11. All the special rights and privileges of the King and his family should be withdrawn.
12. Army, police and administration should be under the people's control.
13. The Security Act and all other repressive acts should be abolished.
14. All the false charges against the people of Rukum, Rolpa, Jajarkot, Gorkha, Kavre, Sindhuphalchowk, Sindhuli, Dhanusha and Ramechhap should be withdrawn and all the people falsely charged by the government should be released.
15. Armed police operations in different districts should immediately be stopped.
16. The government should constitute a special investigating committee to look into the matters of Dilip Choudhary, Bhawan Thapa Magar, Prabhakar Subedi and other people who disappeared from police custody at different times and the culprits should be punished and appropriate compensation given to their families.
17. People, who died during the time of the movement, should be declared as martyrs and their families and those who have been wounded and disabled should be given proper compensation. Strong action should be taken against the killers.
18. Nepal should be declared a secular state.
19. Girls should be given equal property rights to those of their brothers.
20. All kinds of exploitation and prejudice based on caste should be ended. In areas having majority of one ethnic group, that group should have autonomy over that area.
21. The status of dalits as untouchable should be ended and the system of unsociability should be ended once and for all.
22. All languages should be given equal status. Up until middle-high school level (uccha-madhyamic) arrangements should be made for education to be given in the children's mother tongue.

23. There should be guarantee of free speech and free press. The communications media should be completely autonomous.
24. Intellectuals, historians, artists and academicians that engaged in other cultural activities should be guaranteed intellectual freedom.
25. In both the Tarai and hilly regions there is prejudice and misunderstanding in backward areas. This should be ended and the backward areas should be assisted. Good relations should be established between the villages and the cities.
26. Decentralization in real terms should be applied to local areas, which should have local rights, autonomy and control over their own resources.
27. Those who cultivate the land should own it. The land of rich landlords should be confiscated and distributed to the homeless and others who have no land.
28. The property of brokers and commission agents should be confiscated and that money should be invested in industry.
29. All should be guaranteed work and should be given stipend until jobs are found for them.
30. HMG should pass strong laws ensuring that people involved in industry and agriculture should receive minimum wages.
31. The homeless should be given suitable accommodation. Until HMG can provide such accommodation they should not be removed from where they are squatting.
32. Poor farmers should be completely freed form debt. Loans from the Agricultural Development Bank by poor farmers should be completely written off. Small industries should be given loans.
33. Fertilizer and seeds should be easily and cheaply made available, and the farmers should be given a proper market price for their production.
34. Flood and draught victims should be given all necessary help.

35. All should be given free and scientific medical service and education and education for profit (private schools?) should be completely stopped.
36. Inflation should be controlled and labourers' salaries should be raised in direct ratio with the rise in prices. Daily essential goods should be made cheap and easily available.
37. Arrangement should be made for drinking water, goods, roads, and electricity in the villages.
38. Cottage and other small industries should be granted special facilities and protection.
39. Corruption, black marketing, smuggling, bribing, commission, etc. should be stopped.
40. The orphans, the disabled, the elderly and children should be given help and protection.

We offer a heartfelt request to the present coalition government that they should, fulfill the above demands, which are essential for Nepal's existence and for the people's daily lives as soon as possible. If the government doesn't show any interest by Falgun 5,2052, (February 17, 1996) we will be compelled to launch a movement against the government.

Source: Pancha N. Maharjan, "The Maoists Insurgency in Nepal" in Dhrub Kumar (ed.), **Domestic Conflict and Crisis of Governability in Nepal**, CNAS, Kathmandu, 2000: 191-193.

Appendix – V

Origin and Development of CPN (Maoists)

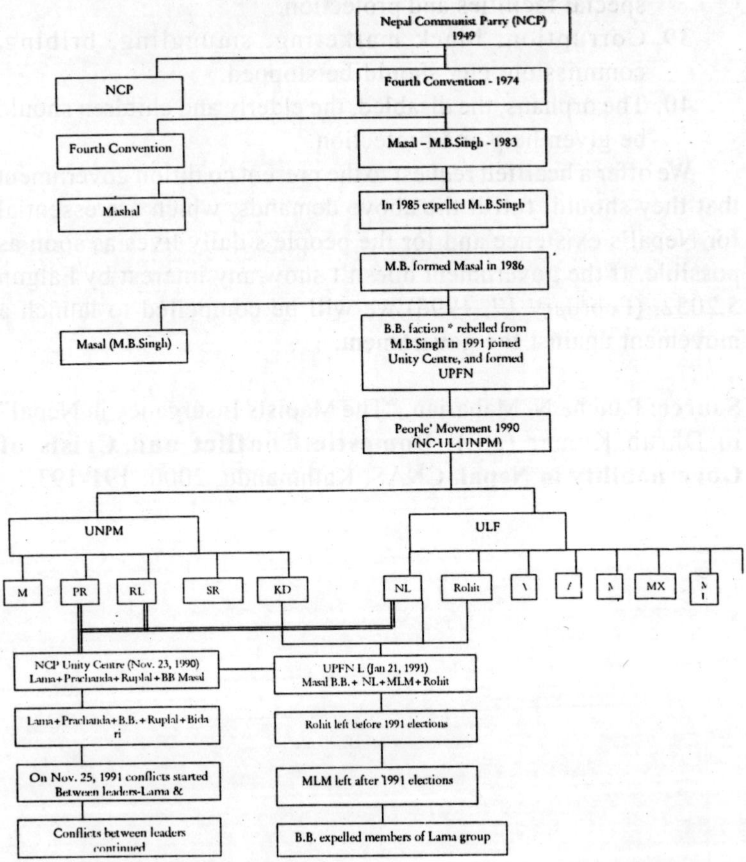

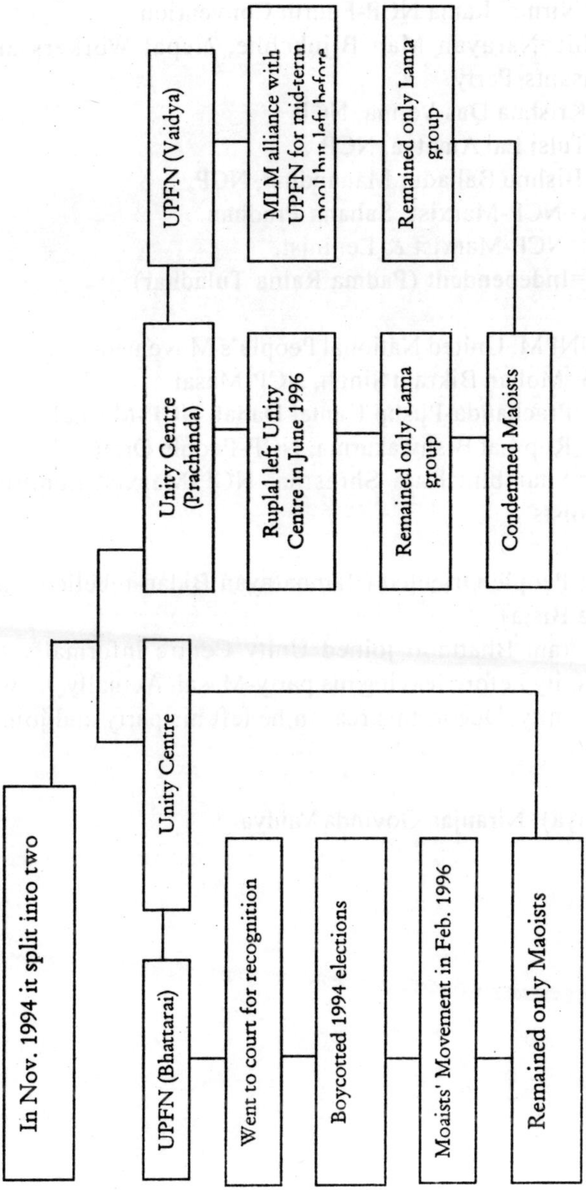
In Nov. 1994 it split into two
Unity Centre
UPFN (Bhattarai)
Unity Centre (Prachanda)
UPFN (Vaidya)
Went to court for recognition
Boycotted 1994 elections
Moaists' Movement in Feb. 1996
Remained only Maoists
Ruplal left Unity Centre in June 1996
Remained only Lama group
Condemned Maoists
MLM alliance with UPFN for mid-term
Remained only Lama group

ULF: United Left Front:

1. NL Nirmal Lama NCP-Fourth Convention
2. Rohit=Narayan Man Bijukchhe, Nepal Workers and Peasants Party
3. V=Krishna Das Verma, NCP
4. A=Tulsi Lal Amatya, NCP
5. M=Bishnu Bahadur Manandhar, NCP
6. MX=NCP-Marxist, Sahana Pradhan.
7. ML=NCP-Marxist & Leninist.
8. Ind=Independent (Padma Ratna Tuladhar)

UNPM: United National People's Movement

1. MB=Mohan Bikram Singh, NCP-Masal
2. PR=Prachanda-Pushp Kamal Dahal, NCP-Mashal
3. RL=Rup Lal Bishwakarma, NCP-People Oriented.
4. SR=Shambhu Ram Shrestha, NCP-Marxist-Leninist-Maoists.

Bidari-NCP-People Oriented (Ramnarayan Bidan-rebelled from Rupchandra Bista)

*B.B.=Baburam Bhattarai joined Unity Centre informally for functional unity before leaving his party-Masal. Actually, he was in for party unity. Due to this reason he left his party and joined Unity Centre

UPFN (Vaidya)=Niranjan Govinda Vaidya

Appendix – VI

12-Point Understanding Between Political Parties and the Maoists (November 22, 2005)

1. There is no possibility of peace, progress and prosperity in the country. Therefore, an understanding has been reached to establish absolute democracy by ending autocratic monarchy, with all forces against the autocratic monarchy centralizing their assault against autocratic monarchy from their respective positions, thereby creating nationwide storm of democratic protests.
2. The seven agitating parties are fully committed to the fact that only by establishing absolute democracy through the restoration of the parliament with the force of agitation, forming all-party government with complete authority, holding elections to a constituent assembly through dialogue and understanding with the Maoists, can the existing conflict in the country be resolved and sovereignty and state power completely transferred to the people. It is the view and commitment of the CPN (Maoists) that the above mentioned goal can be achieved by holding a national political conference of the agitating democratic forces, and through its decision, forming an interim government to hold constituent assembly elections. An understanding has been reached between the agitating seven parties and the CPN (Maoists) to continue dialogue on this procedural work-list and finding a common understanding. It has been agreed that the

force of People's Movement is the only alternative to achieve this.

3. Today, the country has demanded the establishment of permanent peace along with a positive solution to the armed conflict. Therefore, we are committed to end autocratic monarchy and the existing armed conflict, and establishing permanent peace in the country through constituent assembly election sand forward-looking political outlet. The CPN (Maoists) expresses its commitment to move along the new peaceful political stream through this process. In this very context, an understanding has been reached to keep, during the holding of constituent assembly elections after ending autocratic monarchy, the armed Maoists force and the royal army under the supervision of the United Nations or any other reliable international supervision, to conclude the elections in a free and fair manner and accept the result of the elections. We expect reliable international mediation even during the dialogue process.
4. Expressing clearly and making public institutional commitment to the democratic norms and values like the competitive multiparty system of governance, civil liberties, human rights etc, the CPN (Maoists) has expressed commitment to move forward its activities accordingly.
5. The CPN (Maoists) has expressed its commitment to create an environment, allowing the political activists of other democratic parties displaced during the course of the armed conflict to return to their former localities and live there with dignity, return their home, land and property seized in an unjust manner and carry out their activities without hindrance.
6. Undertaking self-criticism and self-evaluation of past mistakes, the CPN (Maoists) has expressed commitment not to repeat such mistakes in future.
7. The seven political parties, undertaking self-evaluation, have expressed commitment not to repeat the mistakes

of the past which were committed while in parliament and in government.

8. In the context of moving the peace process forward, commitment has been expressed to fully respect the norms and values of human rights and press freedom and move ahead accordingly.
9. As the announcement of municipal polls pushed forward with the ill motive of deluding the people and the international community and giving continuity to the autocratic and illegitimate rule of the king, and the talk of elections to parliament are a crafty policy, we announce to actively boycott them and call upon the general public to make such elections a failure.
10. The people and their representative political parties are the real guardians of nationality. Therefore, we are firmly committed to protect the independence, sovereignty and geographical integrity of the country and national unity. Based on the principle of peaceful co-existence, it is our common obligation to maintain friendly relations with all countries of the world and good neighbour relationship with neighboring countries, especially India and China. But we request the patriotic masses to be cautious against the false attempt by the king and (his) loyalists to prolong his autocratic and illegitimate rule and delude the patriotic people by projecting the illusory 'Mundane' nationalism and questioning the patriotism of the political parties and appeal to the international powers and the people to support, in every possible way, the democratic movement against autocratic monarchy in Nepal.
11. We call upon the civil society, professional organizations, various wings of parties, people of all communities and regions, press and intellectuals to actively participate in the peaceful movement launched on the basis of these understandings centered on democracy, peace, prosperity, forward-looking social change and the country's independence, sovereignty, and pride.
12. A common commitment has been expressed to investigate any objection raised by any party over such incidents; inappropriate conducts that took place between the parties

in the past. If found guilty, and to make the action public. An understanding has been reached to settle any problem emerging between the parties through peaceful dialogue at the concerned level or at the leadership level.

Source: Keshav Devkota, **Prachandpath ra Ganatantra**, Suagat Pushtak Parkashan, Kathmandu, 2063.

Appendix – VII

25-Point Cease Fire Code of Conduct Signed Between the Government of Nepal and CPN (Maoists)

Preamble

Respecting the popular mandate expressed through the historic People's Movement for total democracy, progress and peace; Remaining committed towards the Universal Declaration of Human Rights-1948, and fundamental principles and values of international humanitarian law and human rights; Remaining committed to fulfill the 12-points agreement between the SPA and the Maoists; Remaining committed towards democratic values including the concept of competitive multiparty democracy, civic liberties, fundamental rights, human rights of the Nepali people to participate in the process of constitution making through elections to the constituent assembly without any fear, threat and violence; Placing democracy, peace, prosperity, forward-looking social transformation and freedom, sovereignty and dignity of the nation in the centre; and in order to transform the ceasefire between the Government of Nepal and the CPN (Maoists) into permanent peace and resolve the problems through negotiations, a code of conduct has been issued as follows, as per the wishes of the Nepali people:

Guaranteeing Fearless Civilian Life

1. Not to issue any statement or engage in any activities which could provoke each other.

2. Both the parties shall not mobilize, display or use their armed forces in a manner that could spread fear and terror amongst the people.
3. Not to attack or destroy each other's military or security installations, not to lay down mines or ambushes, not to recruit new people in one's military and not to spy against each other.
4. Both sides will extend mutual cooperation in order to maintain peace and security.
5. Discussion and understating will be made as per need regarding the issue of management of arms and armed personnel. Creating an environment of trust among the people.
6. Both the parties will not participate in public meetings, conference or any other political activities in combat dresses or along with arms.
7. No hindrance will be made from either side for political activists and members of social organizations to move around the country and express their views, organize meetings or engage in their organizational works. They will not be subject to any mental or physical pressure.

On Basic Services to the People and Development Activities

8. During the period of ceasefire, activities like 'bandh' (general strike) and 'chakka jam' (transport strike) will not be organized, but peaceful demonstrations may be organized.
9. Essential services and facilities to the people will be allowed to operate without any disruption
10. Not to create hurdles in undertaking regular development works peacefully and other works aimed at people's benefit.
11. Transportation of items like food, medicines, and materials used in development works and daily utility items will not be obstructed or banned.
12. Both the parties will create an environment for the smooth functioning of schools, colleges and universities, hospitals, health centres and industrial institutions. Cooperation from media for peace talks.

13. Use civilized and dignified language while disseminating information about ceasefire, code of conduct and the peace process and other political activities.
14. Nobody should issue statement through media in a manner, which could hamper the talks and peace process. Not to collect donation and other financial assistance forcefully.
15. Donation or financial assistance in cash, kind or in the form of services will not be collected or mobilized against one's will.

Release and Rehabilitation

16. Accusation, claims or cases filed by both the parties against various individuals will be withdrawn and the detainees will be released gradually.
17. Where about of the people who have been disappeared will be publicized immediately.
18. To help in the rehabilitation of and extend cooperation to displaced people to return to their respective houses in a peaceful, comfortable and respectable manner.
19. Return the properties of the leaders of political parties, activists and civilian, which were seized, locked up or prohibited from being used during the period of the conflict, to concerned persons or their families. Problems arising while returning the properties will be resolved through mutual agreement.

Facilitating the Talks

20. No hurdles will be created in the movement and activities of individuals involved in negotiations from both the parties monitoring.
21. On the basis of mutual agreement between the two parties, national and international monitoring teams will be asked to monitor the ceasefire.

Miscellaneous

22. Dispute, if any, in terms of interpretation of this code of conduct, will be resolved on the basis of agreement between the parties.

23. In accordance with the spirit of the preamble of this code, amendments could be made in the code of conduct through mutual agreement.
24. To enforce this code of conduct immediately after it is signed.
25. To make the code of conduct public immediately after it is signed.

Signed by:	Signed by:
Krishna Bahadur Mahara	Krishna Prasad Sitaula
On behalf of the CPN (Maoists)	On behalf of the Government of Nepal

May 25, 2006

Appendix – VIII

The Eight-Point SPA-Maoists Agreement (June 16, 2006)

1. The 12-points understanding reached between the SPA and Maoists in November last year and the 25-points Ceasefire Code of Conduct signed between the SPA government and CPN (Maoists) on May 26, 2006.
2. Both the parties express commitment to democratic norms and values including competitive multiparty system, civic liberties, fundamental rights, human rights, freedom of press and the concept of rule of law and carry out each other's activities in a peaceful manner.
3. Request the United Nations to help in the monitoring and management of the armies and arms of both government and Maoist sides for free and fair elections to the constituent assembly.
4. Guarantee the democratic rights achieved through the 1990 popular movement and the recent historic people's movement; draft an interim constitution based on the 12-points understanding and the Ceasefire Code of Conduct; form an interim government accordingly; announce the dates for constituent assembly elections; dissolve the house of representatives through consensus after making alternative arrangement; dissolve the people's government of CPN (Maoists).
5. Decide issues of national interests having long-term effects through consensus.
6. Guarantee the fundamental rights of the Nepali people to participate in the constituent assembly elections without

any fear, influence, threat and violence. Invite international observation and monitoring during the elections as per the need.

7. Bring about a forward-looking restructuring of the state so as to resolve the class-based, racial, regional and gender-based problems through constituent assembly elections. Transform the ceasefire between Nepal Government and CPN (Maoists) into permanent peace by focusing on democracy, peace, prosperity, forward-looking change and the country's independence, sovereignty and pride and express commitment to resolve the problem through talks.
8. The government and Maoists talk teams have been directed to accomplish all talks related to above-mentioned points without any delay.

Source: Keshev Raj Devkota, Prachanda, **Prachandapath ra Ganatantra**, Suagat Pustak Prakashan, Kathmandu, 2063.

Appendix – IX

Six-points Agreement Between SPA and Maoists (November 7, 2006)

Respecting people's aspiration for democracy, peace and progress expressed through repeated historic people's movement and struggles since 1951.

Reaffirming commitments of the 12-points and eight-points agreements, and 25-points Code of Conduct between the SPA and the Maoists along with other agreements, understanding, code of conducts and letter sent to the United Nations stating similar perspectives by the Maoists and the Nepal government.

Reiterating commitments to competitive multiparty democratic system, civil liberties, fundamental rights, human rights, complete press freedom, rule of law, all other norms and values of democratic system.

Guaranteeing the fundamental rights of the Nepalese people to cast their votes in the constituent assembly polls without any kind of fear.

By putting democracy, peace, prosperity, progressive social and economic transformation, independence, integrity, sovereignty and prestige of the state in the centre-stage and to implement the commitments made by both the sides to hold the elections to constituent assembly by mid-June 2007 in a free and fair manner, the following decisions have been taken from the meeting of the top leaders of the SPA and the Maoists today, November 8, 2006.

I. Relating to the Implementation of the Past Agreements

Implement all the agreement, understandings and the code of conduct signed earlier fully, sincerely and strongly,

Form a high-level commission to investigate and publicize the where about of citizens stated to have been disappeared by the state and the Maoists in the past.

Accelerate the process of returning the houses, land and properties confiscated in the past. Ensure the environment so that displaced people would be able to return to their villages. For this purpose, committees would be formed in districts comprising representatives from both the sides. Complete all these works within one month.

Make public announcement regarding the withdrawal of all accusations and charges leveled by the state at the leaders and the cadres of the CPN (Maoists) and release all political prisoners from both the sides.

II. Relating to Management of Arms and Army

In order to hold the elections to constituent assembly in a peaceful, free and fair environment and for democratization and restructuring of the Nepali Army as per the feelings expressed in 12-points agreement, eight-points understanding, 25-points Code of Conduct and five-points letter sent to the United Nations, the following works would be carried out:

Relating to Maoists Army

As per the commitments expressed in the letter sent to the United Nations by the Nepal government and the Maoists on August 9, the combatants of the Maoists would be sent to following cantonments. The United Nations would do the necessary verification and monitoring of them.

Main camps would be in the following places

1. Kailali, 2. Surkhet, 3. Rolpa, 4. Palpa, 5 Kavre, 6. Sindhuli 7. Ilam. There would be three smaller camps located in the periphery of each of these main camps.

All the arms and ammunitions would be security stored in the camps except those needed for providing security of the camp after the Maoist combatants are sent to the cantonments. They will be put under a single lock system and the concerned side would keep the key of this lock. For the UN to monitor it, a device with siren as well as recording facility will be installed. When there is need to examine the stored arms, the UN would do so in the presence of the concerned side. Prepare the details of technology including camera for monitoring as per the agreement among the Nepal government, the Maoists and the United Nations.

On completion of cantonment of the Maoists combatants, Nepal government would take up the responsibility for providing ration and other facilities to them.

The interim cabinet would form a special committee to carry out monitoring, integration and rehabilitation of the Maoist combatants. Make arrangement for the security of the Maoist leaders as per the agreement with the Nepal government relating to Nepali Army.

The Nepali Army would be confined to the barracks as per the commitments of the letter sent to the United Nations. Guarantee that its arms would not be used for or against any side. Keep similar quantity of arms of the Nepali Army in the store, seal it with single-lock system and give the key to the concerned side. For the UN to monitor it, a device with siren as well as recording facility will be installed. When there is need to examine the stored arms, the UN would do so in the presence of the concerned side. Prepare the details of technology among the Nepal government, the Maoists and the United Nations.

The cabinet would control, mobilize and mange the Nepali Army as per the new Military Act. The interim cabinet would prepare and implement the detailed action plan of democratization of the Nepali Army by taking suggestion from the concerned committee of the interim parliament. This includes works like determination of the right number of the Nepali Army, prepare the democratic structure reflecting the national and inclusive character, and train them on democratic principles and human rights values.

Continue the works of the Nepali Army such as border security, security of the conservation areas, protected areas, banks, airport, power house, telephone tower, central secretariat and security of VIPs.

III. Relating to the Subjects of the Interim Constitution

1. Relating to Interim Constitution

Finalize the interim constitution presented by the interim constitution drafting committee as per the agreements reached today.

The reinstated House of Representatives would promulgate the interim constitution and the newly formed interim legislature would endorse it.

2. Relating to the Monarchy

No rights on state administration would remain with the king.

Bring the properties of the late King Birendra, late Queen Aishwarya and their family members under the control of the Nepal government and use it for the welfare purposes through a trust.

All properties acquired by King Gyanendra by the virtue of him being the king (like palaces of various places, forests and conservation areas, heritage having historical and archeological importance) would be nationalized.

3. Relating to Interim Legislature (Parliament)

The interim legislature would be unicameral of the following type:

(i) There would be 209 members of the SPA and others who are members of the present lower and upper House (excluding those who opposed the People's Movement) Since the Left Front does not have its representation in the current parliament, its representation in the interim parliament would be determined base on understanding.

(ii) 73 members from the side of the Maoists.

(iii) 48 members from among the sister organizations and professional bodies, oppressed ethnic communities and regions and political personalities (to be nominated based on understanding) (total number : 330).

Both those who stood against the people's movement would not be given membership in the interim parliament.

The Reinstated House of Representatives and national assembly would be dissolved once the formation of the interim, parliament is completed.

The people's government, people's court run by the CPN (Maoists) would be dissolved on the day of the formation of the interim parliament.

Run the interim parliament as per the political understanding.

4. Relating to Interim Government

Form the interim cabinet as per the understanding.

Determine the work division and structure of the interim parliament as per understanding.

The interim government would work as per the aspiration of the people's movement, political understanding and culture of cooperation.

5. Relating to Judiciary

Follow the norms and values and concept of the independent judiciary.

Make the judiciary committed to the aspiration of the people's movement, democracy and interim constitution.

Institute a constitutional court to finalize disputes regarding the constituent assembly.

6. Relating to Constitutional Bodies

A new constitutional council will be formed that will include the Prime Minister, Chief Justice and the Speaker of the interim parliament, which will recommend appointments to the constitutional bodies. Such appointments will be based on specific criteria.

The appointments in the Election Commission will be completed on the basis of understanding.

7. Relating to Local Bodies

Interim local bodies will be formed in district, city and village level on the basis of agreement between the SPA and the Maoists.

8. Relating to Citizenship Problem

Distribute citizenship to all Nepalese that have been deprived of their citizenship certificate before the elections of the constituent assembly.

Considering mid-April 1990 as the base (cut off) year, all Nepali citizens who were born before that date and have been continuously living in Nepal since then will be provided with citizen certificate. Other provisions regarding citizenship will be according to the provisions mentioned in the law.

9. Regarding the Elections of the Constituent Assembly

The interim cabinet will be given the authority to ascertain the date to hold the elections of the constituent assembly by mid-June 2007.

The elections of the constituent assembly will be based on mixed electoral system. 205 members will be elected through

First-Past-The-Post System. 204 members will be elected as per the proportional representation system on the basis of votes won by the political parties. A law in this regard will be made after consultation with the Election Commission.

While appointing the candidates, the political parties should ensure proportional representation of oppressed groups, region, Madhesi, Women, Dalits and other groups. 16 members will be nominated by the interim Council of Ministers from among distinguished persons. The total number of members of the constituent assembly will be 425.

Nepalese who are 18 years or above at the time when the interim constitution is promulgated will be eligible to vote.

Monitoring of the election of the constituent assembly will be done by the United Nations.

10. Structure of the State

To end discriminations based on class, ethnicity, lingual, gender, cultural, religion and region and to deconstruct the centralized and unitary structure of the state and to reconstruct it into an inclusive, democratic and forward looking state.

A high level commission will be formed to suggest on the restructuring of the state.

Final decision regarding the restructuring of the state will be made by the constituent assembly.

11. Directive Principles of Socio-Economic Transformation

To end all forms of feudalism, a common minimum programme will be prepared for socio-economic transformation on the basis of mutual agreement and they will be implemented.

Formulate policies to implement scientific land reform programme by doing away with the feudal land ownership. To adopt policies that will protect and promote national industries and resources.

To ascertain the rights of the citizens on sectors like education, health, shelter, employment, and food security.

Policies will be adopted to provide land and socio-economic security to backward groups like landless, bonded labourers, tillers, Haruwa-Charuwa and other such groups, which are socio-economically backward.

To adopt policies to take strict actions against the people who have worked in government positions and have amassed huge amount of properties through corruption.

Prepare a common development concept that will help in socio-economic transformation of the country and will also assist in ensuring the country's prosperity in a short period of time.

Follow policies ascertaining the professional rights of workers and increase investment on sectors like promoting industries, trade and export and increase employment and income generating opportunities.

IV. Relating to the Management of the Conflict Victims

1. Provisions will be made for providing proper relief, respect and resettlement for the family members of the people who have died due to the conflict and for the ones who have been disabled.
2. Provide relief to the family members of the people who have been disappeared on the basis of the report presented by the investigation commission.
3. Carry out special programme to rehabilitate the people who have been displaced due to the conflict; to provide relief in case of destruction of private and public properties; and to reconstruct the destroyed infrastructures.

4. Conduct investigation about those who were involved in gross violation of human rights at the time of the conflict and those who committed crime against humanity. Form a high level Truth and Reconciliation Commission to create an environment for social reconciliation.

V. Miscellaneous

1. A high-level committee will be formed as per understanding to monitor if the agreement has been implemented.
2. The government will take action against anyone involved in acting against the code of conduct, agreement and laws.
3. At the time of the elections of the constituent assembly, the political parties will be free to present their policies regarding republic, socio-economic transformation, referendum, election system and other such issues in which an agreement has not been reached now.

VI. Time Schedule

1. To conclude comprehensive peace agreement between Nepal government and the CPN (Maoists) by November 16, 2006.
2. That all the Maoist combatants would gather into the camps by November 21, 2006 as stated in 2(1) and store the arms. The United Nations would do their verification and monitoring.
3. As stated in 2(5), the Nepali Army would remain confined in barracks by November 21, 2006, keep the specified number of arms in the store and the United Nations would conduct its monitoring.
4. To complete the interim constitution by November 21, 2006.
5. To promulgate the interim constitution by November 26, 2006, establish the interim legislature and dissolve the House of Representatives and National Assembly.

6. Form the interim cabinet by December 1, 2006.

Prachanda
Chairman, CPN (Maoists)

Girija Prasad Koirala
Prime Minister and President of the Nepali Congress

Madhav Kumar Nepal
General-Secretary of CPN (UML)

Sher Bahadur Deuba
President of Nepali Congress (Democratic)

Amik Sherchan
Deputy Prime Minister and Chairman of People's Front Nepal

Bharat Bimal Yadav
Vice President of NSP (Anandi Devi)

Narayan Man Bijukchhe
President of NWPP
C.P. Mainali Chairman of Left Front

November 8, 2006

Note of dissent by the UML

Agreeing for the implementation of the subjects stated above as all other parties have agreement on those, our party has following differences:

1. The UML believes that the issue of whether to keep the monarchy or not should be determined through the referendum along with the election to constituent assembly.

2. The MUL believes that it would be most democratic to adopt the proportional system for elections to the constituent assembly.

Source: Udhav P. Pyakurel, **Maoists Movement in Nepal: A Sociological Perspective**, Delhi, 2007: 166-174.

Appendix – X

Comprehensive Peace Accord Held Between Government of Nepal and CPN (Maoists)

Preamble

Respecting the popular mandate of Nepali people expressed in favour of democracy, peace and progress through the historical struggle and people's movements, time and again, from 2007 BS and even before till now;

Reaffirming the full commitment towards the 12-points agreement reached between SPA, CPN (Maoists), eight-points consensus, 25-points Code of Conduct held between Government of Nepal and CPN (Maoists), decision made in the meeting held between apex leaders of SPA and CPN (Maoists) held on November 8, 2006 including all agreement, consensus, Code of Conduct reached between Government of Nepal, and CPN (Maoists), and letters of similar viewpoints sent to United Nation;

Expressing determination for progressive restructuring of the state to resolve existing problems in the country, based on class, caste, region, and sex;

Reiterating the full commitment towards democratic value and acceptance including competitive multiparty democratic system of governance, civil liberty, fundamental right, human rights, full press freedom and concept of rule of law;

Remaining committed towards Universal Declaration of Human Rights, 2048, international humanitarian laws and basic principles and acceptance relating to human rights;

Keeping democracy, peace, prosperity, progressive economic and social change and independence, indivisibility, sovereignty, and self-respect of the country at center;

Expressing commitment to hold elections to Constituent Assembly in free and fair manner till the end of the month of Jeth 2064 BS;

Declaring the beginning of a new chapter of peaceful collaboration by ending armed struggle continued in the country from 2052 BS through political consensus between the two parties to ensure sovereignty of Nepali people through Constituent Assembly, forward-looking political resolution, democratic restructuring of the state and economic-social and cultural transformation;

This comprehensive peace agreement has been reached between Government of Nepal and CPN (Maoists) with commitment to transform ceasefire between Government of Nepal and CPN (Maoists) into sustainable peace.

1 Preliminary

1.1 The name of this agreement is 'Comprehensive Peace Agreement'. In short the agreement shall be called Peace Agreement.

1.2 The agreement shall come into force after public declaration by the government and Maoists side.

1.3 Both the sides shall give necessary directives to all the agencies under their control for immediate implementation of this agreement and to abide by it and implement it and get it implemented.

1.4 All the agreement, consensus and decisions reached between SPA, the government and Maoists that are (enclosed in annex) shall be integral part of this agreement.

1.5 The consensus and agreement to be reached hereafter for the implementation of this agreement shall also be the integral part of this agreement.

2 Definition: Unless the Subject and Context Mean Otherwise, in This Agreement

(a) 'Ceasefire' means the acts to negate all forms of aggressions, kidnappings, disappearances, taking into custody aimed at each other and between Government of Nepal and CPN (Maoists), mobilization and strengthening of armed forces, destruction in the society by any means including aggression and activities of violence and acts of incitement and instigation.

(b) 'Interim Constitution' means 'Interim Constitution of Nepal 2063' to be issued until drafting and enforcement of the new constitution by constituent assembly.

'Interim Council of Ministers' means 'Interim Council of Ministers' to be formed according to 'Interim Constitution'.

'Both the Parties' means the party of government of Nepal and the party of Communist Party of Nepal (Maoists).

'Prevailing Law' means Interim Constitution of Nepal 2063 and prevailing Nepal Laws that are not inconsistent with it. But this definition shall not obstruct legal arrangement existed before enforcement of Interim constitution 2063.

'Verification' means the subject of verification and true record keeping of military, combatant and arms by United Nations.

3 Political-Economic-Social Transformations and Conflict Management

Both the parties are in agreement to adopt following policy

and programme for political-economic and social transformation and to affirmatively resolve existing conflict in the county:

3.1 To ensure forward moving political economic and social transformation on the basis of decision made in summit meeting between SPA and CPN (Maoists) held on November 8, 2006.

3.2 To guarantee sovereignty inherent in Nepalese people in practice by forming interim legislature – parliament according to interim constitution and by holding elections to constituent assembly in free and fair manner till the Month of Jetha, 2064 BS by Interim government.

3 3 To not allow any authority regarding affairs of governance of the country to remain with the king. To bring the properties of late King Birendra, late queen Aishwarya and their family under Government of Nepal and to make use of the property in the interest of the state by forming a trust. To nationalize all the properties (like palaces situated in different places, forest and parks, heritages with historical and archeological importance) received by King Gyanendra in his capacity as the king. To decide the issue of whether or not to retain the monarchy by simple majority in the first meeting of constituent assembly.

3.4 To adopt a political system that complies with universally accepted fundamental human rights, multiparty competitive democratic system, sovereignty inherited in people, supremacy of the people, constitutional check and balance, rule of law, social justice, equality, independent judiciary, periodic elections, monitoring by civil society, complete press freedom, people's right to information, transparency and accountability in the activities of political parties, people's participation, impartial, competent, and fair concept of bureaucracy.

3.5 To address the problems related to women, Dalits, indigenous people, Janajatis, Madhesi, oppressed, neglected, minorities and the backward by ending discrimination based on class, caste, language, sex, culture, religion, and region and to restructure the state on the basis of inclusiveness, democracy and progression by ending present centralized and unitary structure of the state.

3.6 To keep implementing at least programs of common consensus for the economic and social transformation to end all forms of feudalism.

3.7 To adopt the policy to implement scientific land reform programme by ending feudalistic system of land holding.

3.8 To follow the policy for the protection and promotion of national industries and resources.

3.9 To adopt policy to establish rights of all citizens in education, health, housing, employment and food reserve.

3.10 To adopt policy to provide land and the other economic protection to landless squatters, Kamaiya, Halia, Harwa, Charwa and economically backward sections.

3.11 To adopt policy to severely punish people amassing properties by means of corruption while remaining in government posts.

3.12 To form common development concept for economic and social transformation and justice and to make the country developed and economically prosperous, at the earliest.

3.13 To follow the policy to increase investment in industries, trade and export promotion in order to increase opportunities for income generation by ensuring professional rights of the labourers.

4 Management of Army and Arms

In order to hold elections to constituent assembly in a free and fair manner and for the democratic restructuring of the army to proceed with the following works according to 12-points agreement, eight-points consensus, 25-points Code of Conduct, five-points letter sent to United Nations and decision taken by summit meeting held on November 8, 2006.

Relating to the 'Maoists' Army

4.1 As per the commitment expressed in the letter sent on behalf of the Government of Nepal and the CPN (Maoists) to the United Nations on August 9, 2006, the Maoists' Army Combatants shall remain within the following cantonments. The UN shall verify and monitor them.
The Main cantonments shall remain at the following locations: 1. Kailali 2. Surkhet 3. Rolpa 4. Nawalparasi 5. Chitwan 6. Sindhuli 7. Ilam.
Three sub-cantonments shall be placed in the periphery of each of these main cantonments.

4.2 After placing the Maoist combatants within the cantonments, all the arms and ammunition except those required for providing security to the cantonments shall be securely stored and the keys to the single lock shall remain with the side concerned. The UN shall monitor the process of placing the weapons under the single lock by keeping records and fitting a device along with siren. In case of need to examine the weapons placed under the single lock, the UN shall do so under the presence of concerned side. All the technical details along with camera monitoring shall bc prepared under the joint agreement of the UN, CPN (Maoists) and the Government of Nepal.

4.3 The Government of Nepal shall make all the necessary arrangements including ration needed for the Maoist combatants after placing them within the cantonments.

4.4 The Interim Council of Ministers shall form a special committee in order to inspect, integrate and rehabilitate the Maoist combatants.

4.5 The government shall be taking care of security arrangements of the Maoist leaders.

Relating to the Nepali Army

4.6 As per the commitment expressed in the letter sent to the UN, the Nepali Army shall be confined within the barracks. Guarantee that the arms shall not be used for or against any side. The Nepali Army shall store the same amount of arms in accordance with that of the Maoists and seal it with single-lock and give the key to the concerned side. In case of need to examine the stored arms, the UN would do so in the presence of the concerned side. Prepare the details of technology including camera for monitoring as per the agreement among the Government of Nepal, the Maoists and the UN.

4.7 The Council of Ministers shall control, mobilize and manage the Nepali Army as per the new Military Act. The Interim Council of Ministers shall prepare and implement the detailed action plan of democratization of the Nepali Army by taking suggestions from the concerned committee of the interim parliament. This shall include tasks such as determining the right number of the Nepali Army, preparing the democratic structure reflecting the national and inclusive character and training them as per the democratic principles and values of the human rights.

4.8 Nepali Army shall be giving continuity to tasks such as border security, security of the conservation areas, protected areas, banks, airport, power house, telephone tower, central secretariat and security of VIPs.

5 Ceasefire

5.1 Termination of Military Action and Armed Mobilization

5.1.1 Both sides shall express commitment to refrain form carrying out following activities:

(a) Direct or indirect use of any type of weapon or acts of attack against each other.

(b) Searching or confiscating weapons belonging to other side with or without weapons at the place where the arms have been stored as per the understanding reached between both sides.

(c) Hurt or render mental pressure against any individual.

(d) Set up ambush targeting any side.

(e) Involve in murder or violent activities.

(f) Involvement in kidnap / detention / imprisonment / disappearance.
(g) Arial attack or bombardment.
(h) Mining and sabotaging.
(i) Spying military activities of any side.

5.1.2 Both sides shall not recruit additional armed forces or conduct military activities, including transporting weapons, ammunitions and explosives.

However, the security forces deployed by the interim government shall have authority to conduct routine patrol, explore in order to prevent illegal trafficking of the weapons, explosives or raw materials used in assembling weapons at the international border or custom points and seize it.

5.1.3 No individual or group shall bear any illegal weapons, ammunitions or explosives while traveling.

5.1.4 Both sides shall assist each other to mark the landmines and booby-traps used during the time of armed conflict by providing necessary information within 30 days and defuse and excavate it within 60 days.

5.1.5 Armies of both sides shall not bear arms or show their presence wearing combat fatigue during any public programme, political meeting or civil assembly.

5.1.6 Nepal Police and Armed Police Force (APF) shall give continuity to the task of maintaining legal system and law and order other along with criminal investigation as per the norms and sentiments of the Jana Andolan and peace accord as well as prevailing law.

5.1.7 Both sides shall issue circular to its respective armed bodies or personnel to stop addressing any armed personnel of opposite side by the term 'enemy' or behave in similar manner.

5.1.8 Both sides agree to maintain a record of the government, public, private building, land and other property seized, locked up or not allowed to use in course of the armed conflict and return them back immediately.

5.2 Situation Normalization Measures

5.2.1 Collection of cash or kind and tax collection against one's wish and against the existing law shall not be allowed.

5.2.2 Both sides agree to make public the status of the people under one's custody and release them within 15 days.

5.2.3 Both sides also agree to make public within 60 days of signing of the agreement the real name, caste and address of the people made 'disappeared' or killed during the conflict and also inform the family members about it.

5.2.4 Both sides agree to constitute a National Peace and Rehabilitation Commission and carry out works through it to normalize the adverse situation arising as a result of the armed conflict, maintain peace in the society and run relief and rehabilitation works for the people victimized and displace as a result of the conflict.

5.2.5 Both sides agree to set up a High-level Truth and Reconciliation Commission as per the mutual consensus in order to prove about those involved in serious violation of human rights and crime against humanity in course of the armed conflict and develop an atmosphere for reconciliation in the society.

5.2.6 Both sides pledge to abandon all types of war, attack, counter-attack, violence and counter-violence in the country with a commitment to ensure democracy, peace and forward-looking change in the Nepali society. It is also agreed that both the sides would assist one another in the establishment of peace and maintaining of law and order.

5.2.7 Both sides guarantee to withdraw accusations, claims, and complaints and under –consideration cases leveled against various individuals due to political reasons and immediately make public the state of those imprisoned and immediately release them.

5.2.8 Both sides express the commitment to allow, without any political prejudice, the people displaced due to the armed conflict to return back voluntarily to their respective ancestral or former residence, reconstruct the infrastructure destroyed as a result of the conflict and rehabilitate and reintegrate the displaced people into the society.

5.2.9 Both sides agree to the individual and collective responsibility of resolving, with also the support of all political parties, civil society and local institutions, any problems arising in the aforementioned context on the basis of mutual consensus and creating an atmosphere conducive for normalization of mutual relations and for reconciliation.

5.2.10 Both sides express the commitment not to discriminate against or exert any kind of pressure on any member of the family of the two sides or on the basis of being related to one another.

5.2.11 Both sides agree not to create any kind of obstacle and allow any kind of obstruction to be created in the independent traveling, assuming of duties and executing of work by the Government of Nepal and public bodies' employees and assist them in their work.

5.2.12 Both sides agree to allow unrestricted travelling as per the law within the state of Nepal to the United Nations, International Donors Agencies and Diplomatic Missions based in Nepal, National and International Non-Government Organizations, press, human rights activists, election observers and foreign tourists.

5.2.13 Both sides are committed to operating publicity programmes in a decent and respectable manner.

6 End of Conflict

6.1 On the basis of the historical agreement reached between the SPA and the CPN (Maoists) on.November 8, 2006, we declare an end to the armed conflict ongoing in the country since 1995 by giving permanency to the ongoing ceasefire between the Government and the Maoists.

6.2 The decisions taken by the meeting on November 8, 2006 of the senior leaders of the SPA and the CPN (Maoists) would be the main policy basis for long-term peace.

6.3 Following the arrival of the Nepali Army in the barracks and the Maoist Army combatants in temporary camps, holding, display and use of violence and arms for creating fear and terror and in any form against the agreement and law would be legally punishable.

6.4 Army of both the sides would not be allowed to publicize for or against any side and support or protest any side. But they shall not be deprived from their right to vote.

7 Human Rights, Fundamental Rights and Adherence to Humanitarian Law

By remaining committed to the Universal Declaration of Human Rights, 1948, the International Humanitarian Law and fundamental principles and standards of human rights, both sides expressed their agreement to the following issues:

7.1 Human Rights

7.1.1 Both sides reiterate their commitment to the respect and protection of human rights and to international humanitarian law and accept that nobody should be discriminated on the basis of colour, gender, language, religion, age, race, national and social origin, wealth, disability, birth and other status, thought or belief.

7.1.2 Both sides agree to create an atmosphere where the Nepali people can enjoy their civil, political, economic, social and cultural rights and are committed to ensuring that such rights are not violated under any circumstances in the future.

7.1.3 Both sides express the commitment that impartial investigation and action as per the law would be carried out against the people responsible in creating obstructions to the exercising of the rights envisaged in the letter of agreement and guarantee not to encourage impunity. Apart from this, they shall also guarantee the right to relief of the families of the conflict and torture victims and the disappeared.

7.1.4 Both sides would not be involved in the acts of torture, kidnapping and forcing the civilians in any work and take necessary action to discourage such acts.

7.1.5 On the basis of norms and values of secularism, both sides shall respect the social, cultural, religious sensitivity, religious rite and the religious faith of the individual.

7.2 Right to Life

7.2.1 Both sides respect and protect the fundamental rights to life of an individual. Nobody shall be deprived of these fundamental rights and no law shall be formulated to award death penalty.

7.3 Right to Individual Dignity, Freedom and Mobility

7.3.1 Both sides respect and protect the right to individual dignity. In this connection, no person including those deprived of enjoying freedom as per the law would be subjected to torture or any other cruel, inhuman or degrading behavior or punishment. The citizens' rights to confidentiality shall be respected.

7.3.2 Both sides fully respect the individual's right to freedom and security and shall not be allowed to keep anyone under arbitrary or illegal detention, kidnap or hold captive. Both sides agree to make public the status of every individual made 'disappeared' and held captive and inform about this to their family members, legal advisor and other authorized person.

7.3.3 Both sides shall respect and protect the citizen's right to free mobility and the freedom to choose within legal norms the location of one's residence and express the commitment to respect the right of the people displaced by the conflict and their families to return back to their homes or to settle in any other location of their choice.

7.4 Civil and Political Rights

7.4.1 Both sides are committed to respect the individual's freedom of speech, expression, setting up organizations and holding peaceful gathering and right to freedom or exploitation.

7.4.2 Both sides respect the right of every citizen to take part directly or through one have selected representative in issues of public concern, to vote, to be elected and equality in joining of public services.

7.4.3 Both sides are committed to respect the individual's right to be informed.

7.5 Economic and Social Rights

7.5.1 Both sides are committed to respect and protect the individual's right to livelihood through employment of their choice or acceptance.

7.5.2 Both sides are committed to respecting and guaranteeing the rights of food security of all the people. They guarantee that there would be no interference in the transportation, use and distribution of food, food products and food-grains.

7.5.3 Both sides identify with the fact that the citizens' right to health should be respected and protected. Both sides will not create hurdles in the supply of medicines and in health assistance and campaigns, and express commitment for treatment and rehabilitation of the people injured in course of the conflict.

7.5.4 With the realization of the fact that the right to education should be guaranteed and respected, both sides are committed to maintaining a conducive academic environment in the educational institutions. Both sides agree to guarantee that the right to education would not be impeded. They agree to put to an end, on an immediate basis, activities like taking the educational institutions under control and making them to disappear, and to not to establish barracks in a way that it would impede them.

7.5.5 Both sides agree that the private property of any individual would not be seized or usurped, except permitted by the laws.

7.5.6 Both sides believe in the fact that the industrial climate in the country should not be disturbed and production should be given continuity and that the right of collective bargaining and social security should be respected. They also believe in the fact that if any problem arises between the business houses and labourers, they should be encouraged to resolve the problem in a peaceful manner. Both sides respect the right to work prescribed by the International Labour Organization.

7.6 Women and Child Rights

7.6.1 Both sides fully agree to protect the rights of the women and children in a special way, to immediately stop all types of violence against women and children, including child labor as well as sexual exploitation and abuse. They also fully agree not to include or use children who are 18 years old and below in the armed force. Children thus affected would be instantaneously rescued and necessary and suitable assistance would by provided for their rehabilitation.

7.7 Right to Personal Liberty

7.7.1 Both sides agree to the freedom of opinion and expression; freedom to assemble peacefully and without arms; freedom of movement; freedom to practice any profession, or to carry on any occupation, industry or trade; press and publication rights; the freedom to take part in peaceful political activities; the right to equality before the law; and to implement and have a tolerable system of justice implemented.

8 Dispute Settlements and Implementation Mechanism

8.1 Both sides agree to become responsible and accountable in a personal and collective way and not to repeat in future mistakes committed in the past and also to correct these mistakes on a gradual basis.

8.2 The National Peace and Rehabilitation Commission can set up mechanism as per the need for making the campaign for peace successful. The composition and working procedures of the commission would be as determined by the interim council of ministers.

8.3 Both sides are committed to settle all kinds of present or possible future mutual differences or problems through mutual talks, understanding, consensus and dialog.

8.4 Both sides express commitment that the Interim Council of Ministers can constitute and determine the working procedures of the National Peace and Rehabilitation Commission, the Truth and Reconciliation Commission, the High-level State Restructuring Recommendation Commission and other mechanisms as per the need to implement this agreement, the Interim Constitution and all the decisions, agreements and understandings reached between the SPA, the Government of Nepal and the CPN (Maoists).

9 Implementation and Follow-up

Both sides have agreed to make the following arrangements for the implementation of the understandings mentioned in this agreement and for their follow-up:

9.1 Both sides agree to give continuity to the task of monitoring of the human rights provisions mentioned in this agreement by the United Nations Office of the High Commissioner for Human Rights, Nepal.

9.2 Both sides agree for the monitoring of the management of arms and the armies by the United Nations Mission in Nepal as mentioned in the five-points letter send to the UN earlier and in the present agreement.

9.3 Both sides agree to get the United Nations supervise the elections to the constituent assembly.

9.4 The National Human Rights Commission shall also carry out works related to the monitoring of human rights as mentioned in this agreement together with the responsibility assigned to it as per the laws. In connection with carrying out its works, the Commission can take the help of national and international human rights organizations after maintaining necessary coordination with them.

9.5 Both sides agree to accept the reports submitted by the above-mentioned bodies, to provide the information requested by them, and to implement the suggestions and recommendations given by them on the basis of consensus and dialogue.

10 Miscellaneous

10.1 Both sides agree not to operate parallel or any form of structure in any areas of the state or government structure as per the letter of the decisions of November 8 and the spirit of the peace agreement.

10.2 Both sides accept to sign any complementary agreements, as necessitated, for the implementation of the present agreement.

10.3 This agreement can be revised any time with the consent of both sides. Both sides agree to provide to each other prior written information if they wish to make any changes. The amendments could be made to the agreement with the consent of both sides after receiving the information. The provisions to be made by such an amendment would not be below the minimum standards of the accepted international human rights and humanitarian laws.

10.4 If any disputes arise in the interpretation of this agreement, a joint mechanism comprising both sides shall make the interpretation on the basis of the preamble and the documents included in the schedule of this agreement, and this interpretation would be final.

10.5 The concept of 'two sides' as mentioned in this agreement would automatically cease to exist after the constitution of the Interim Legislature-Parliament. Thereafter, all the responsibility shall be as per the arrangements made by the Interim Council of Ministers. It would be the duty and responsibility of all the political parties to extend cooperation in the compliance and implementation of the agreement.

10.6 We heartily appeal to one and all to extend cooperation for resolving their problems and demands through talks and dialog and for holding the elections to the Constituent Assembly and maintaining the law and order, at a time when the entire country is focused on the main campaign of the election of the Constituent Assembly.

10.7 We heartily appeal to the civil society, the professional groups, the class organizations, the media, the intellectual community and all the Nepali people to actively participate in this historic campaign of building a new Nepal and establishing lasting peace through the elections of the Constituent Assembly by ending the armed conflict.

10.8 We heartily urge all the friendly countries and the United Nations, as well as the international community to extend support to Nepal in this campaign of establishing full democracy and lasting peace.

Cognizant of the responsibility of the future of the country and the people, and becoming fully committed to this comprehensive peace agreement, we, on behalf of the Government of Nepal and the Communist Party of Nepal (Maoists), hereby make public this comprehensive peace agreement after signing it.

Prachanda	Girija Prasad Koirala
President	Prime Minister
Communist Party of Nepal (Maoists)	Government of Nepal

Signed on November 21, 2006

Source: Uddhap P. Pyakural, **op. it.**

Bibliography

Books

Adhikari Neelamsekhar, *Nepal ma Jatiya Andolan, Arakshan, Swasasan ra Sanghiya Rajyatarf* (Nepali), Kathmadnu, 2000.

Apter David, *Introduction to Political Analysis*, Printicehall of India, New Delhi, 1978.

Brown Louise T., *The Challenge to Democracy in Nepal: A Political History*, Rutledge, London, 1996.

Bista Dor Bahadur, *Fatalism and Development: Nepal's Struggle for Modernization*, Orient Longmans, Calcutta, 1991.

Baral Lok Raj (ed.) *Nepal, Political Parties and Parliament*, Adroit Publishers, Delhi, 2006.

Baral Lok Raj (ed.), *Leadership in Nepal*, Adroit Publishers, Delhi, 2001.

Baral Lok Raj (ed.), *Nepal: Facets of Maoist Insurgency*, Adroit, Delhi, 2006.

Baral Lok Raj, Nepal: *Quest For Participatory Democracy*, Adroit Publishers, Delhi, 2006.

Bhattarai Babu Ram, *Yudha ra Barta*, Janadhwani Prakashan, Kathmandu, 2063.

Bhattarai Babu Ram, *Rajtantra ra Loktantrik Ganatantra*, Jandhwani Prakashan, Kathmandu, 2063.

Bishakarma Padmalal & Malla Sunder K. (eds.), *The Concept of State Restructuring: Issues of Dalits and Madhesis*, National Forum Against Racial Discrimination, Kathmandu, 2006 March.

Bhattachargee G.P., *India and the Politics of Modern Nepal*, Minerva Associates, Bombay, 1970.

Chand Diwakar, *Essays on Development of Nepal*, Chandni Publications, Kathmandu, 2003.

Coplan Lionel, *Land and Social Change in East Nepal*, Himal Books, Kathmandu, 2000.

Devkota Keshavraj, *Prachanda, Prachandapath ra Ganatantra*, Saogat Pustak Prakashan, Kathmandu, 2063.

Dahal Dev Raj, *Conflict Situation in Nepal*, FES, Kathmandu, 2004.

Dhakal Ameet, "Koirala Advocates Ceremonial Monarchy", *The Hindu*, June 15, 2006.

Dhakal Dharendra Purush, *Jan Andolan* (Nepali), Kathmandu, 1990.

Ebenstein William, *Great Political Thinkers*, Oxford or IBH, New Delhi, 1960.

Fukie H. (ed.), *Political Parties of Asia & the Pacefic* Vol. II, Greenwood Press, Westpost, 1985.

Gurung Harka Bahadur, Aditya Anand et.al., *An Overview of Recent Armed Conflict in Nepal*, New ERA, Kathmandu, 2001.

Gurung Harka B., *Nepal, Social Demography and Expressions*, New ERA, Kathmandu, 2005.

Gittings J., *The Role of the Chinese Army*, Oxford University Press, Oxford, 1967.

Gupta Anirudha, *Politics in Nepal, A Study of Post Rana Political Developments and Party Politics*, Allied Publications, Bombay, 1964.

Ghimre Bhumika, *Human Rights Report on Nepal*, US State Department, March 31, 2006.

Gaige Fredrick H., *Regionalism and National Unity in Nepal*, University of California Press, California, 1975.

Guevora Che, *Guerrilla Warfare*, Penguin, London, 1967.

Gyawali Pradeep, *Prachandapath: Vichar ko Kendrikaran ki Bhrastikaran*, Kathmandu, 2001.

Gellner David N., et.al., (eds.), *Nationalism and Ethnicity in a Himalayan Kingdom, The Politics of Culluire in Contemporary Nepal*, Harvard Academic Publishers, Amestardam, 1997.

Hachhethu Krishna, *Party Building in Nepal, Organization, Leadership and People*, Mandala Book Point, Kathmandu, 2002.

Hachhethu Krishna, *State and Democracy in Nepal*, SDSA, Kathmandu, 2004.

Hutt Michael (ed.), *Nepal in the Nineties*, Oxford University Press, Delhi, 1993.

Hoftn Martin et.al. (eds.), *People, Politics and Ideology, Democracy and Social Change in Nepal*, Mandala Book Point, Kathmandu, 1999.

Harris Peter B., *Foundation of Political Science*, Hutchusion London, 1976.

International Crises Group, *Nepal's Maoists: Their Aims, Structure and Strategy*, Asia Report No. 104, 27 October 2005.

Mehta Ashok, *The Royal Nepal Army: Meeting the Maoist Challenges*, Rupa Books, New Delhi, 2005.

International Crises Groups, *Nepal's Troubled Tarai Region*, Asia Report No. 136, July 9, 2007.

International Crises Groups, *Nepal's Maoists: Pursuits or Pragmatists*, Asia Report No. 132, May 18, 2007.

International Crises Groups, *Nepal's Peace Agreement: Making it Work*, Asia Report No. 128, December 15, 2006.

International Crises Groups, *Nepal's Constitutional Process*, Asia Report No. 128, February 26, 2007.

Thapa Deepak & Sijapati Bandita, *A Kingdom Under Siege Nepal's Maoist Insurgency 1996 – 2003*, Printhouse, Kathmandu, 2003.

Joshi Bhuwan Lal & Rose Leo E., *Democratic Innovations in Nepal, A Case of Political Acculturation*, University of California Press, California, 1960.

Jha Hari Bansh, *The Tarai Community or National Integration in Nepal*, CETS, Kathmandu, 1993.

Jacobes and Baerwald (eds.), *Chinese Communism, Selected Documents*, New York, 1963.

Krishan Ram Bahadur, *Nepal ma Dalit Jatiyi Mukts Andolan*, Jan Utthan Pratisthan, Kathmandu, 2002.

Khadka Narayan, *Foreign Aid, Poverty and Stagnation in Nepal*, New Delhi, 1991.

Karan Pradyumna P. & Jankins William M., *Nepal, A Cultural and Physical Geography*, Lexington, 1960.

Karki Arjun & Saddon David (eds.), *The People's War in Nepal, Left Perspective*, Adroit Publishers, Delhi, 2003.

Lane Robet, *Political Ideology: Why the American Common Man Believes What He Does*, New York, 1962.

Lawati Mahendra, *Towards a Democratic Nepal: Inclusive Political Institutions for a Multicultural Society*, SAGE, New Delhi, 2005.

Mahan Agragami Chhalang : Itihas Ko Apariharya Avashyakta, Central Publication Division of the Party, 2001.

Muni S.D., *Insurgency in Nepal, The Challenges and the Response*, Rupa, New Delhi, 2003.

Mahat Ram Sharan, *In Defence of Democracy: Dynamics and Fault Lines of Nepal's Political Economy*: Adroit, Delhi, 2005.

Manchanda Rita, "Politics in Nepal: Women Now Swelling the Ranks of Maoists", *httpllwww.chasque.netlps-onglnotes*.

Mojumdar Kanchanmoy, *Political Relations Between India and Nepal*, New Delhi, 1970.

Majumdar Kanchanmoy, *Nepal and the Indian Nationalist Movement*, Firma M.L.Mukhopandyoy, Calcutta, 1975.

Ogura Kiyoko, *Kathmandu Spring : The People's Movement of* 1990, Himal Books, Kathmandu, 2001.

Pokharel Shankar, *Maovadi Ugravampanth ra Prajatantrik Nikas*, Akaissaon Shatabdi Masik, Kathmandu, 2058.

Parvati, "Women's Participation in the People's War" in Karki Arjun & Seddon David, *The People's War in Nepal, Left Perspective*, Adroit, Delhi, 2003.

Prachanda, *Problems and Prospects of the Revolution in Nepal*, Janadesh Publication, 2004.

Phadnis Urmila, *Ethnicity and National Building in South Asia*, SAGE Publications, New Delhi, 1990.

Pandey Devendra Raj, *Nepal's Failed Development: Reflections on the Mission and the Maladies*, Nepal South Asia Centre, Kathmandu, 1999.

Pndey Nichal Nath, *Nepal's Maoist Movement and Implications for India and China*, Manohar, Delhi, 2005.

Pyakuru Uddhav P., *Maoists Movement in Nepal*, Adroit, Delhi, 2007.

Rawal Bhim, *Nepal Ma Samyavadi Aandolan, Udbhav ra Bikas*, Pairavia Prakashan, Kathmandu, 1990.

Shrestha Anand Prasad & Upreti Hari (eds.), *Critical Barries to the Negotiation of Armed Conflict in Nepal*, Nepal Foundation for Advance Studies, Kathmandu, 2005.

Shaha Rishikesh, *Politics in Nepal* 1980 – 90, Manohar, Delhi, 1990.

Shaha, Rishikesh, *Madern Nepal, A Political History* I – II Vol., Manohar, Delhi, 1990.

Shaha Rishikesh, *Nepali Politics, Retrospect and Prospect*, Oxford University Press, New Delhi, 1978.

Schwar B., *Chinese Communism and the Rise of Mao*, Harvard University Press, Massachusetts, 1958.

Shrestha N.R. *In the Name of Development: A Reflection on Nepal*, Educational Enterprises, Kathmandu, 1997.

Stiller Ludwing F., *The Rise of the House of Gorkha, A Study in the Unification of Nepal*, Manjushri Publishing House, New Delhi, 1973.

Seliger Martin, *Ideology and Politics*, The Free Press, New York, 1976.

Shrivastava Kashi Prasad, *Nepal Ka Itihas*, Atmaram & Sons, Delhi, 1986.

Some Important Documents of Communist Party of Nepal (Maoist) Janadesh Publications, Kathmandu, 2004.

Surendra KC, *Nepal Ma Communist Andolan Ko Itihas* (Nepali) Kathmandu, 1991.

Scalppino Robert L., *The Communist Revolution in Asia*, Printice Hall, New Jersey, 1965.

Sharma Prayag Raj, *The State and Society in Nepal, Historical Foundations and Contemporary Trends*, Himal Books, Kathmandu, 2004.

Thapa Manjushree, *An Elegy for Democracy, Forget Kathmandu*, PENGUIN, India, 2005.

Tiwari Satwanta Chaube, *Democratic Movement in Nepal and the Indian Left*, Kalinga Publications, Delhi, 2001.

Upreti Bishnu Raj, *The Price of Neglect: From Resource Conflict to Maoist Insurgency in the Himalayan Kingdom*, Bhrikuti Academic Publications, Kathmandu, 2004.

Upreti B.C. et.al. (eds.), *Globalization and South Asia*, Sumit Enterprises, New Delhi, 2008.

Upreti B.C., *The Nepali Congress, An Analysis of the Party's Performance in the General Elections and its Aftermath*, Nirala Publications, Delhi, 1993.

Upreti B.C, *Nepal, Dilemmas of Development and Change in Far Western Hills*, Indus Publishing House, New Delhi, 2006.

Upreti B.C., *Nepal, Democracy at Crossroads, Post 1990 Dynamics, Issues and Challenges*, Kanishka Publishers Distributors, New Delhi, 2007.

Upreti B.C. & Upadhyay Shashi (eds.), *State and Democracy in South Asia*, Sumit Enterprises, New Delhi, 2008.

Upreti B.C., *Contemporary South Asia*, Kalinga Publications, Delhi, 2004.

Upreti Bishnu Raj, *Armed Conflict and Peace Process in Nepal, The Maoist Insurgency, Past Negotiations and Opportunities for Conflict Transformation*, Adroit, Delhi, 2006.

UNDP, *Nepal Human Development: Environment and Poverty Reduction*, UNDP Nepal, Kathmandu, 2004.

Vishkarma Hiralal, *A Strategy for the Upliftment and Empowerment of Dalits*, Kathmandu, 1996.

Wasby Stephen L., *Political Science, The Discipline and the Dimensions*, Scientific Book Agency, Calcutta, 1970.

Articles

Adhikari Indira, "Women in Conflict : The Gender Perspective in Maoist Insurgency", in Baral Lok Raj (eds.), *Nepal, Facets of Maoist Insurgency*, Adroit, Delhi, 2006

Nickson Andrew R., "Democratization and the Growth of Communism in Nepal: A Peruvian Scenario in the Making", *Journal of Commonwealth and Comparative Politics*, Vol.30, No.3, November 1992.

Bhattarai Babu Ram, "Royal Regression and the Question of a Democratic Republic in Nepal", *Economic and Political Weekly*, April 9, 2005.

Bhattachan Krishna B., "Possible Ethnic Revolution or Insurgency in a Predatory, Unitary Hindu State", in Kumar Dhrub (ed.), *Domestic Conflict and Crises of Governability in Nepal*, CNAS, Kathmandu, 2000.

Bhattarai Babu Ram, "Politico – Economic Rationale of the People's War in Nepal", www.http//insef.org.

Baral Sitaram, "San AK 47 Ko", *Samay* (Kathmandu), May 13, 2004.

Bhattarai Babu Ram, "Dosro Rashtriya Sammelan Ka Yugantkari Mahatva", *Kantipur* (Kathmandu), March 1, 2001.

Burghart Bichard, "The Formation of the Concept of Nation State in Nepal", in Burghart Richard (ed.), *The Conditions of Listening*, Oxford University Press, Delhi, 1996.

Bhattarai Krishna B., "Ethno – Politics and Ethno – Development: An Emerging Paradigm in Nepal", in Kumar Dhrub (ed.), *Domestic Conflict and Crisis of Governability in Nepal*, CNAS, Kathmandu, 2000.

Bennet Lynn, "Diversity and Inclusion: Contesting Hierarchy in Nepali Democracy", *World Bank Development Report* 2000/01.

Balker Steven C., "Nepal's Maoist Insurgency", *Front Page Magazine.com*, July 25, 2003.

Chandhary Nilobia Roy, "The Great Indian Balancing Act", *The Hindustan Times*, April 23, 2006.

Chamalgai Abi Narayan, "Politics of State Restructuring in Nepal", *Nepali Journal of Contemporary Studies*, Vol.VI, No.2, September, 2006.

Chamalgai Abi Narayan, "Maoist Insurgency: An Ideological Diagnosis", in Baral Lok Raj (ed.), *Nepal Facets of Maoist Insurgency*, Adroit Publishers, Delhi, 2006.

Dahal Dilli Ram, "Ethnic Calandron, Demography and Minority Politics: The Case of Nepal", in Kumar Dhrub (ed.), *State, Leadership and Politics in Nepal*, CNAS, Kathmandu, 1995.

Dinesh, "Janamukti Sena Ko Vikas ra Rjanitik Karya", *Janadesh*, August 10, 2004.

Dahal Dilli Ram, "Madhesi Regionalism and National Integration: A Case of the Nepal Tarai, *Nepali Journal of Contemporary Studies*, 2:1, 2002.

Giri Saroj, "Social Transformation and Political Power, Maoists in Nepal", *Economic and Political Weekly*, May 27, 2006.

Gurung Harka Bahadur, "The Land in Shamsher Pashupati JBR and Malla Kamal P. (eds.), *Nepal in Perspective*, Kathmandu, 1973.

Jha Sanjay K., "Maoist Linkages With North – East Insurgents Growing Concerns", Art 1374, *httpl/www.saag,org*.

Koirala Bidya Nath, "Restructuring the Nepali State: Gender and Dalit Perspectives", *Nepali Journal of Contemporary Studies*, Vol.VII, No.1, March 2007.

Kumar Dhrub, "Military Dimensions of the Maoist Insurgency", in Baral Lok Raj (ed.), *Nepal, Facets of Maoist Insurgency*, Adroit, Delhi, 2006.

Lama Mahendra P., "The Maoist Movement in Nepal: The Economic Implications", in Khatri Sridhar K. & Kueck Gert W. (eds.), *Terrorism in South Asia: Impact on Development and Democratic Process*, Shipra Publication, Delhi, 2003.

Lancaster John, "Concern Grows Over Nepal's Child Fighters", *The Washington Post*, June 14, 2005.

Muni S.D., "Sounding the red Alert", *The Hindustan Times*, September 20, 2007.

Muhammad Ayaz, "Nepal: Jana Andolan and its Challenges", *Nepali Journal of Contemporary Studies*, Vol.VI, No.2, September 2006.

Maharjan Panchanan, "Role of the Extra – Parliamentary Political Party in Multi – Party Democracy: A Study of the CPN Unity Centre", *Contributions to Nepalese Studies*, Vol. 20, No.2, 1993.

Maharjan Panchanan, "The Maoist Insurgency and the Crisis of Governability in Nepal", in Kumar Dhrub (ed.), *Domestic Conflict and Crisis of Governability in Nepal*, CNAS, Kathmandu, 2000.

Mathur R.C., "India Factor to the Fore in Nepal", *The Hindustan Times*, May 12, 1991.

Muni S.D., "India Factor in Nepal's Elections", *The Times of India*, May 6, 1991.

Malla Kamal, "Bahunvad : Myth or Reality" *Himal*, Vol.V, No.3, May-June, 1992.

Mikesell Stephen L., "The Paradoxical Support of Nepal's Left for Comrade Gonzalo", *Himal*, March – April, 1993.

Nayak Nihar, "Arms Management in Nepal", *World Focus*, July, 2007.

Onesto Li., "Inside the Revolution", Karki Arjun & Seddon David (eds.), *The People's War in Nepal, Left Perspective*, Adroit, Delhi, 2003.

Pathak Bishnu, *Politics of People's War and Human Rights in Nepal*, Benipa Publications, Kathmandu, 2005.

Ranakant & Upreti B.C., "Regionalism in Nepal, A Case of Tarai in Ranakant (ed.), *Regionalism in South Asia*, Aalekh Publishers, Jaipur, 1984.

Rose Leo E., "Communist Under High Atmospheric Condition: The Party in Nepal: in Robert A. Scalpino (ed.), *The Communist Revolution in Asia*, Prentice Hall, New York, 1969.

Sinha J.K., "Misreading the Mood, India Fails to Understand Maoist Crisis in Nepal", *Times of India*, November 12, 2005.

Shaha Rishikesh, "Idea and Reality, Nepal and Rolpa", *Himal South Asia*, July, 1996.

SubRananian Nerupama, "India and Nepal's Insurgency", *The Hindu*, August 9, 2004.

Galtuing, "Transformation of Conflict in Nepal: A Human Rights Perspective", in Adhikari Bipin (ed.), *Conflict: Human Rights and Peace Challenges Before Nepal*, NHRC, Kathmandu, 2004.

Shah Sudhir, "The Maoist Movement : An Evolutionary Perspective, in Thapa Deepak (ed.), *Understanding the Maoist Movement of Nepal*, Martin Chautari & CSDR, Kathmandu, 2005.

Shakya Sujata, "The Maoist Movement in Nepal : An Analysis from the Women Perspective in Karki Arjun & Seddon David (eds.), *The People's War in Nepal, Left Perspective*, Adroit, Delhi, 2003.

Sharma Mandira & Prasain Dinesh, "Gender Dimensions of the People's War" in Hutt Michael (eds.), *Himalayan People's War : Nepal's Maoist Rebellion*, Hurst & Co., London, 2004.

Shakya Keshba Raj, "Nationalities Movements and Nepali State", *Nepali Journal of Contemporary Studies*, Vol.VII, No.1, March, 2007.

Thapa Deepak, "Erosion of the Nepali World", *Himal South Asia*, April, 2002.

Thapa Manjushree, "Nepal's Troubled Kingdom", *The Hindu*, April 23, 2006.

Upreti B.C., "Democracy in Nepal: Bumpy Ground and Road Blocks", in Kulwant Kaur et.al. (eds.), *South Asia, Dynamics of Polity, Society and Economy*, Knowledge World, New Delhi, 2006.

Upreti B.C., "Nepal: In Search of Good Governance", *Asian Studies* (Calcutta), Vol.XIX, No.2. July – December, 2001.

Upreti B.C., "Ethnicity and Politics in Nepal: Emerging Patterns of Socio – Political Mobilization and Alignments", *South Asian Studies*, Vol.37, No.1, January – July, 2002.

Upreti B.C., "The Maoist Insurgency in Nepal: Nature, Growth and Impact, *South Asian Survey*, Vol.13, No.1, 2006.

Upreti Bishnu Raj, "Restructuring Nepali Army: A Conflict Transformation Perspective", *Nepali Journal of Contemporary Studies*, Vol.VII, No.1, March 2007.

Upreti B.C., "Nagarikta Ko Rajniti", in Thapa Basant & Mainali Mohan (eds.), *Madhes, Samasya ra Sambhavana*, Social Science BAHA, Kathmandu, 2006.

Upreti Bishnu Raj, "Nepal on Fire : A Tragedy of Betrayal", *South Asian Journal*, Vol.7, December, 2004.

Upreti B.C., "Regional Movements and Madhese Politics in Nepal", *Nepali Journal of Contemporary Studies* (Kathmandu) Vol.VII, No.1, March, 2007.

Upreti B.C., "Will Monarchy Survive", *SEMINAR* (New Delhi), 546, April, 2005.

Upreti B.C., "Politics in Nepal: Governmental Stability Party Cleavages and Crisis of Democracy in the Post – 1990

Period", *Asian Panorama* (Delhi), Vol.3, No.1&2, December 2004.

Venkateshwara Shyam and Sherchan Sanjeev M., "Let We Shut Our Eyes Off Nepal", *Indian Express*, August 11, 2006.

Vardarajan Sidharth, "In Nepal the Begmising of the End", *The Hindu*, April 22, 2006.

Yechury Sita Ram, "Learning from Experience, An Analysis of Contrasting Approaches of Maoists in Nepal and India", *Economic and Political Weekly*, July 22, 2006.

Yechury Sita Ram, "Till Kingdom Goes", *The Hindustan Times*, April 20, 2006.

Index

N

O

P